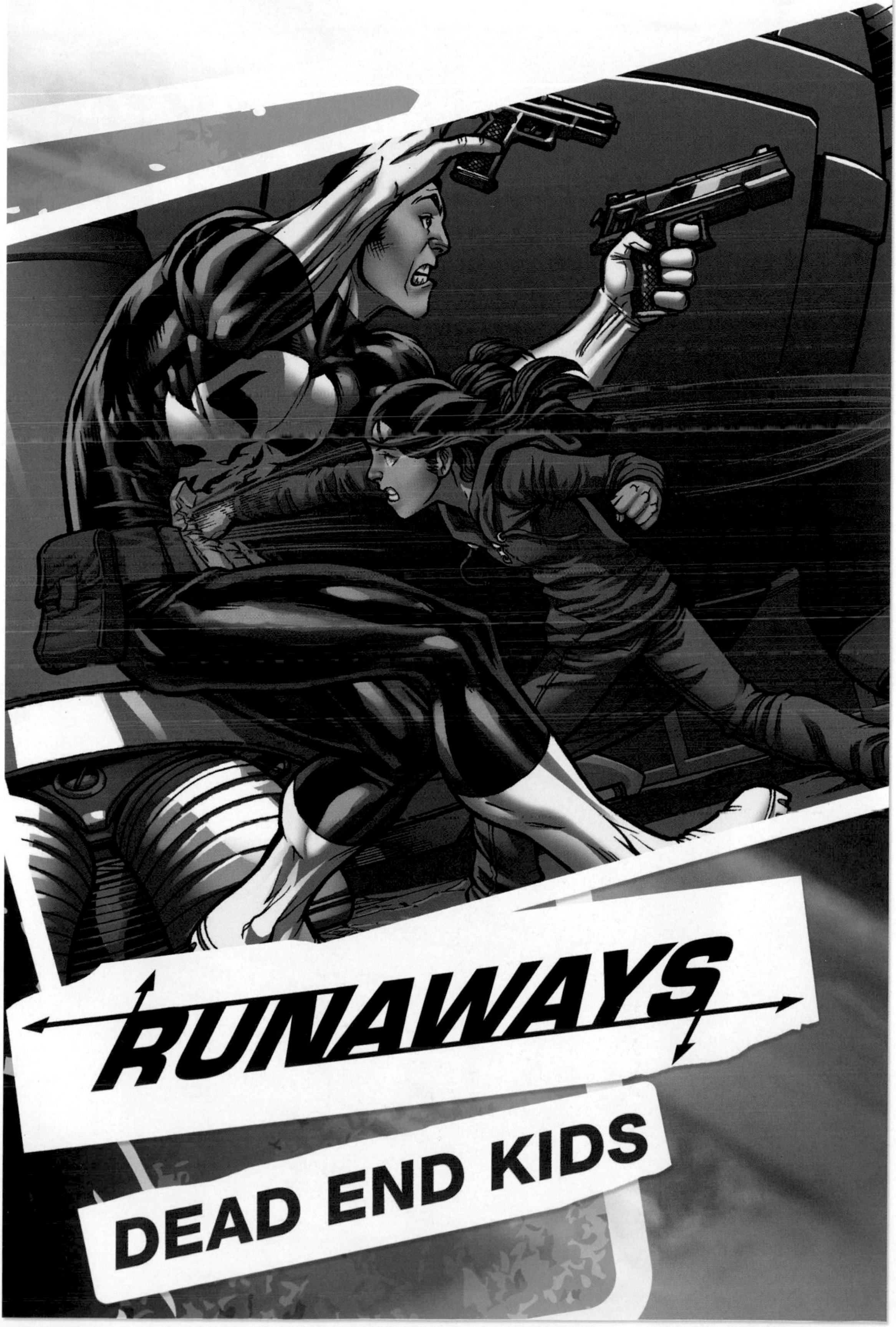
RUNAWAYS
DEAD END KIDS

RUNAWAYS

DEAD END KIDS

WRITER: **JOSS WHEDON**
PENCILER: **MICHAEL RYAN**
INKER: **RICK KETCHAM** WITH **JAY LEISTEN, ANDREW HENNESSY, VICTOR OLAZABA & ROLAND PARIS**
COLORIST: **CHRISTINA STRAIN**
LETTERER: **VC'S RANDY GENTILE, JOE CARAMAGNA & CORY PETIT**
COVER ARTIST: **JO CHEN**
ASSISTANT EDITOR: **DANIEL KETCHUM**
EDITOR: **NICK LOWE**

RUNAWAYS CREATED BY
BRIAN K. VAUGHAN & **ADRIAN ALPHONA**

COLLECTION EDITOR: **JENNIFER GRÜNWALD**
ASSISTANT EDITORS: **CORY LEVINE** & **JOHN DENNING**
EDITOR, SPECIAL PROJECTS: **MARK D. BEAZLEY**
SENIOR EDITOR, SPECIAL PROJECTS: **JEFF YOUNGQUIST**
SENIOR VICE PRESIDENT OF SALES: **DAVID GABRIEL**
PRODUCTION: **JERRY KALINOWSKI**
BOOK DESIGNER: **RODOLFO MURAGUCHI**

EDITOR IN CHIEF: **JOE QUESADA**
PUBLISHER: **DAN BUCKLEY**

RUNAWAYS: DEAD END KIDS. Contains material originally published in magazine form as RUNAWAYS #25-30. First printing 2008. ISBN# 978-0-7851-2853-3. Published by MARVEL PUBLISHING, INC., a subsidiary of MARVEL ENTERTAINMENT, INC. OFFICE OF PUBLICATION: 417 5th Avenue, New York, NY 10016. Copyright © 2007 and 2008 Marvel Characters, Inc. All rights reserved. $19.99 per copy in the U.S. and $21.00 in Canada (GST #R127032852); Canadian Agreement #40668537. All characters featured in this issue and the distinctive names and likenesses thereof, and all related indicia are trademarks of Marvel Characters, Inc. No similarity between any of the names, characters, persons, and/or institutions in this magazine with those of any living or dead person or institution is intended, and any such similarity which may exist is purely coincidental. **Printed in the U.S.A.** ALAN FINE, CEO Marvel Toys & Publishing Divisions and CMO Marvel Entertainment, Inc.; DAVID GABRIEL, SVP of Publishing Sales & Circulation; DAVID BOGART, SVP of Business Affairs & Talent Management; MICHAEL PASCIULLO, VP of Merchandising & Communications; JIM O'KEEFE, VP of Operations & Logistics; DAN CARR, Executive Director of Publishing Technology; JUSTIN F. GABRIE, Director of Editorial Operations; SUSAN CRESPI, Editorial Operations Manager; OMAR OTIEKU, Production Manager; STAN LEE, Chairman Emeritus. For information regarding advertising in Marvel Comics or on Marvel.com, please contact Mitch Dane, Advertising Director, at mdane@marvel.com. For Marvel subscription inquiries, please call 800-217-9158.

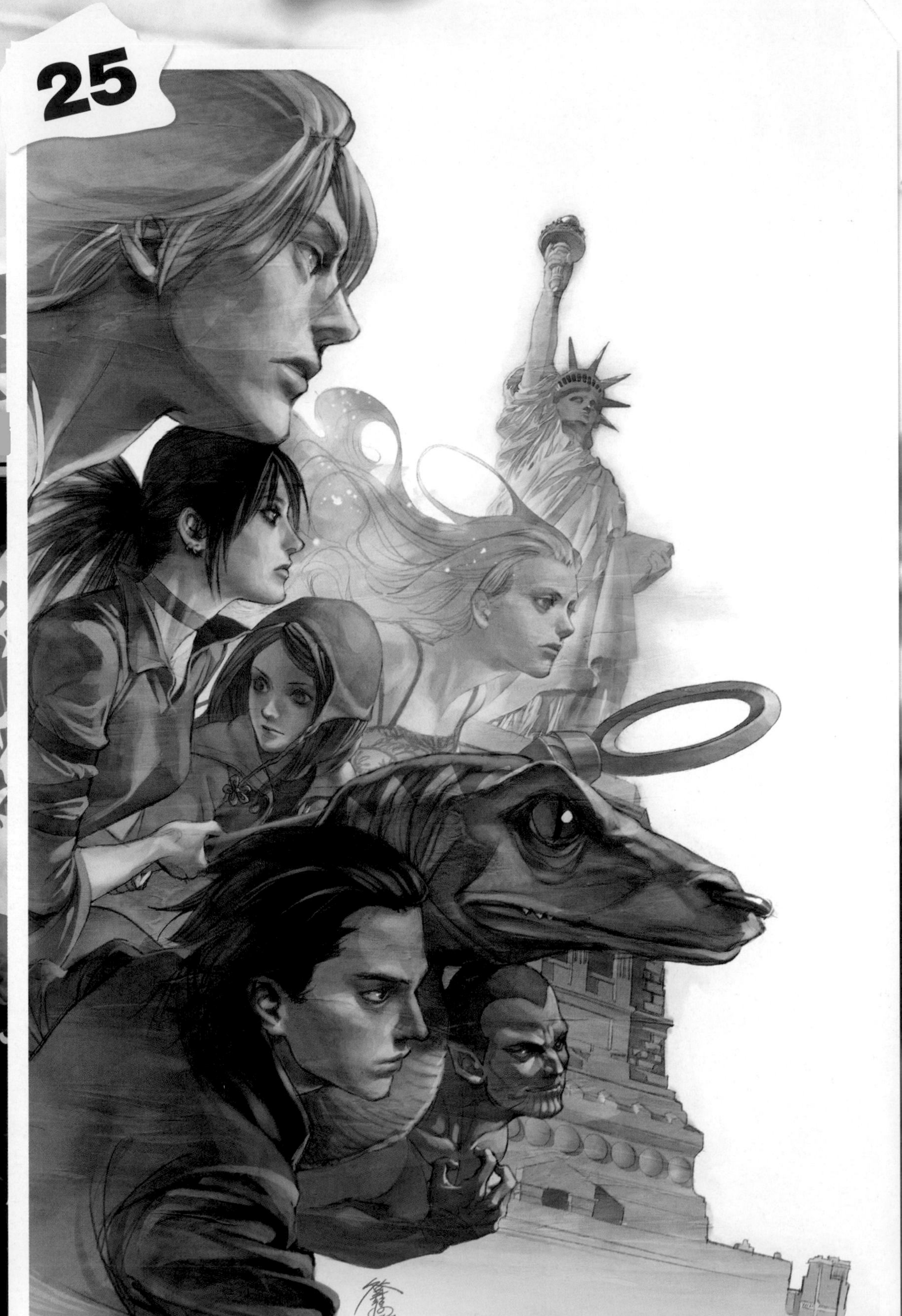
25

DEAD-END KIDS

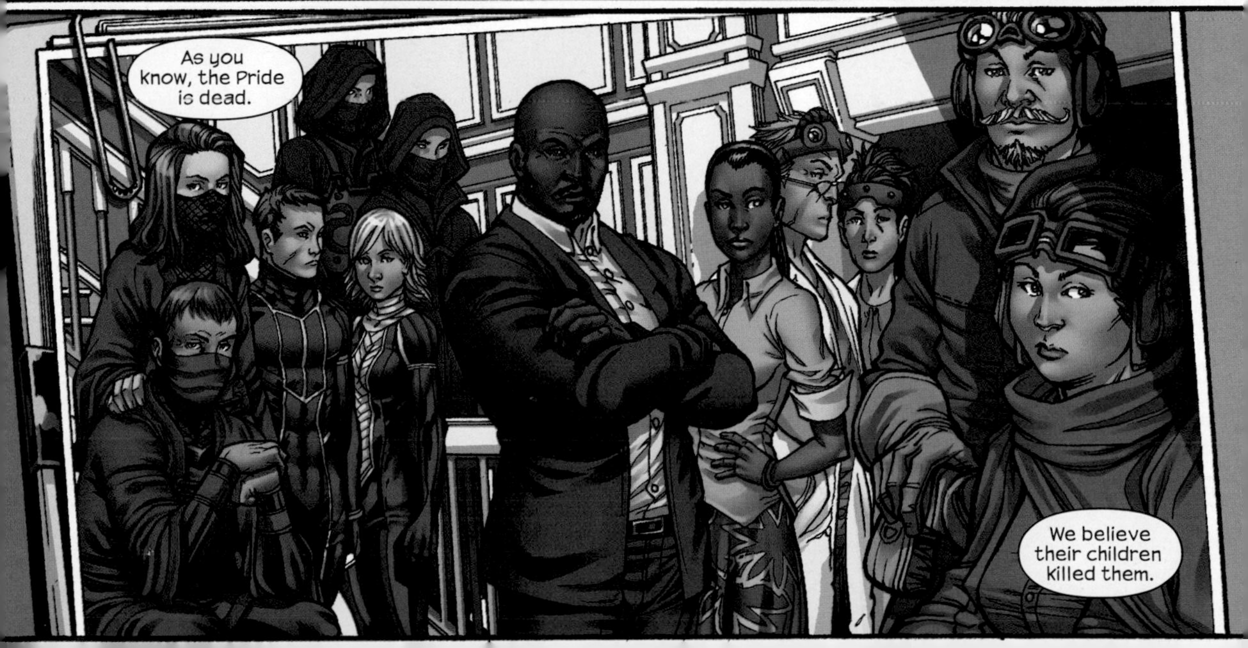
As you know, the Pride is dead.
We believe their children killed them.

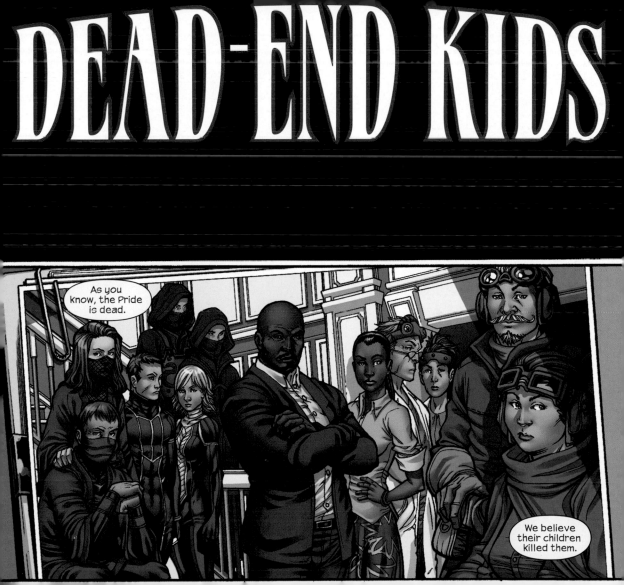

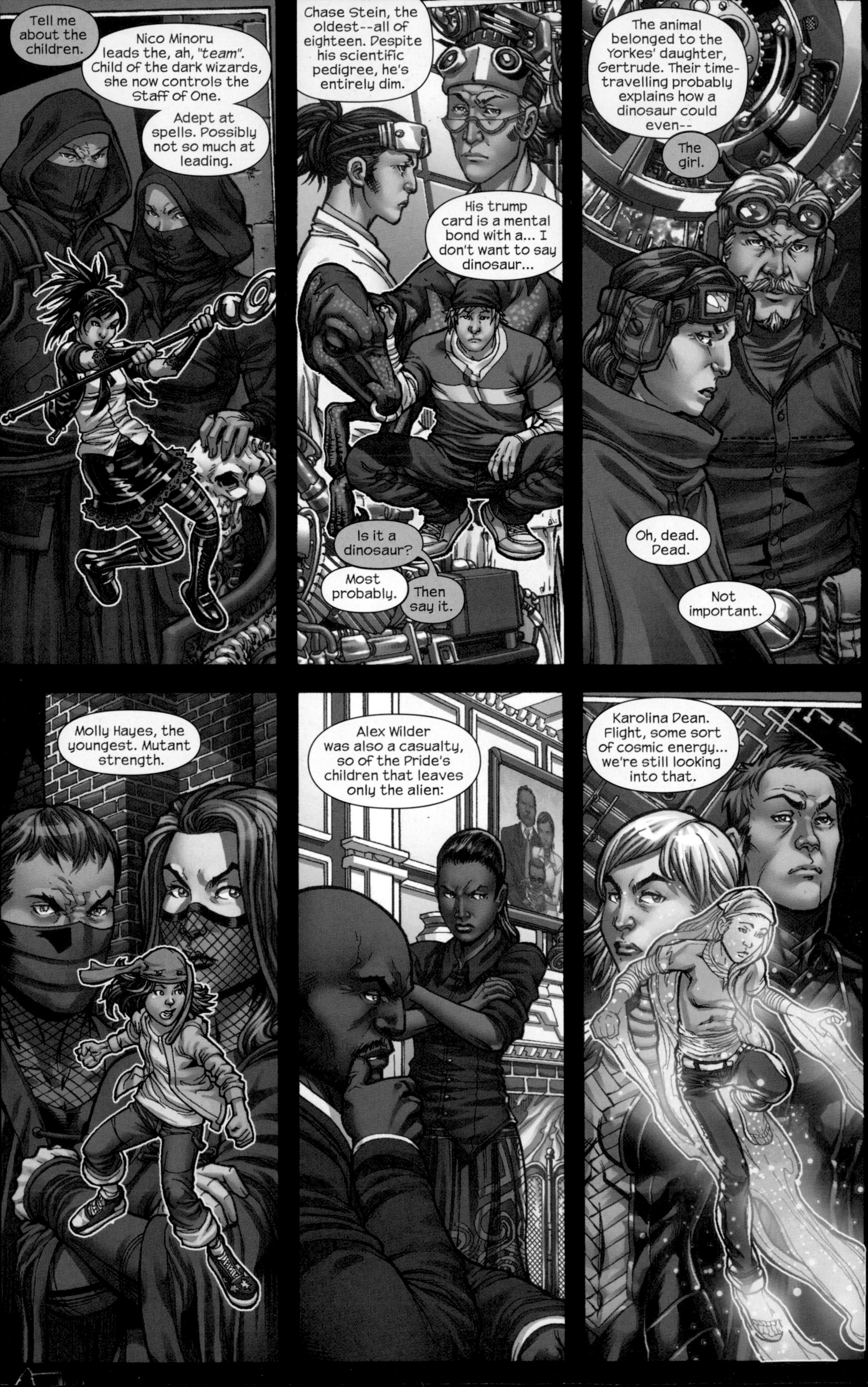
Tell me about the children.
Nico Minoru leads the, ah, *"team"*. Child of the dark wizards, she now controls the Staff of One.
Adept at spells. Possibly not so much at leading.
Chase Stein, the oldest--all of eighteen. Despite his scientific pedigree, he's entirely dim.
His trump card is a mental bond with a... I don't want to say dinosaur...
Is it a dinosaur?
Most probably.
Then say it.
The animal belonged to the Yorkes' daughter, Gertrude. Their time-travelling probably explains how a dinosaur could even--
The girl.
Oh, dead. Dead.
Not important.
Molly Hayes, the youngest. Mutant strength.
Alex Wilder was also a casualty, so of the Pride's children that leaves only the alien:
Karolina Dean. Flight, some sort of cosmic energy... we're still looking into that.

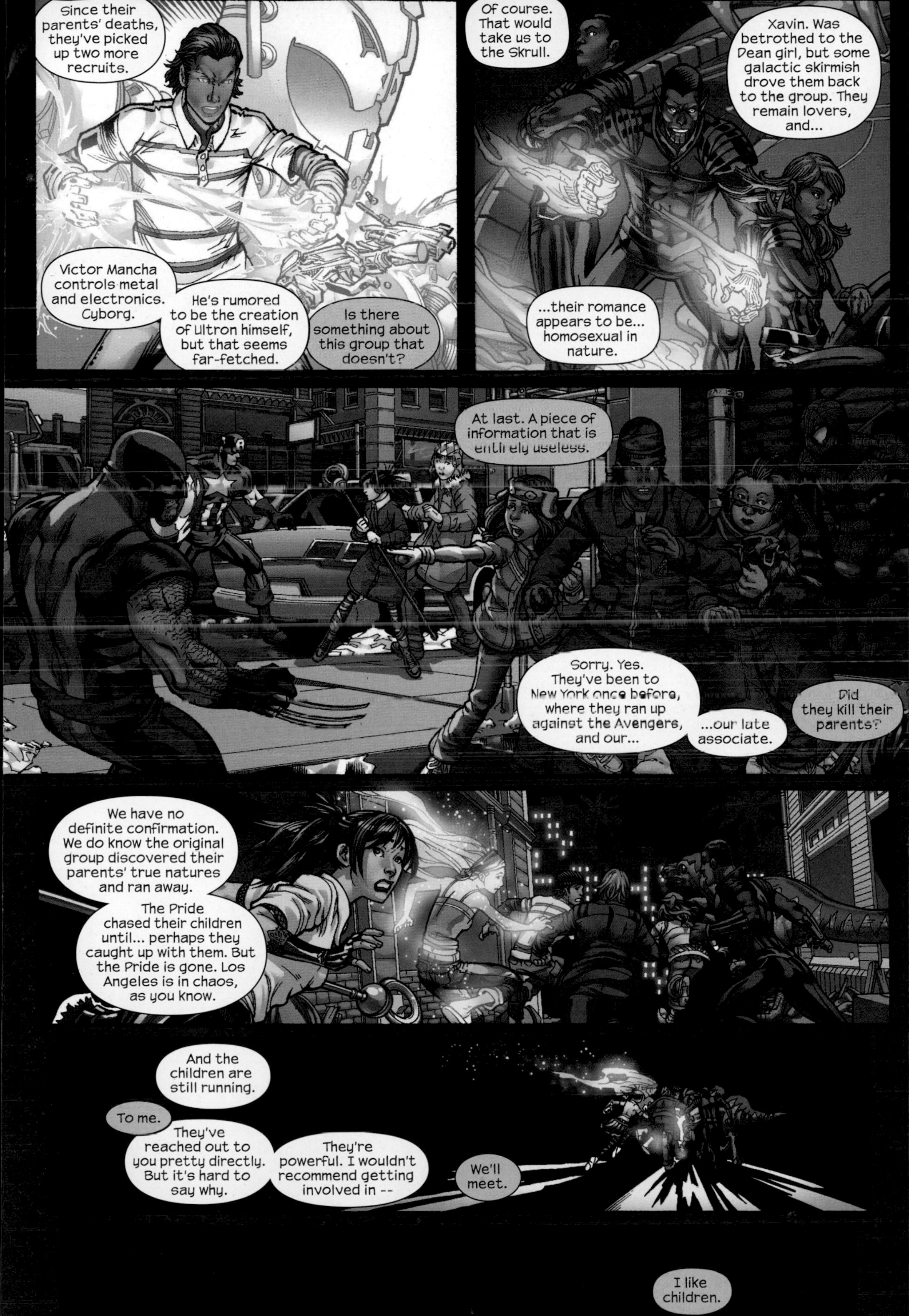
Since their parents' deaths, they've picked up two more recruits.
Victor Mancha controls metal and electronics. Cyborg.
He's rumored to be the creation of Ultron himself, but that seems far-fetched.
Is there something about this group that doesn't?
Of course. That would take us to the Skrull.
Xavin. Was betrothed to the Dean girl, but some galactic skirmish drove them back to the group. They remain lovers, and...
...their romance appears to be... homosexual in nature.
At last. A piece of information that is entirely useless.
Sorry. Yes. They've been to New York once before, where they ran up against the Avengers, and our...
...our late associate.
Did they kill their parents?
We have no definite confirmation. We do know the original group discovered their parents' true natures and ran away.
The Pride chased their children until... perhaps they caught up with them. But the Pride is gone. Los Angeles is in chaos, as you know.
And the children are still running.
To me.
They've reached out to you pretty directly. But it's hard to say why.
They're powerful. I wouldn't recommend getting involved in --
We'll meet.
I like children.

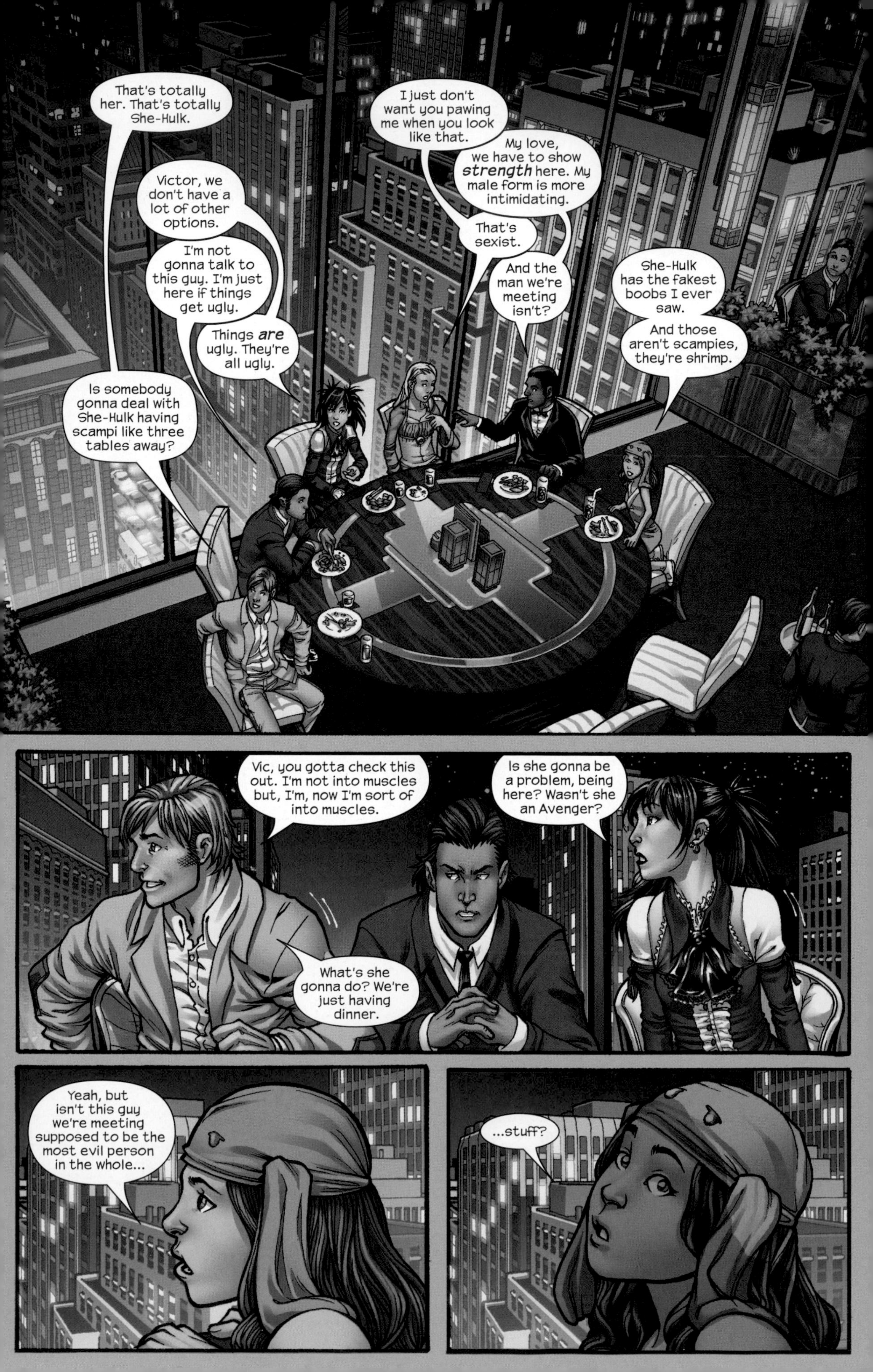
That's totally her. That's totally She-Hulk.
I just don't want you pawing me when you look like that.
My love, we have to show *strength* here. My male form is more intimidating.
Victor, we don't have a lot of other options.
That's sexist.
I'm not gonna talk to this guy. I'm just here if things get ugly.
And the man we're meeting isn't?
Things *are* ugly. They're all ugly.
She-Hulk has the fakest boobs I ever saw.
And those aren't scampies, they're shrimp.
Is somebody gonna deal with She-Hulk having scampi like three tables away?
Vic, you gotta check this out. I'm not into muscles but, I'm, now I'm sort of into muscles.
Is she gonna be a problem, being here? Wasn't she an Avenger?
What's she gonna do? We're just having dinner.
Yeah, but isn't this guy we're meeting supposed to be the most evil person in the whole...
...stuff?

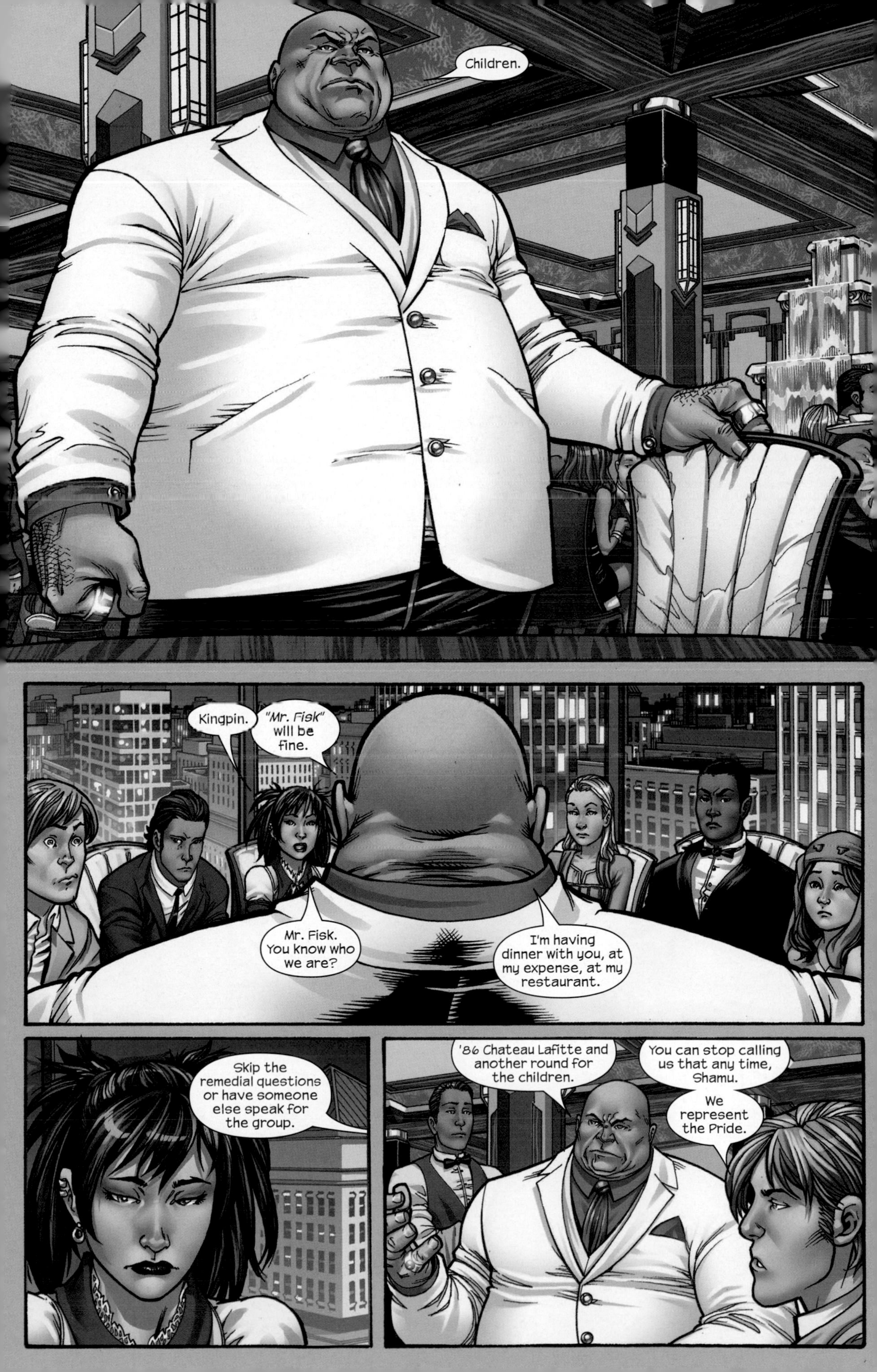
Children.
Kingpin.
"Mr. Fisk" will be fine.
Mr. Fisk. You know who we are?
I'm having dinner with you, at my expense, at my restaurant.
Skip the remedial questions or have someone else speak for the group.
'86 Chateau Lafitte and another round for the children.
You can stop calling us that any time, Shamu.
We represent the Pride.

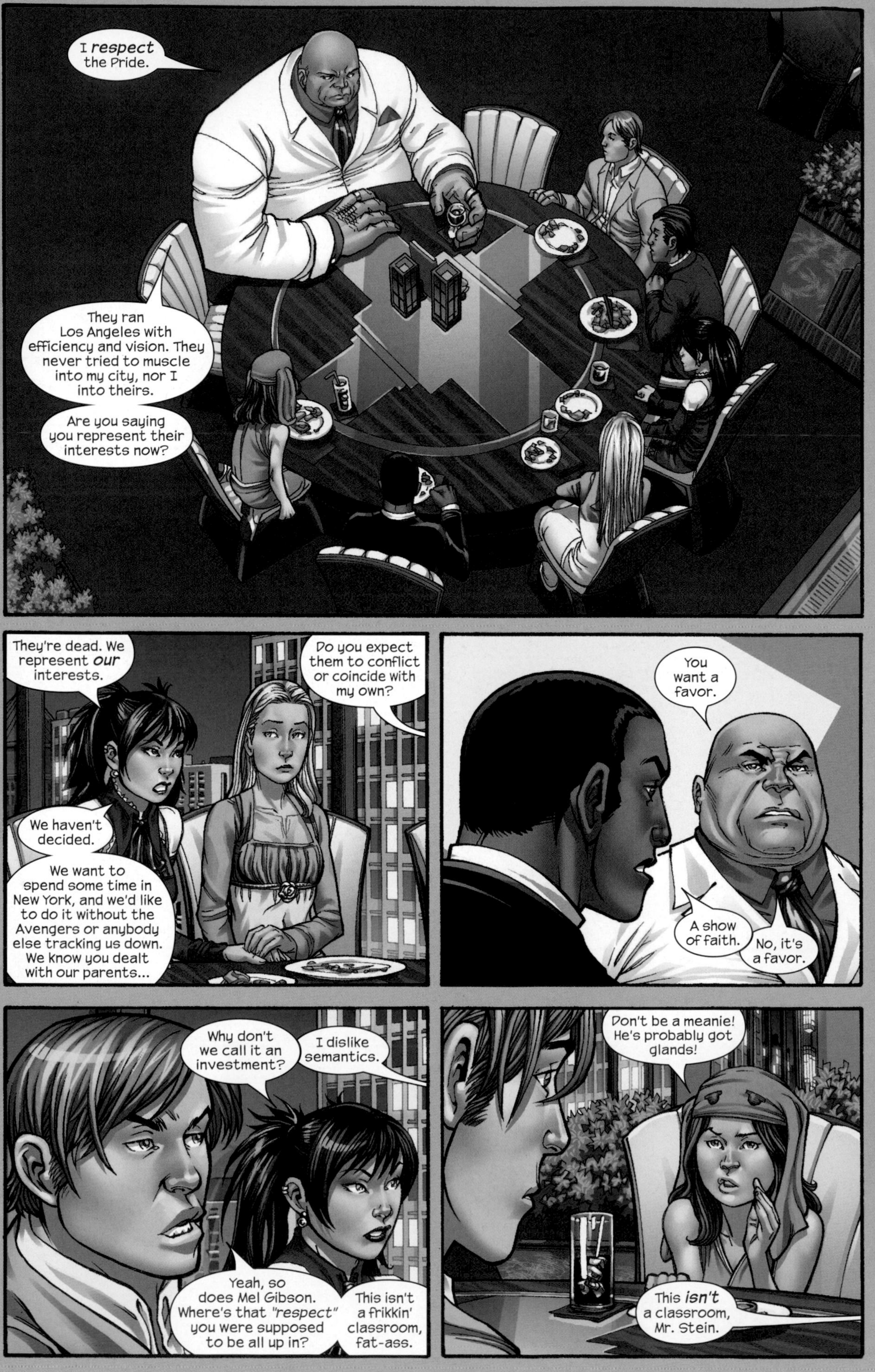
I *respect* the Pride.
They ran Los Angeles with efficiency and vision. They never tried to muscle into my city, nor I into theirs.
Are you saying you represent their interests now?
They're dead. We represent *our* interests.
Do you expect them to conflict or coincide with my own?
We haven't decided.
We want to spend some time in New York, and we'd like to do it without the Avengers or anybody else tracking us down. We know you dealt with our parents...
You want a favor.
A show of faith.
No, it's a favor.
Why don't we call it an investment?
I dislike semantics.
Yeah, so does Mel Gibson. Where's that *"respect"* you were supposed to be all up in?
This isn't a frikkin' classroom, fat-ass.
Don't be a meanie! He's probably got glands!
This *isn't* a classroom, Mr. Stein.

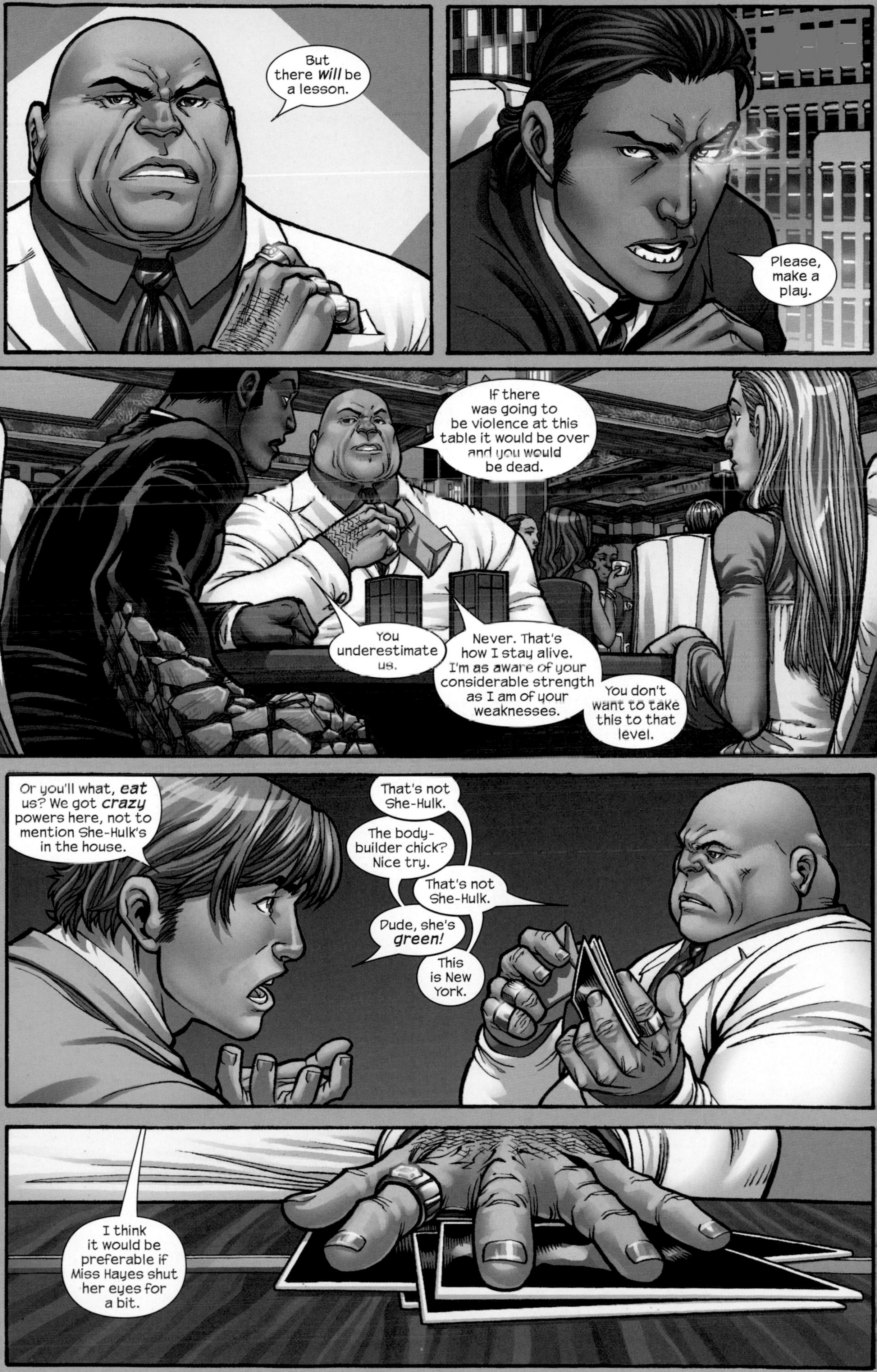

But there *will* be a lesson.
Please, make a play.
If there was going to be violence at this table it would be over and you would be dead.
You underestimate us.
Never. That's how I stay alive. I'm as aware of your considerable strength as I am of your weaknesses.
You don't want to take this to that level.
Or you'll what, *eat* us? We got *crazy* powers here, not to mention She-Hulk's in the house.
That's not She-Hulk.
The body-builder chick? Nice try.
That's not She-Hulk.
Dude, she's *green!*
This is New York.
I think it would be preferable if Miss Hayes shut her eyes for a bit.

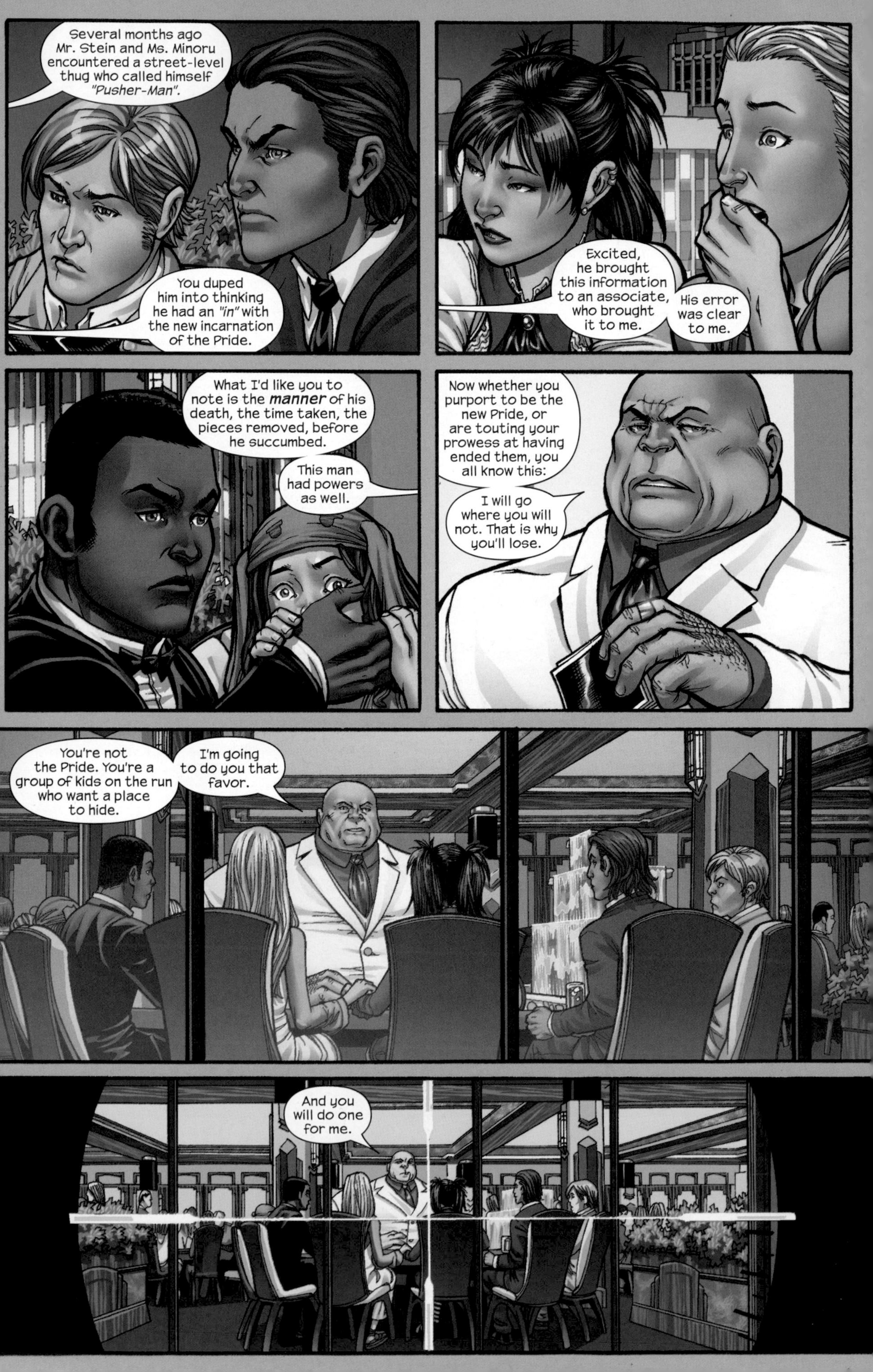

Several months ago Mr. Stein and Ms. Minoru encountered a street-level thug who called himself "Pusher-Man".
You duped him into thinking he had an "in" with the new incarnation of the Pride.
Excited, he brought this information to an associate, who brought it to me.
His error was clear to me.
What I'd like you to note is the manner of his death, the time taken, the pieces removed, before he succumbed.
This man had powers as well.
Now whether you purport to be the new Pride, or are touting your prowess at having ended them, you all know this:
I will go where you will not. That is why you'll lose.
You're not the Pride. You're a group of kids on the run who want a place to hide.
I'm going to do you that favor.
And you will do one for me.

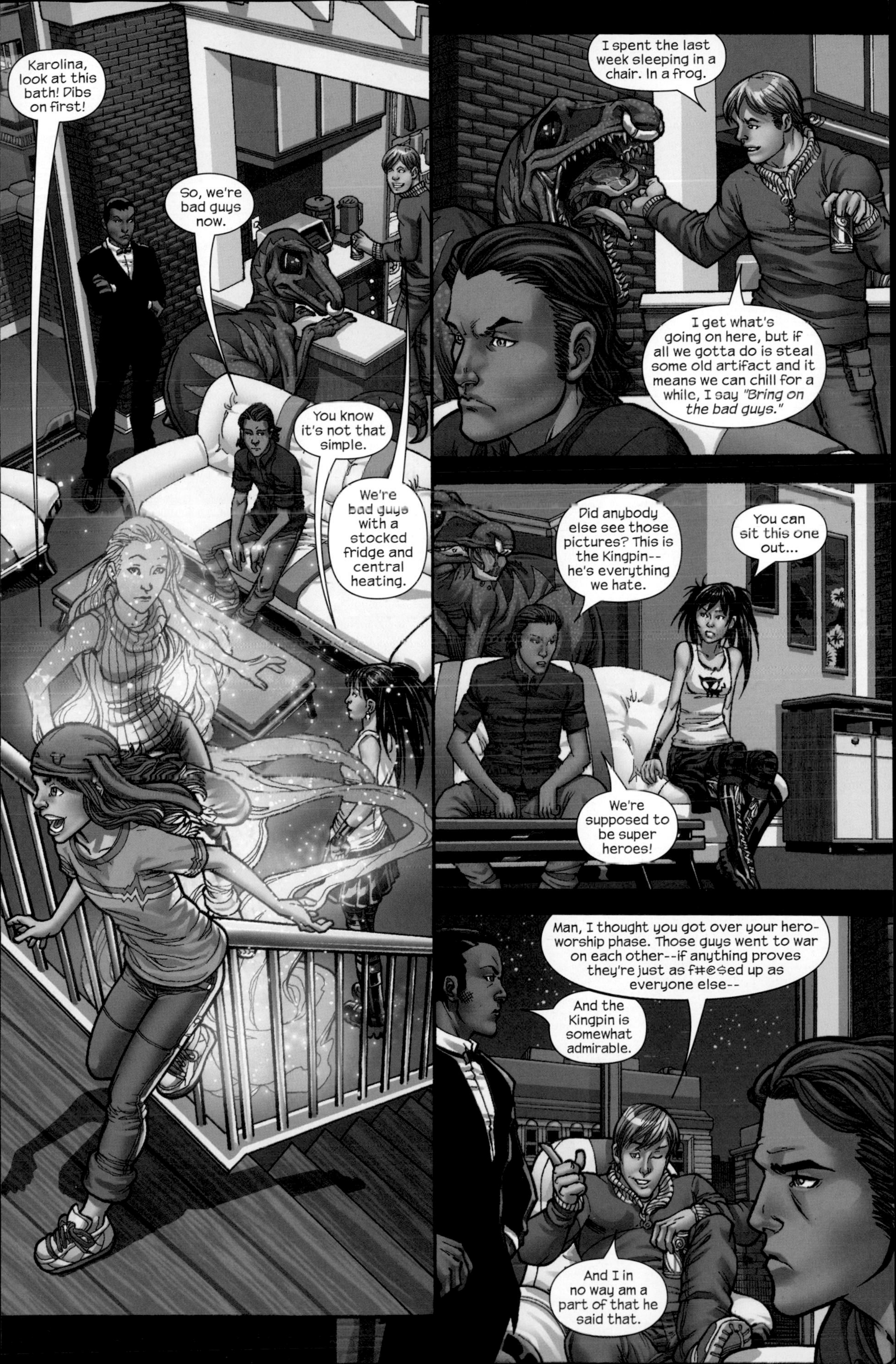
Karolina, look at this bath! Dibs on first!
So, we're bad guys now.
You know it's not that simple.
We're bad guys with a stocked fridge and central heating.
I spent the last week sleeping in a chair. In a frog.
I get what's going on here, but if all we gotta do is steal some old artifact and it means we can chill for a while, I say "Bring on the bad guys."
Did anybody else see those pictures? This is the Kingpin-- he's everything we hate.
You can sit this one out...
We're supposed to be super heroes!
Man, I thought you got over your hero-worship phase. Those guys went to war on each other--if anything proves they're just as f#@$ed up as everyone else--
And the Kingpin is somewhat admirable.
And I in no way am a part of that he said that.

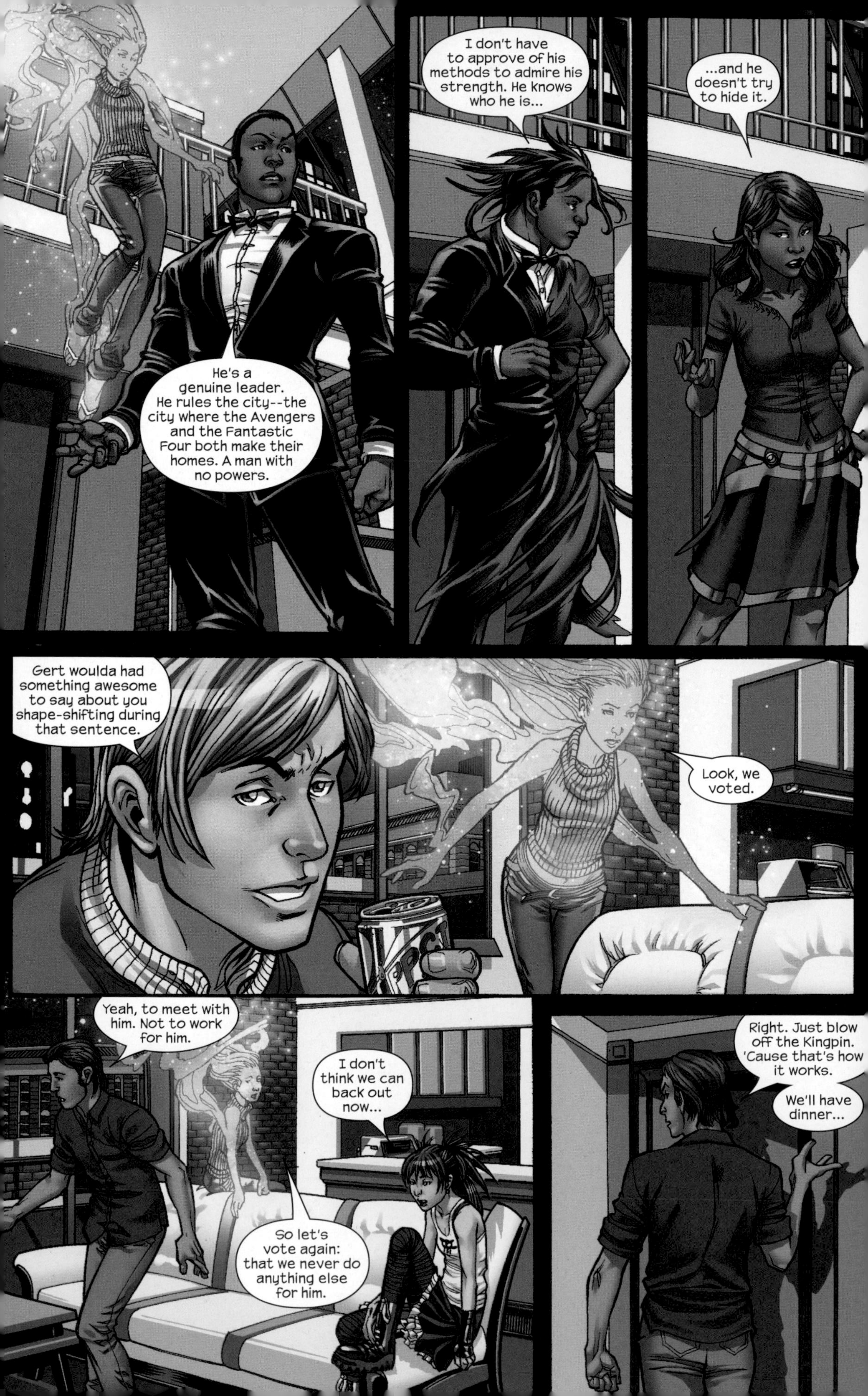
He's a genuine leader. He rules the city--the city where the Avengers and the Fantastic Four both make their homes. A man with no powers.
I don't have to approve of his methods to admire his strength. He knows who he is...
...and he doesn't try to hide it.
Gert woulda had something awesome to say about you shape-shifting during that sentence.
Look, we voted.
Yeah, to meet with him. Not to work for him.
I don't think we can back out now...
So let's vote again: that we never do anything else for him.
Right. Just blow off the Kingpin. 'Cause that's how it works.
We'll have dinner...

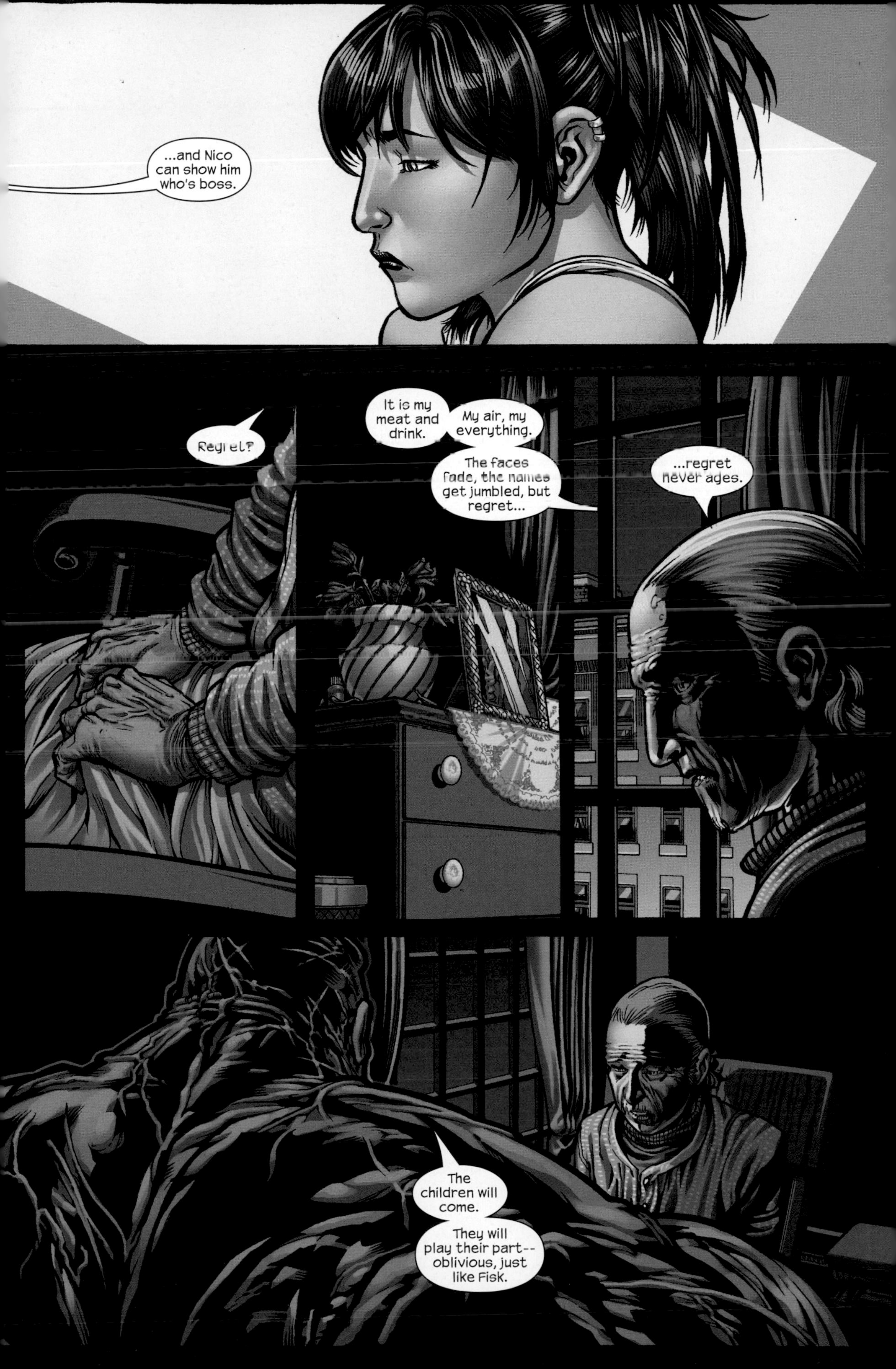
...and Nico can show him who's boss.
Regret?
It is my meat and drink.
My air, my everything.
The faces fade, the names get jumbled, but regret...
...regret never ages.
The children will come.
They will play their part-- oblivious, just like Fisk.

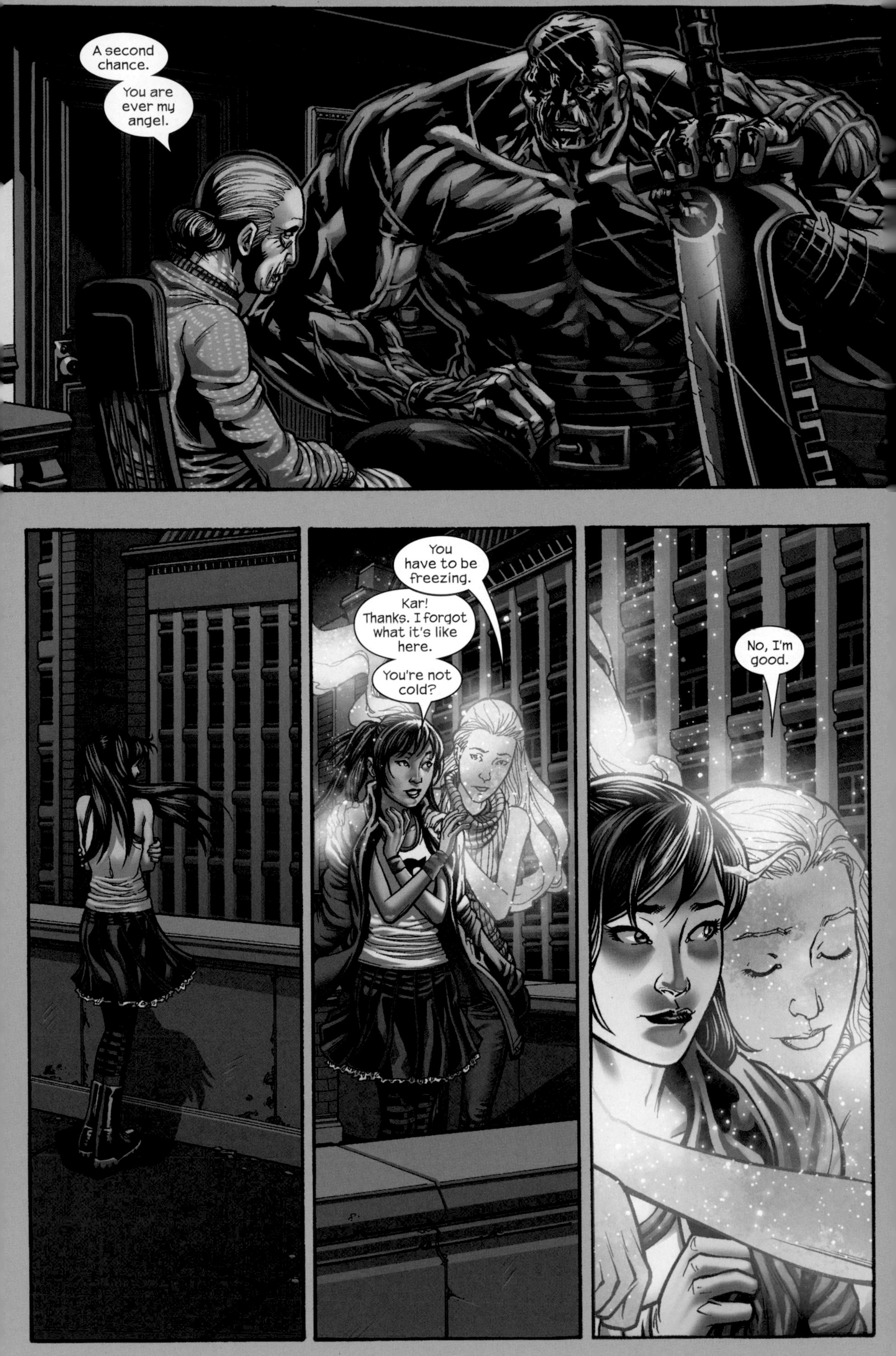
A second chance.
You are ever my angel.
You have to be freezing.
Kar! Thanks. I forgot what it's like here.
You're not cold?
No, I'm good.

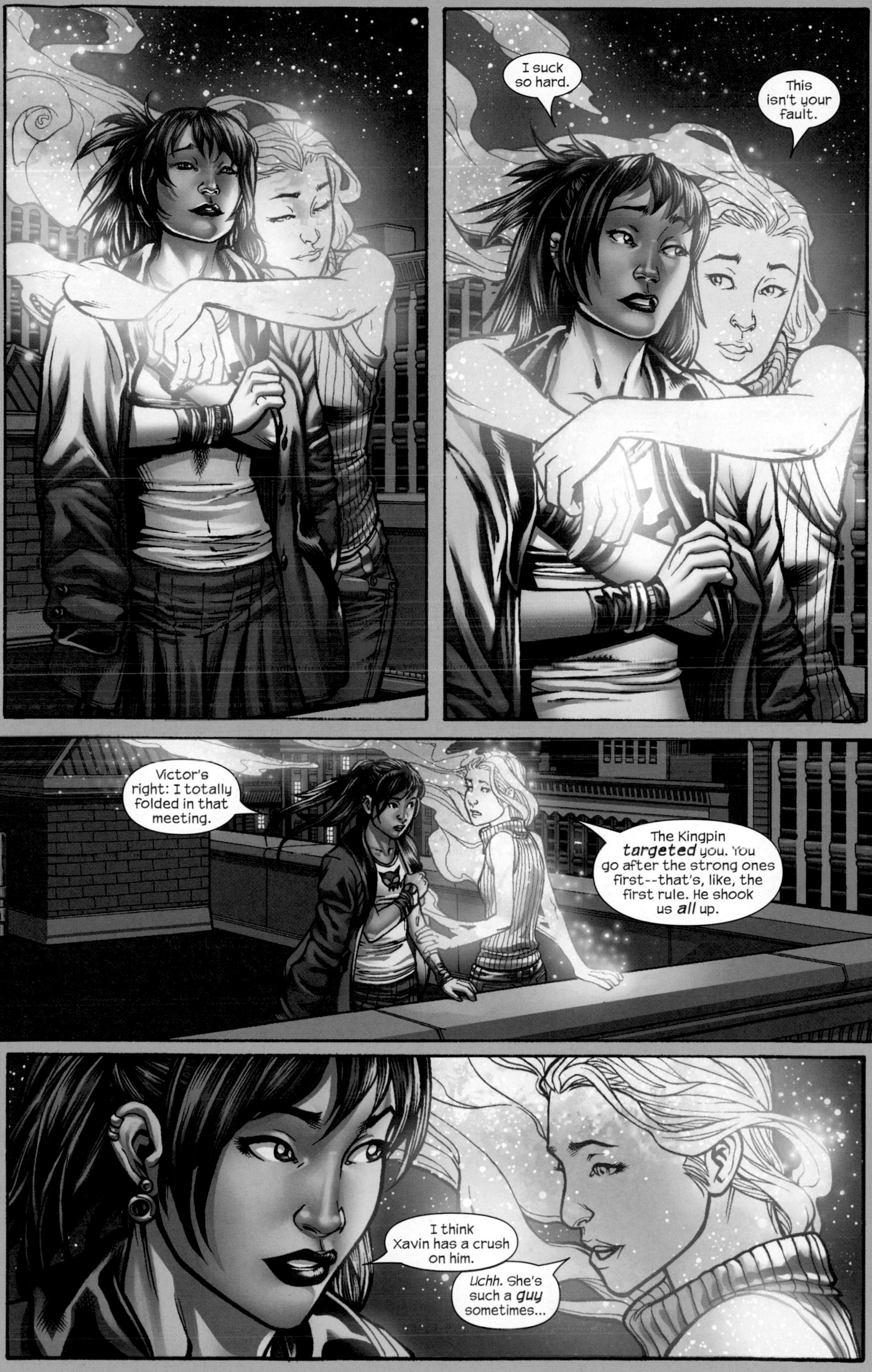
I suck so hard.
This isn't your fault.
Victor's right: I totally folded in that meeting.
The Kingpin *targeted* you. You go after the strong ones first--that's, like, the first rule. He shook us *all* up.
I think Xavin has a crush on him.
Uchh. She's such a *guy* sometimes...

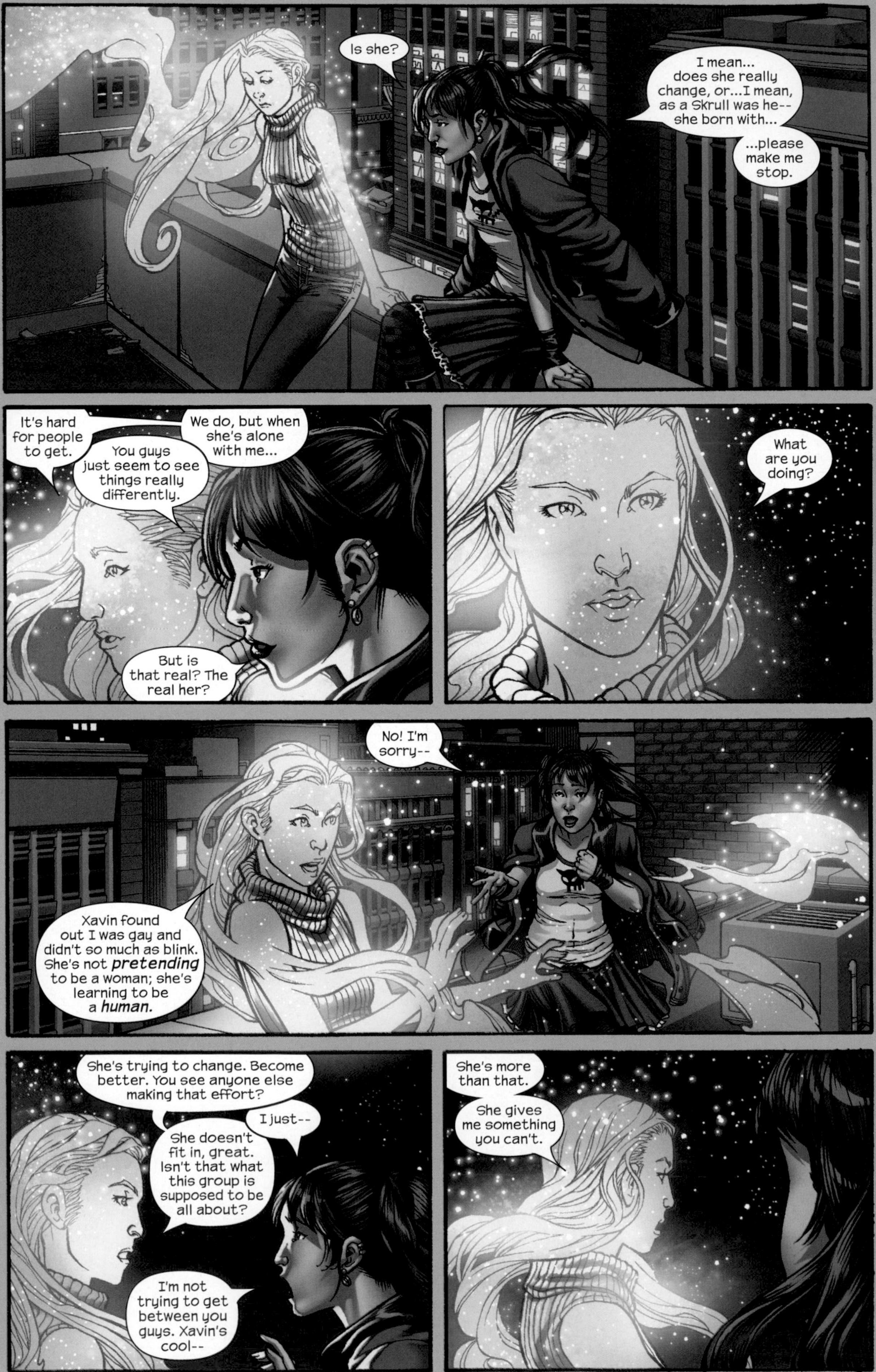
Is she?
I mean... does she really change, or...I mean, as a Skrull was he--she born with...
...please make me stop.
It's hard for people to get.
You guys just seem to see things really differently.
We do, but when she's alone with me...
But is that real? The real her?
What are you doing?
No! I'm sorry--
Xavin found out I was gay and didn't so much as blink. She's not *pretending* to be a woman; she's learning to be a *human.*
She's trying to change. Become better. You see anyone else making that effort?
I just--
She doesn't fit in, great. Isn't that what this group is supposed to be all about?
I'm not trying to get between you guys. Xavin's cool--
She's more than that.
She gives me something you can't.

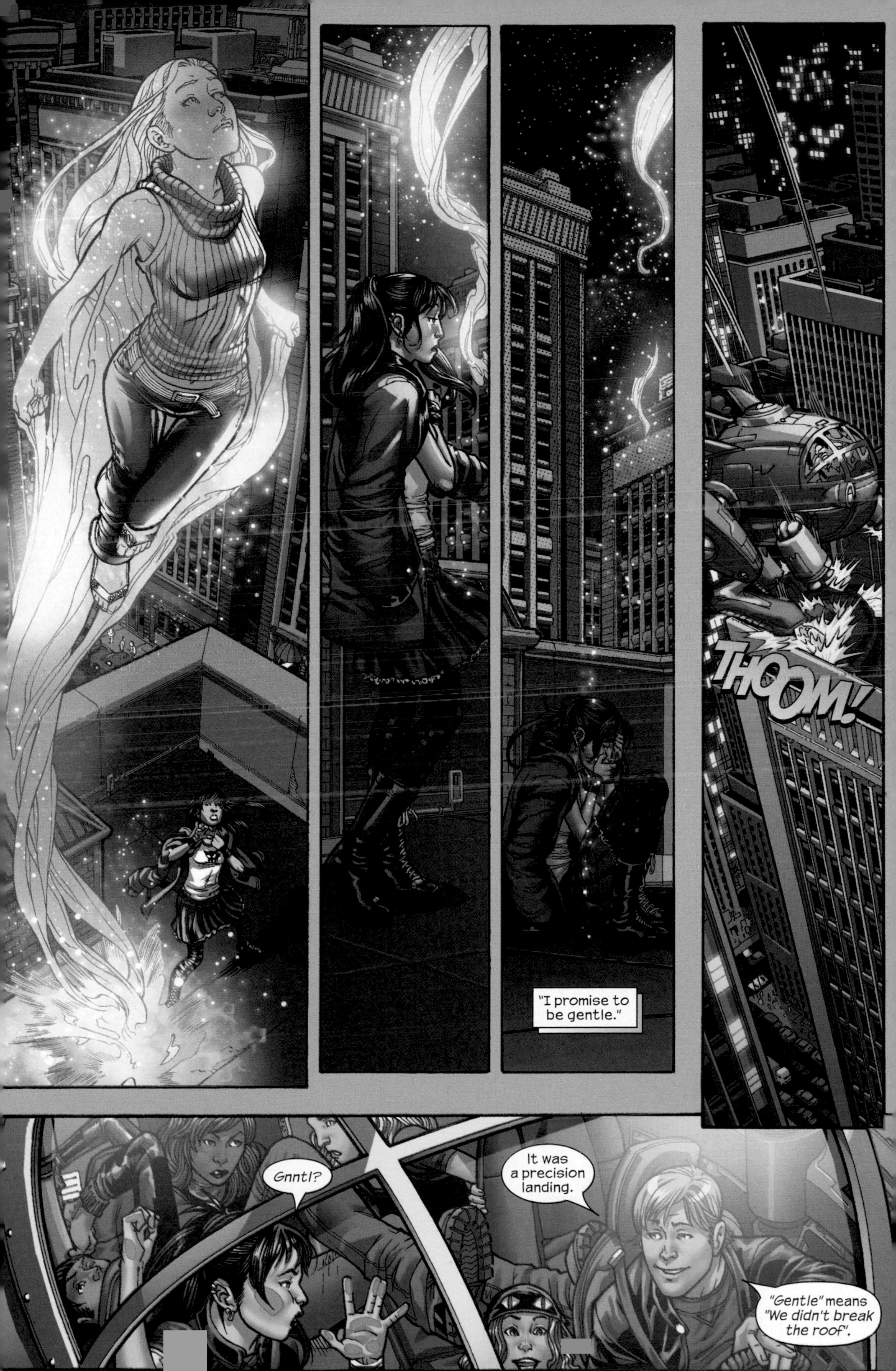
"I promise to be gentle."
THOOM!
Gnntl?
It was a precision landing.
"Gentle" means "We didn't break the roof".

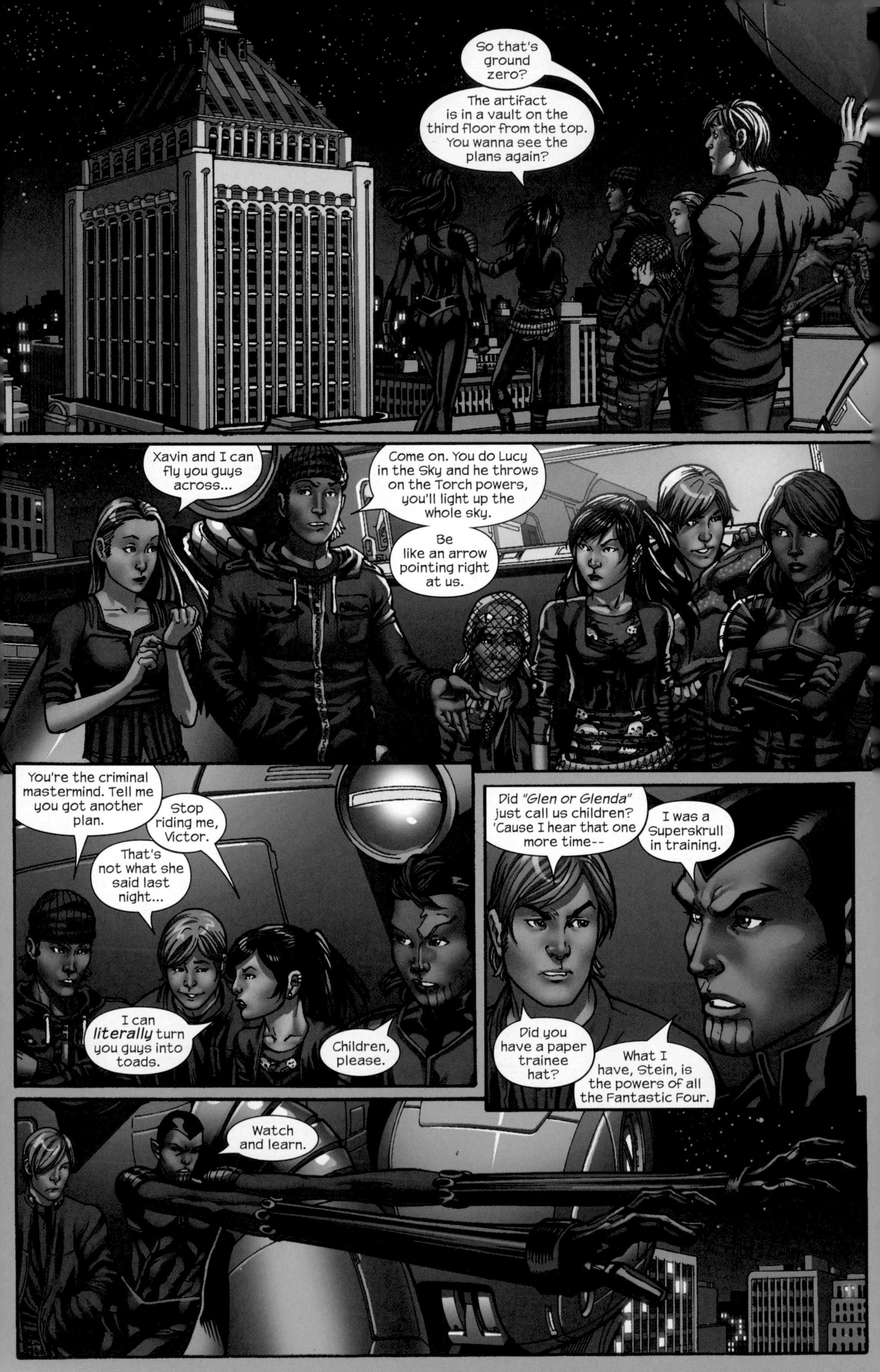
So that's ground zero?
The artifact is in a vault on the third floor from the top. You wanna see the plans again?
Xavin and I can fly you guys across...
Come on. You do Lucy in the Sky and he throws on the Torch powers, you'll light up the whole sky.
Be like an arrow pointing right at us.
You're the criminal mastermind. Tell me you got another plan.
Stop riding me, Victor.
That's not what she said last night...
I can *literally* turn you guys into toads.
Children, please.
Did "*Glen or Glenda*" just call us children? 'Cause I hear that one more time--
I was a Superskrull in training.
Did you have a paper trainee hat?
What I have, Stein, is the powers of all the Fantastic Four.
Watch and learn.

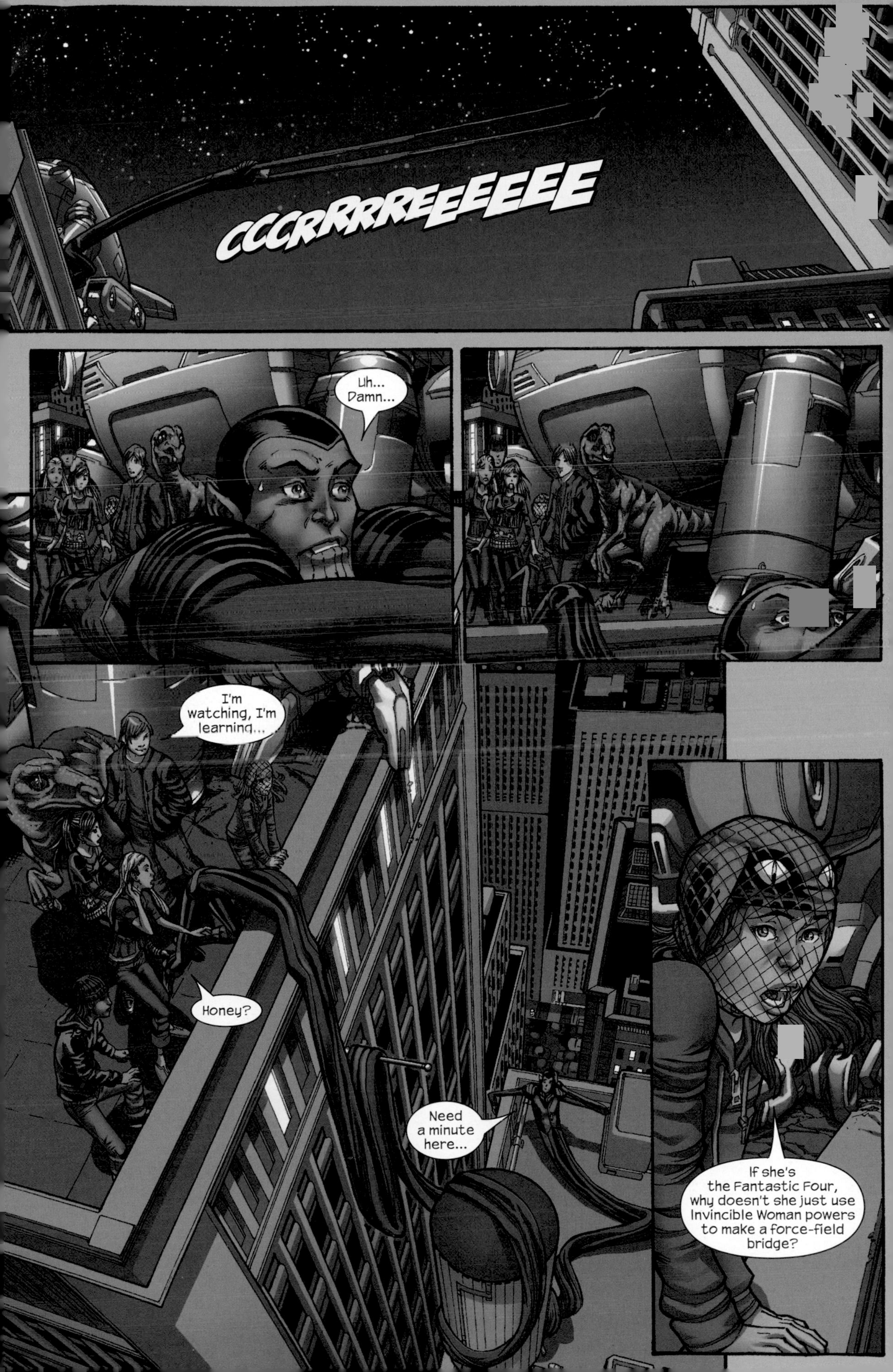
CCCRRRRREEEEEEE
Uh... Damn...
I'm watching, I'm learning...
Honey?
Need a minute here...
If she's the Fantastic Four, why doesn't she just use Invincible Woman powers to make a force-field bridge?

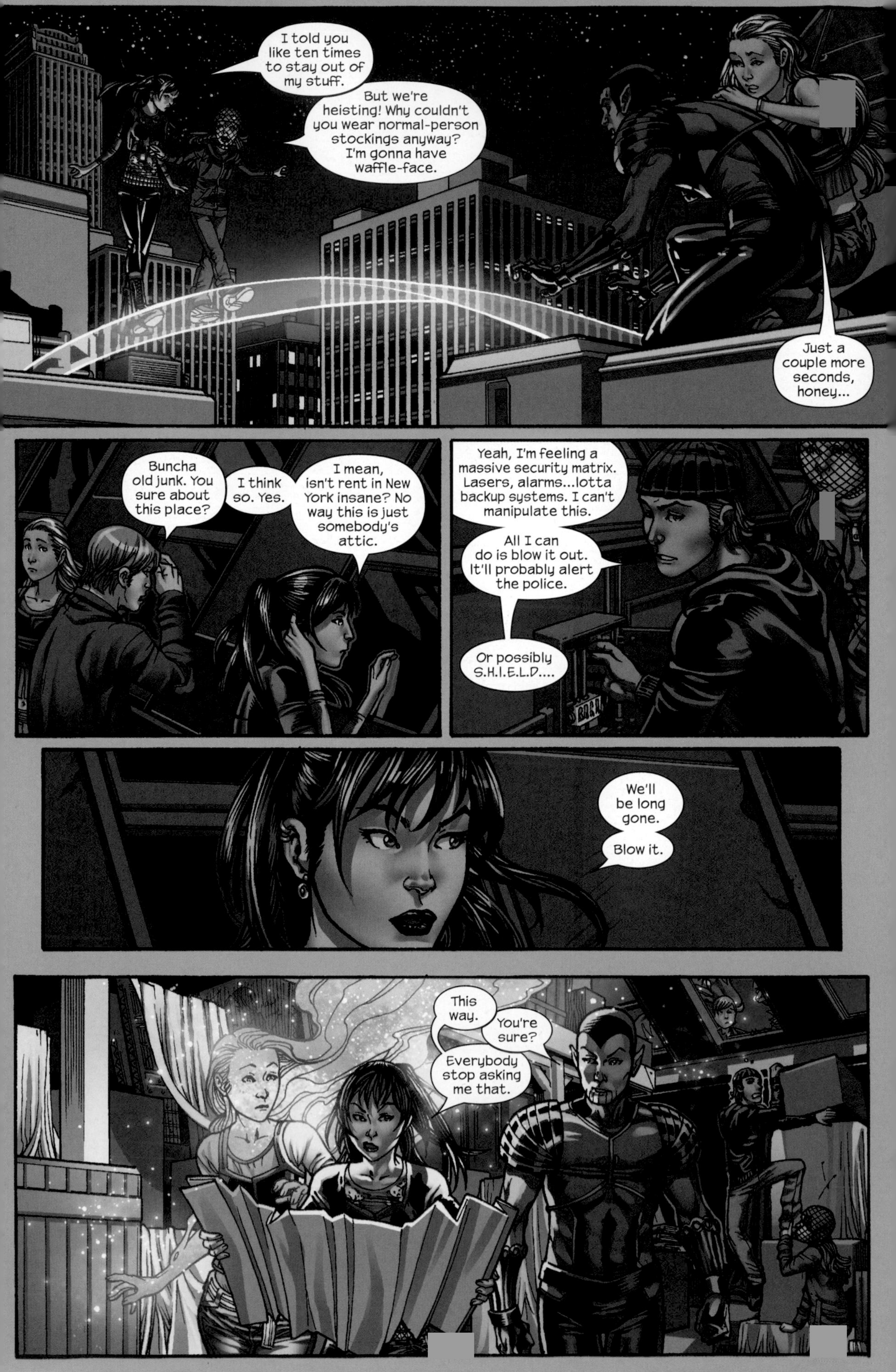
I told you like ten times to stay out of my stuff.
But we're heisting! Why couldn't you wear normal-person stockings anyway? I'm gonna have waffle-face.
Just a couple more seconds, honey...
Buncha old junk. You sure about this place?
I think so. Yes.
I mean, isn't rent in New York insane? No way this is just somebody's attic.
Yeah, I'm feeling a massive security matrix. Lasers, alarms...lotta backup systems. I can't manipulate this.
All I can do is blow it out. It'll probably alert the police.
Or possibly S.H.I.E.L.D....
We'll be long gone.
Blow it.
This way.
You're sure?
Everybody stop asking me that.

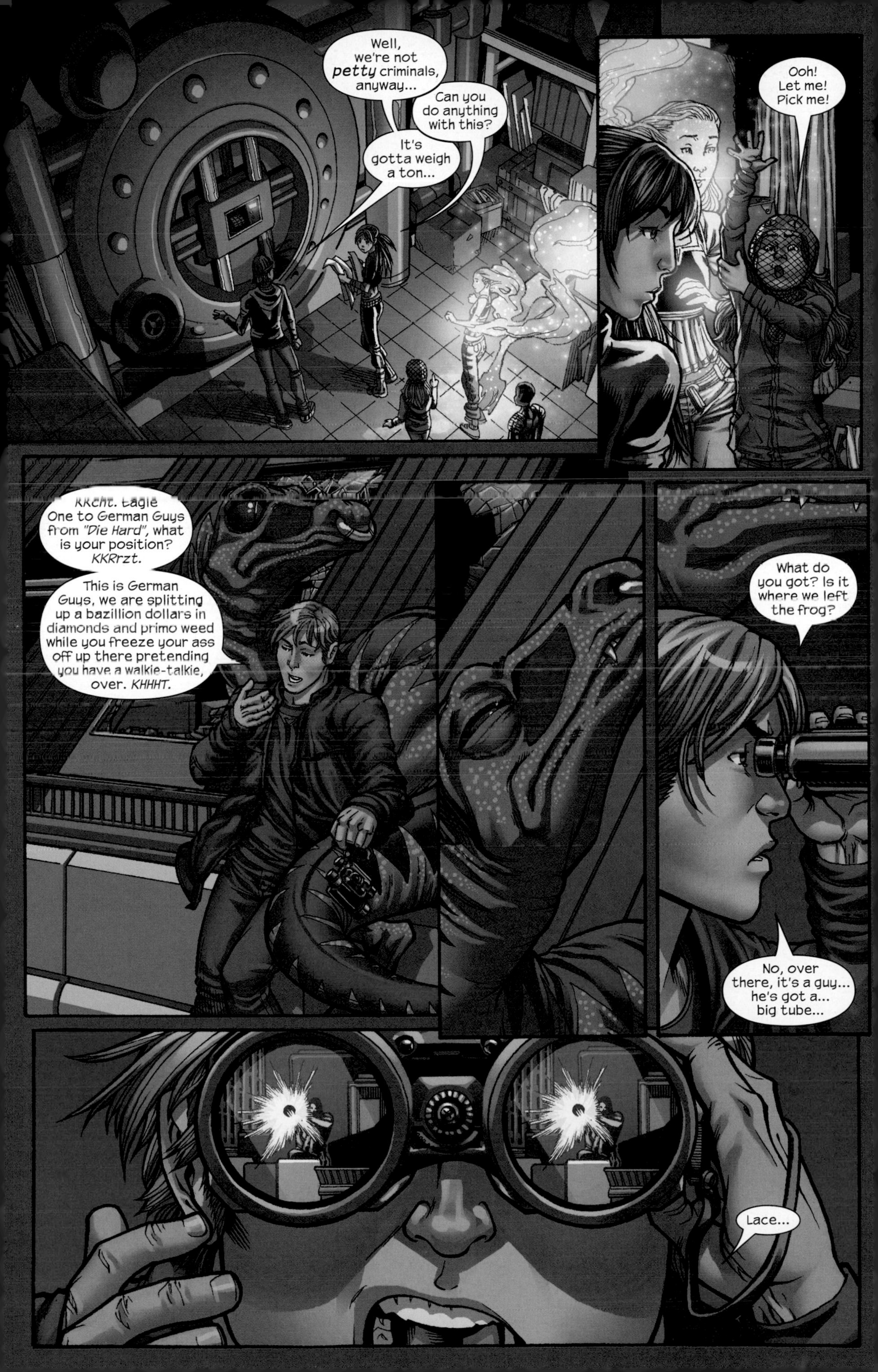

Well, we're not *petty* criminals, anyway...
Can you do anything with this?
It's gotta weigh a ton...
Ooh! Let me! Pick me!
KKcht. Eagle One to German Guys from *"Die Hard"*, what is your position? *KKRrzt.*
This is German Guys, we are splitting up a bazillion dollars in diamonds and primo weed while you freeze your ass off up there pretending you have a walkie-talkie, over. *KHHHT.*
What do you got? Is it where we left the frog?
No, over there, it's a guy... he's got a... big tube...
Lace...

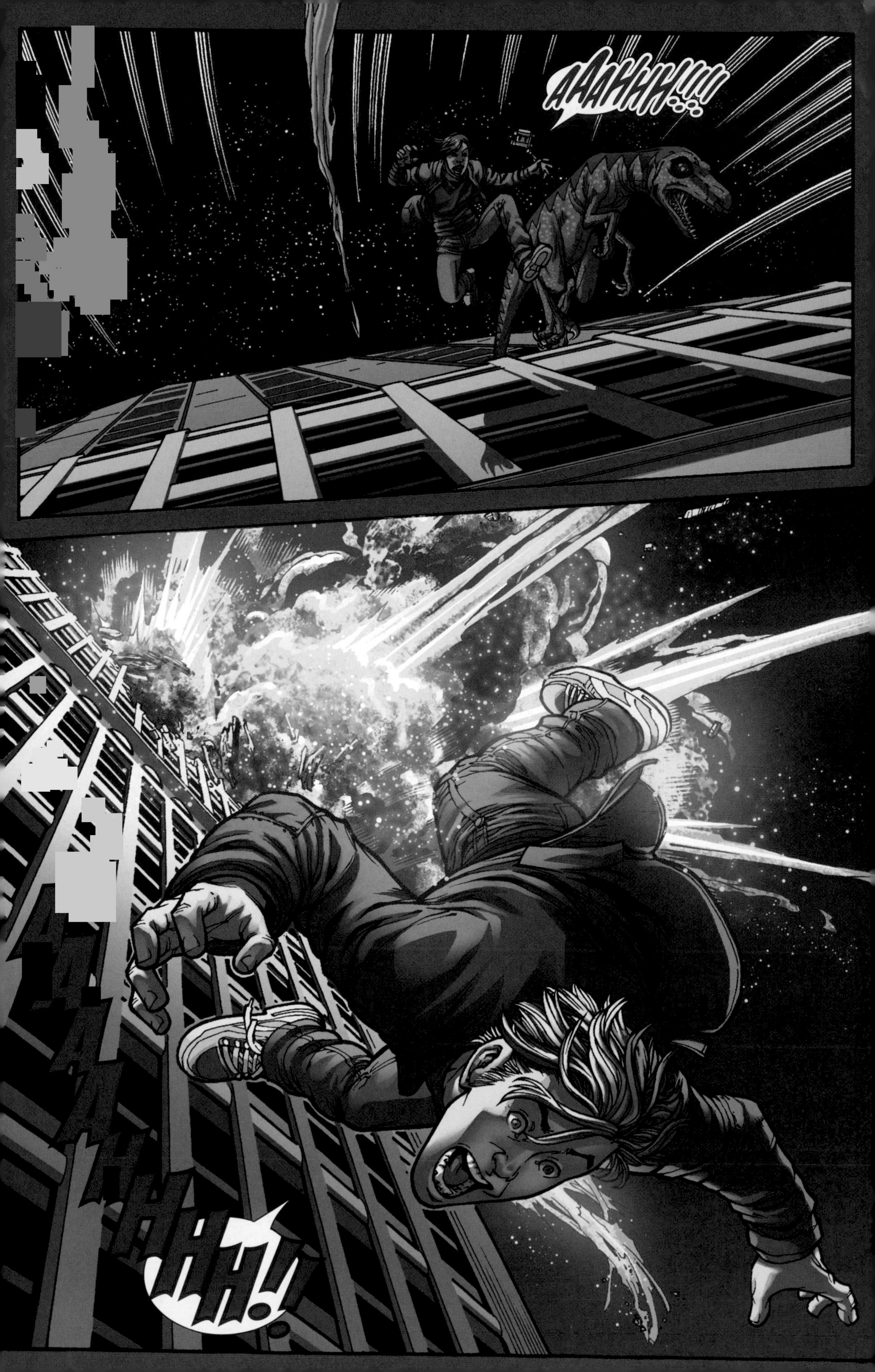
AAAHHH!!!...
AAAHHHH!

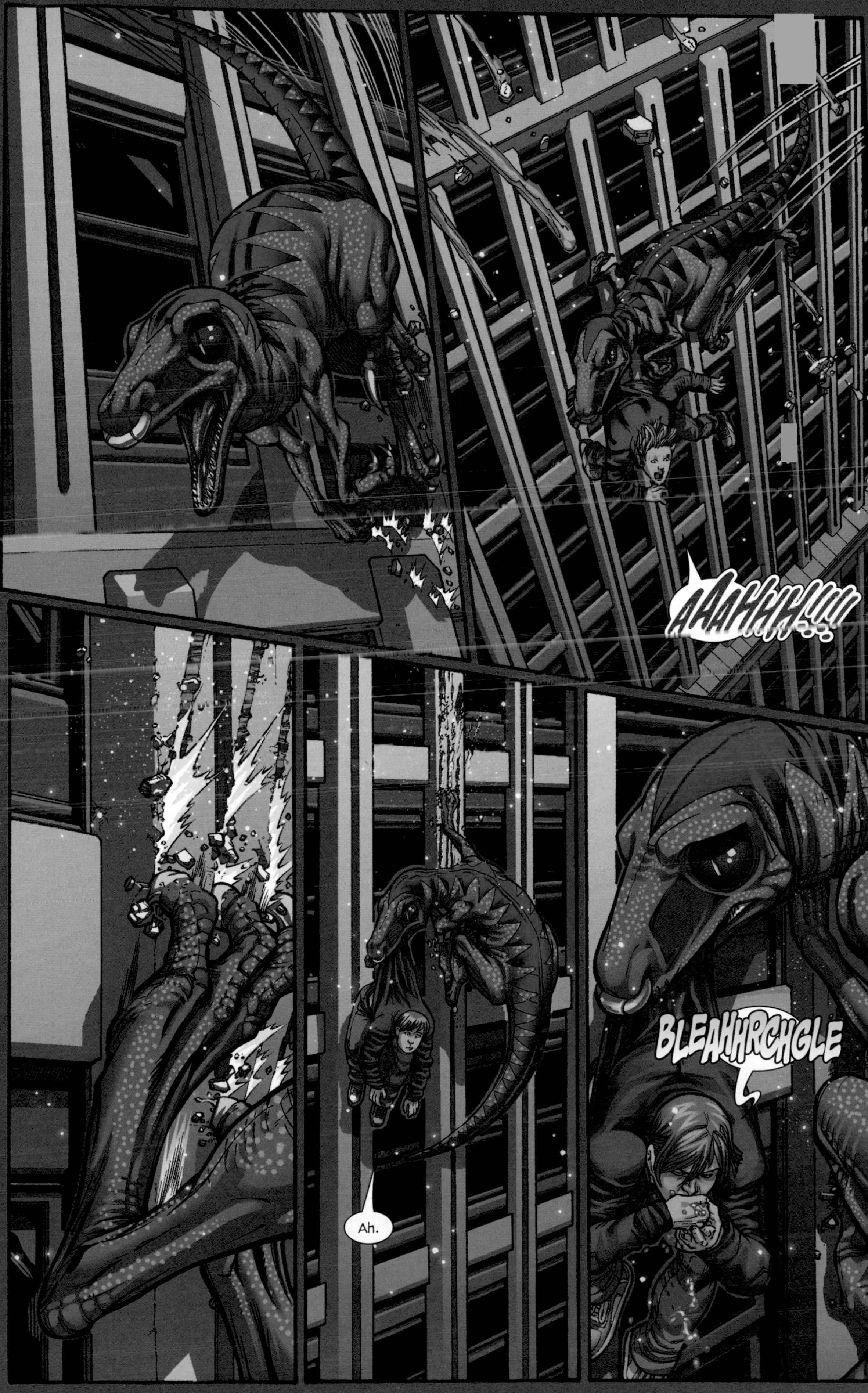
AAAHHHH!!!!
Ah.
BLEAHHRCHGLE

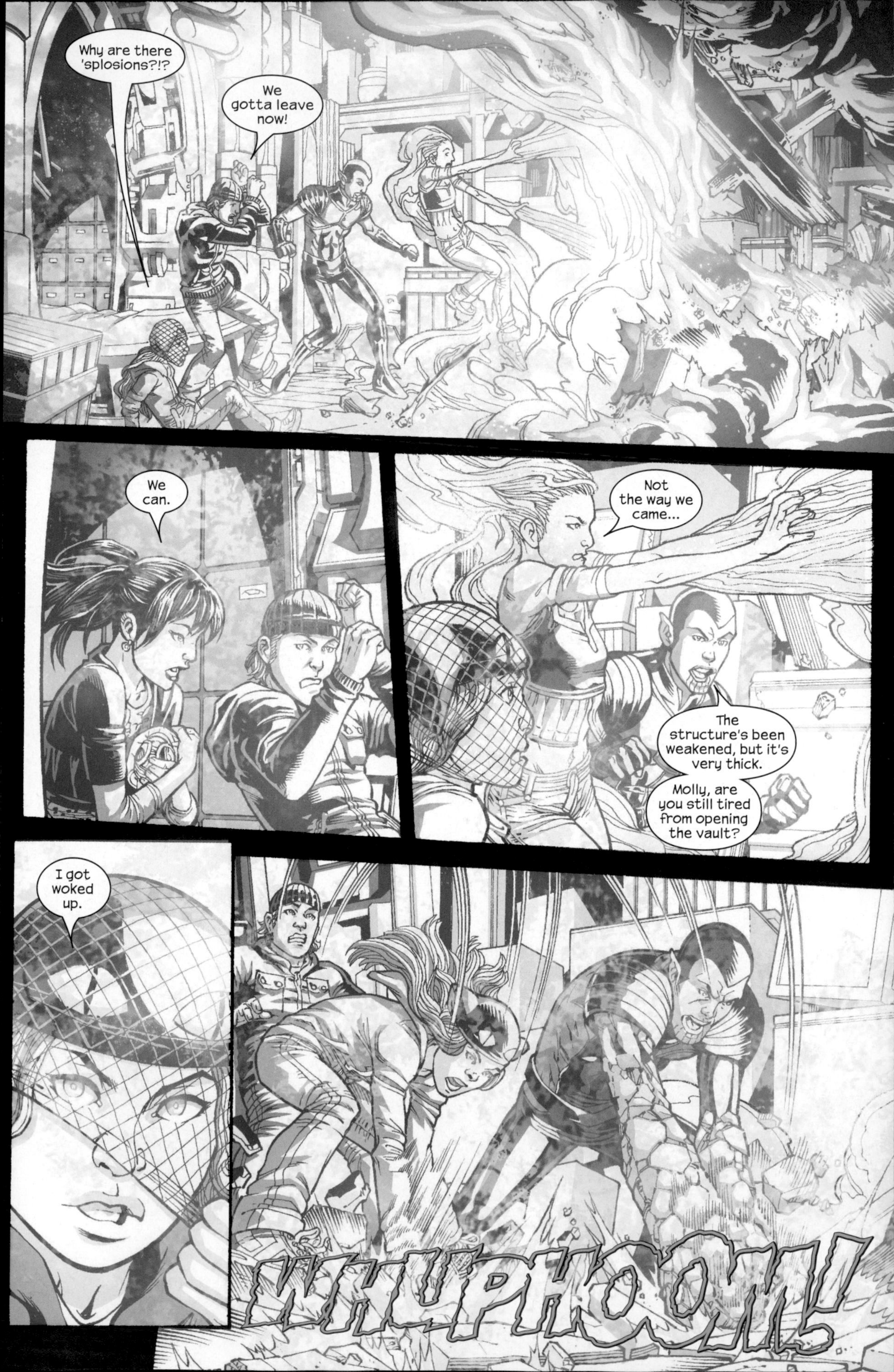
Why are there 'splosions?!?
We gotta leave now!
We can.
Not the way we came...
The structure's been weakened, but it's very thick.
Molly, are you still tired from opening the vault?
I got woked up.
WHUPHOOM!

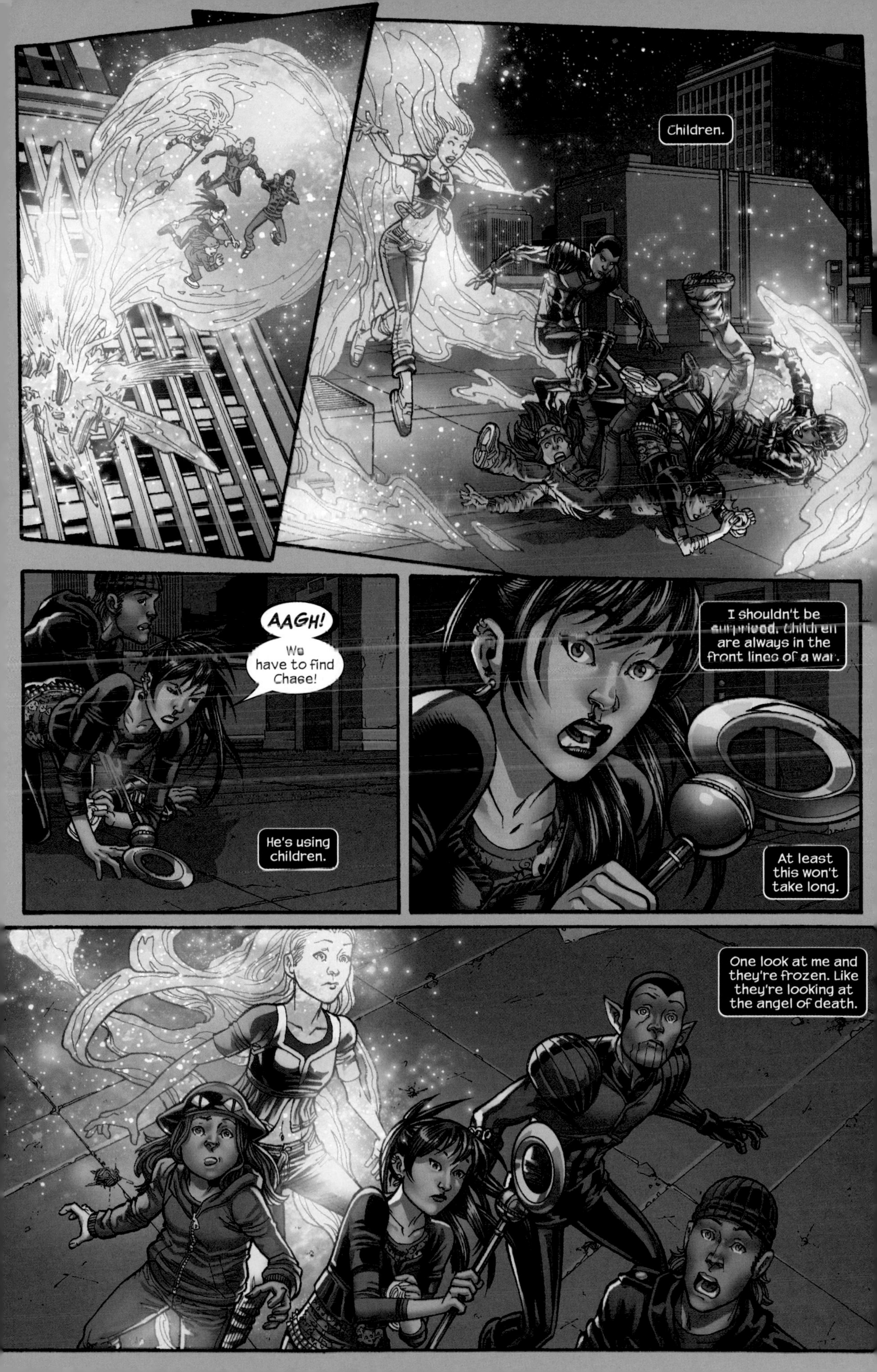
Children.
AAGH!
We have to find Chase!
He's using children.
I shouldn't be surprised. Children are always in the front lines of a war.
At least this won't take long.
One look at me and they're frozen. Like they're looking at the angel of death.

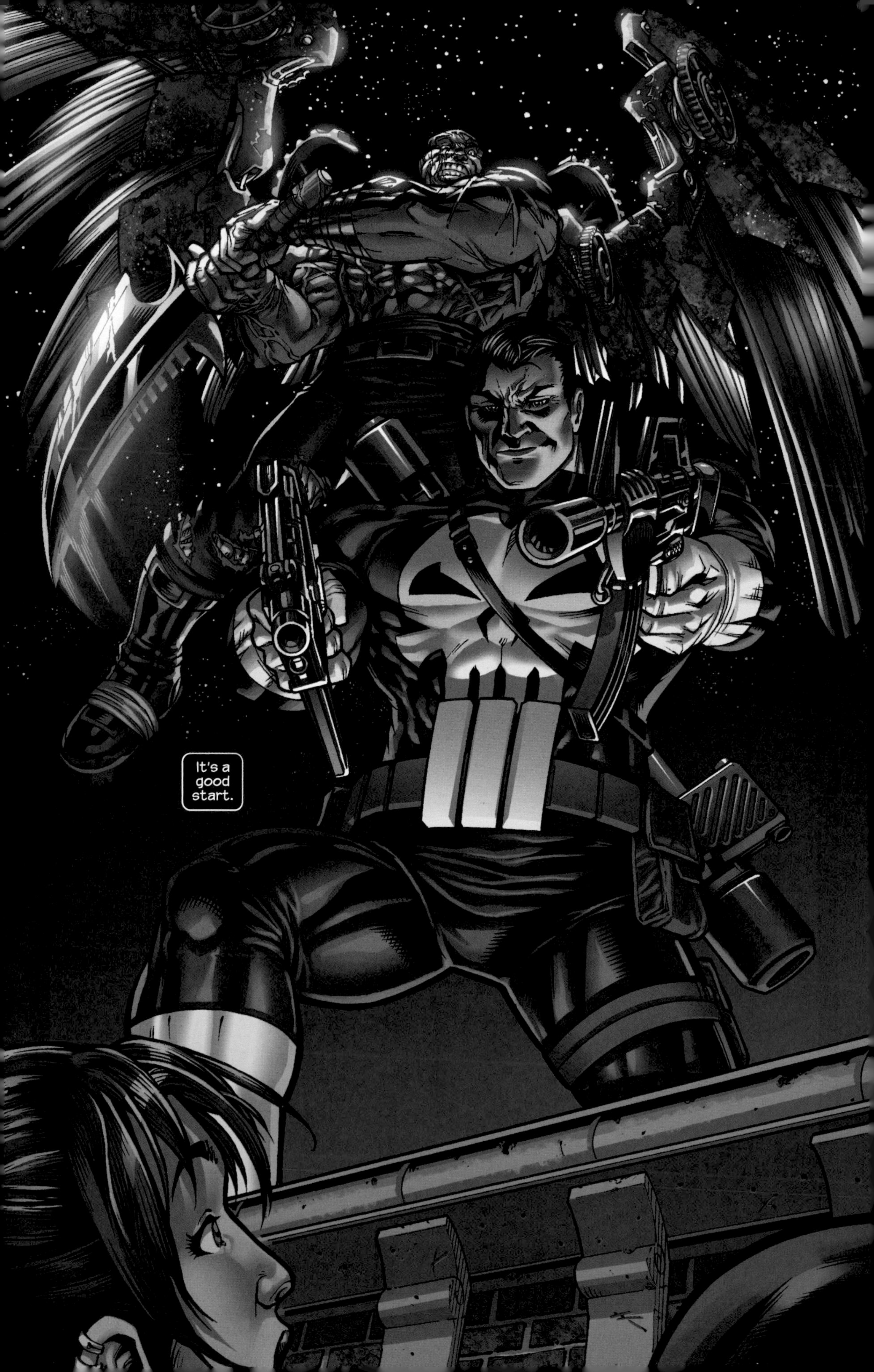
It's a good start.

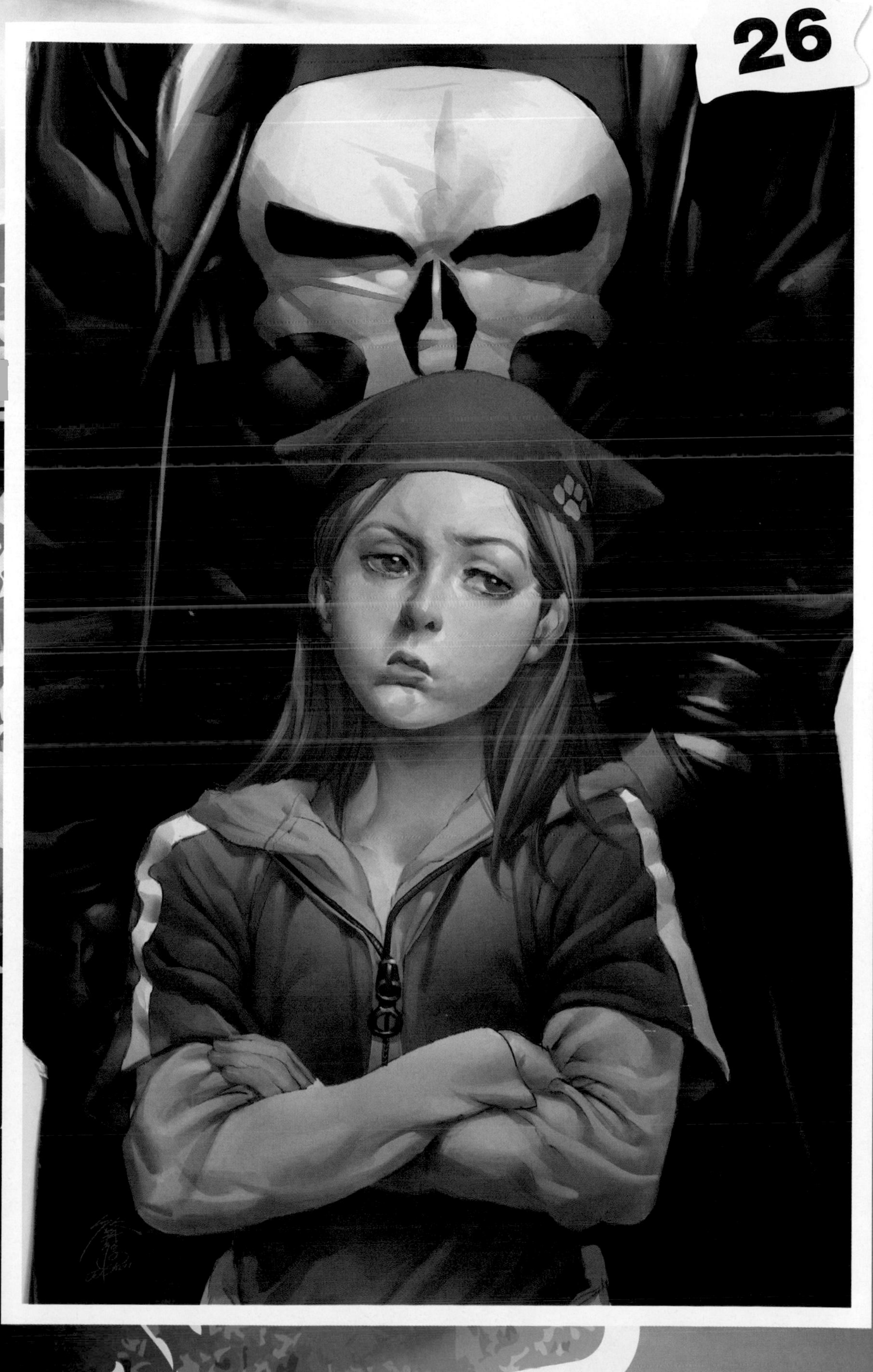
26

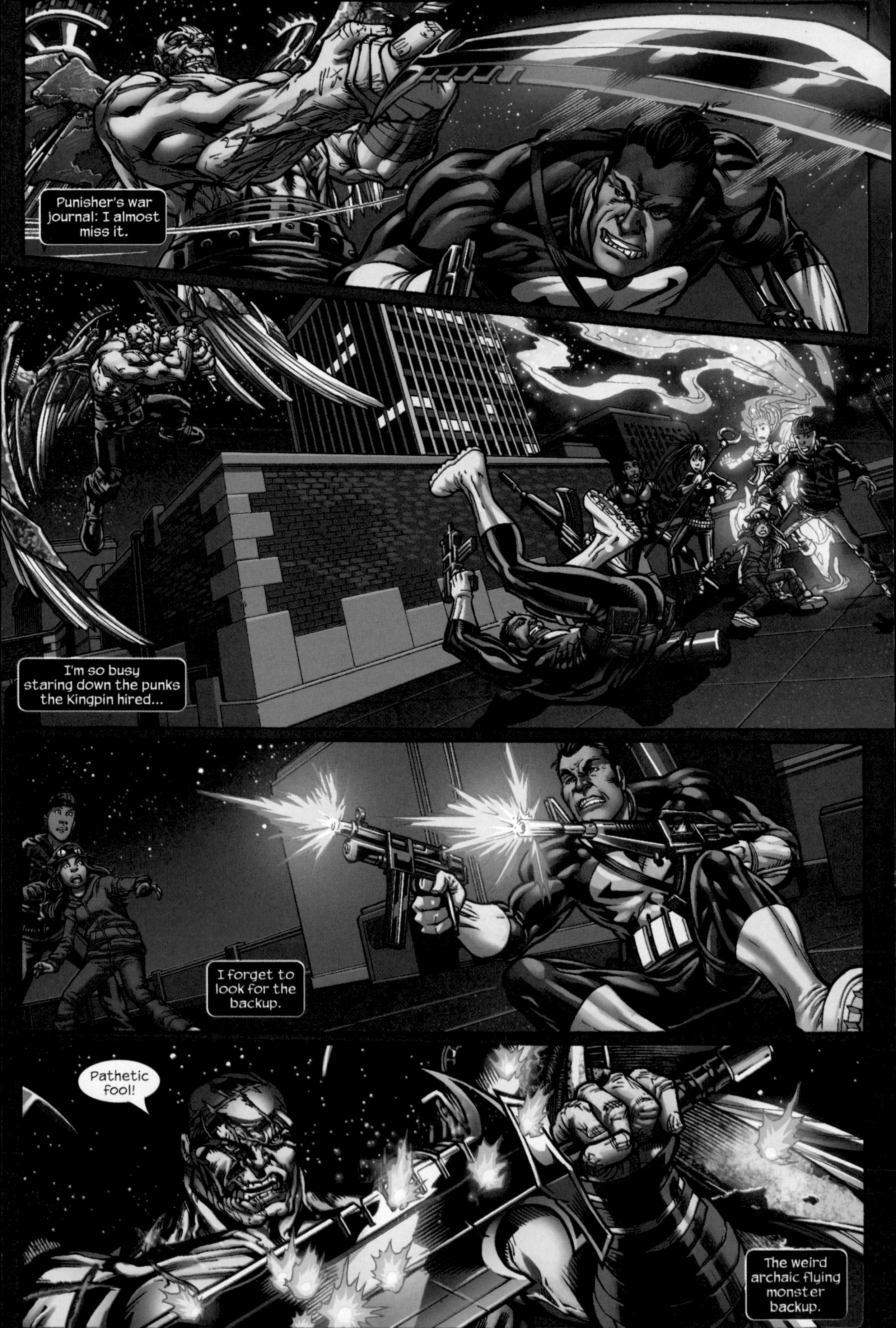

Punisher's war journal: I almost miss it.
I'm so busy staring down the punks the Kingpin hired...
I forget to look for the backup.
Pathetic fool!
The weird archaic flying monster backup.

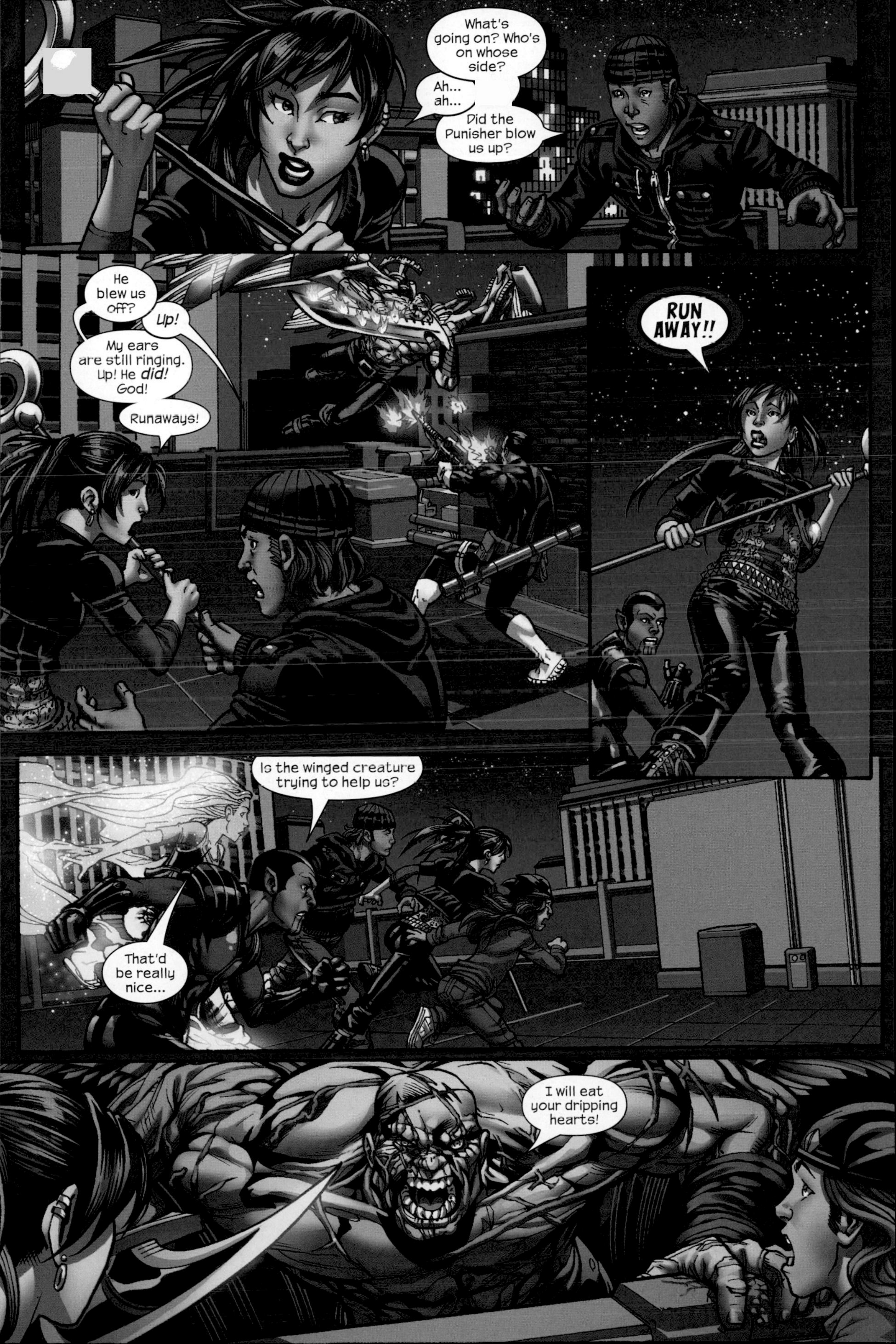

What's going on? Who's on whose side?
Ah... ah...
Did the Punisher blow us up?
He blew us off?
Up!
My ears are still ringing. Up! He *did!* God!
Runaways!
RUN AWAY!!
Is the winged creature trying to help us?
That'd be really nice...
I will eat your dripping hearts!

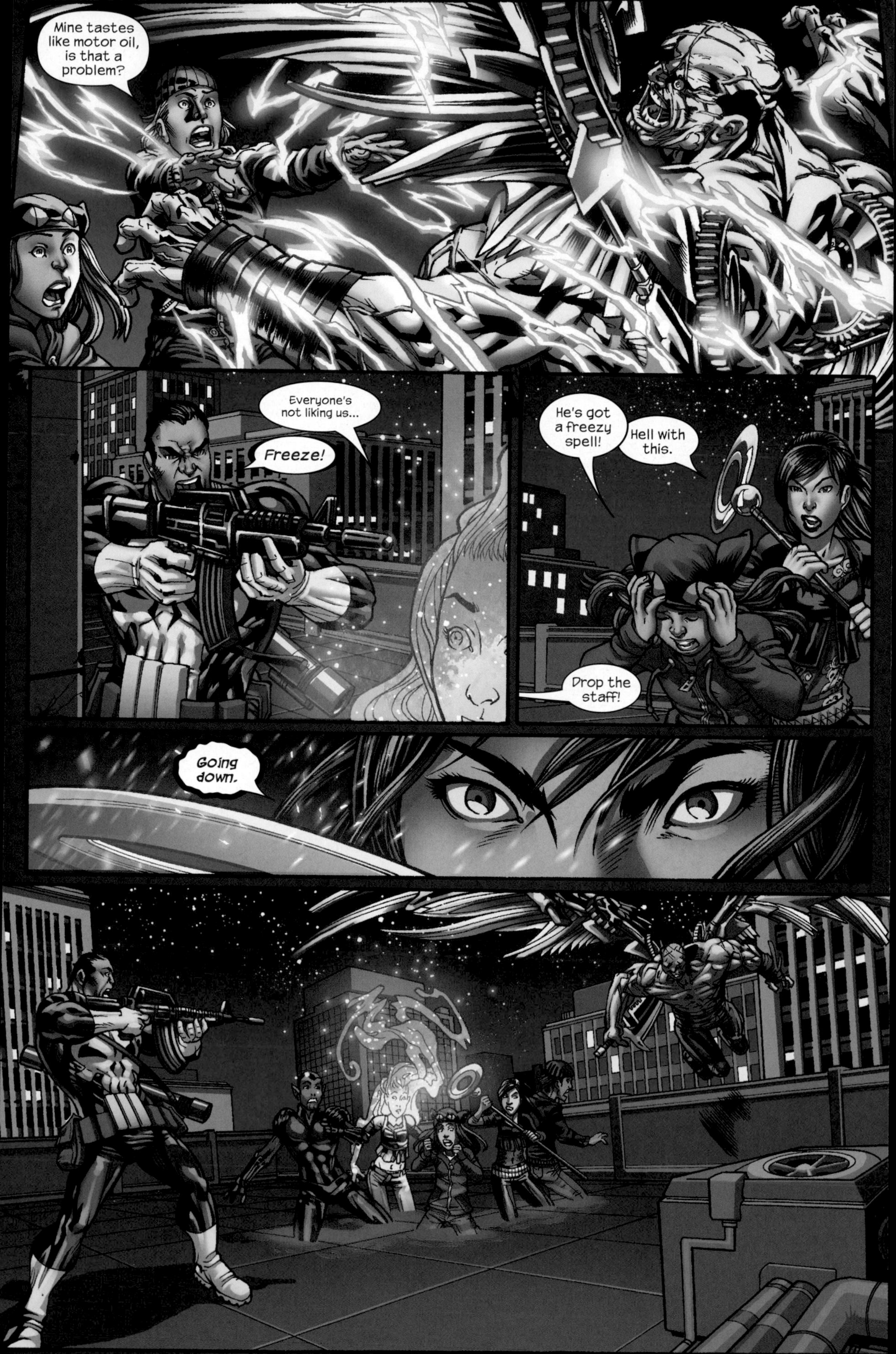

Mine tastes like motor oil, is that a problem?
Everyone's not liking us...
Freeze!
He's got a freezy spell!
Hell with this.
Drop the staff!
Going down.

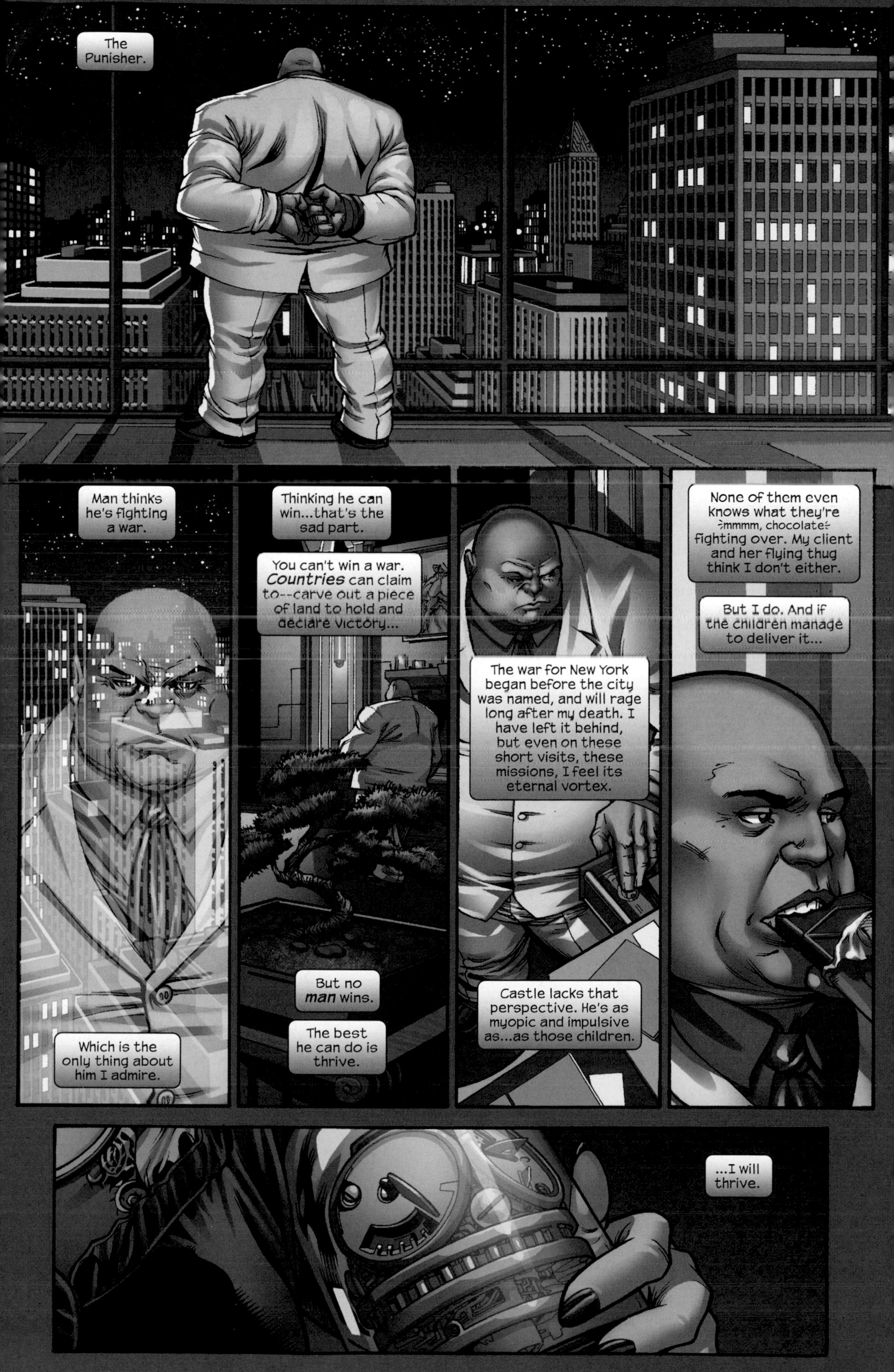

The Punisher.
Man thinks he's fighting a war.
Thinking he can win...that's the sad part.
You can't win a war. *Countries* can claim to--carve out a piece of land to hold and declare victory...
The war for New York began before the city was named, and will rage long after my death. I have left it behind, but even on these short visits, these missions, I feel its eternal vortex.
None of them even knows what they're ÷mmmm, chocolate÷ fighting over. My client and her flying thug think I don't either.
But I do. And if the children manage to deliver it...
Which is the only thing about him I admire.
But no *man* wins.
The best he can do is thrive.
Castle lacks that perspective. He's as myopic and impulsive as...as those children.
...I will thrive.

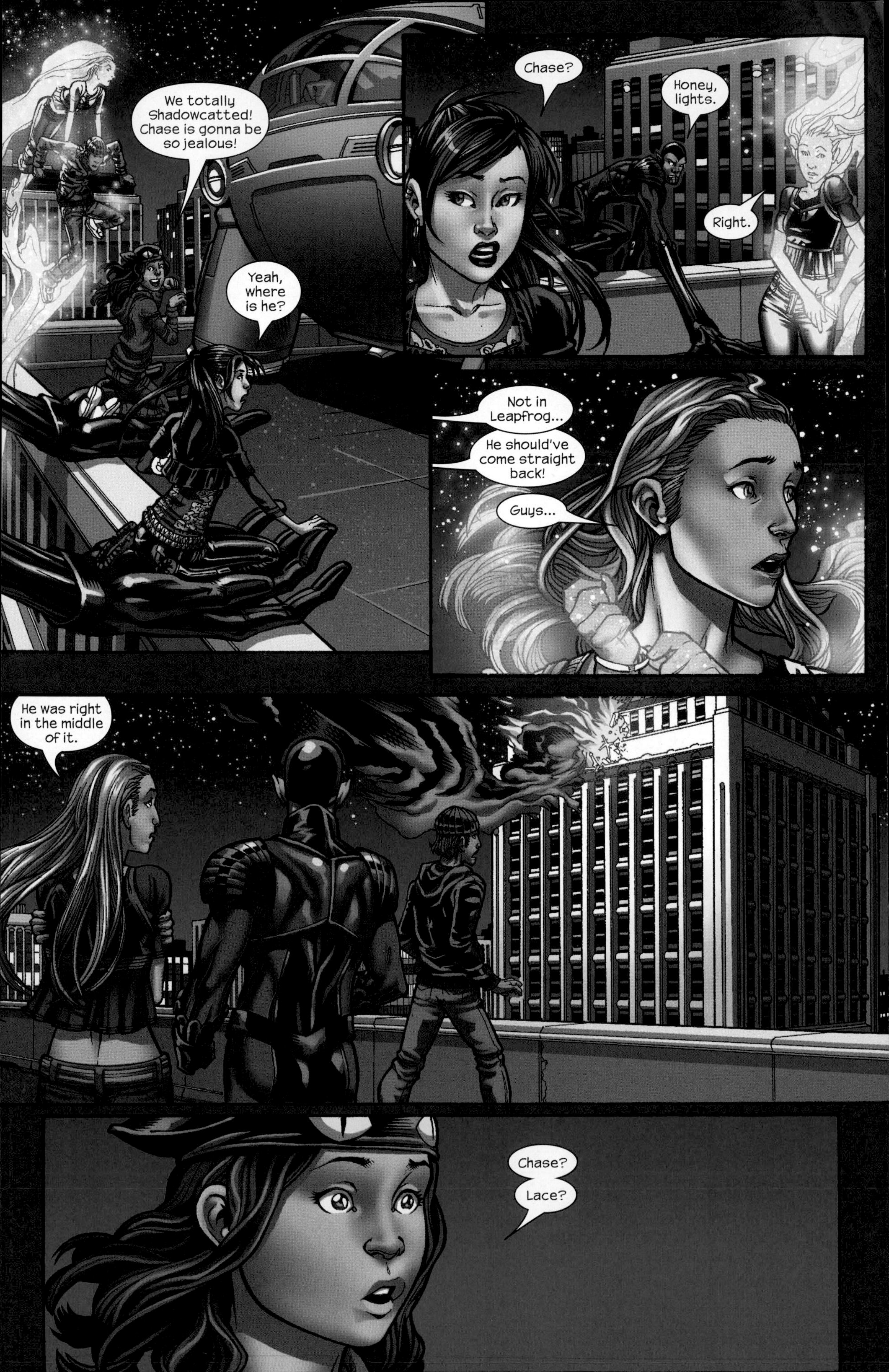

We totally Shadowcatted! Chase is gonna be so jealous!
Yeah, where is he?
Chase?
Honey, lights.
Right.
Not in Leapfrog...
He should've come straight back!
Guys...
He was right in the middle of it.
Chase?
Lace?

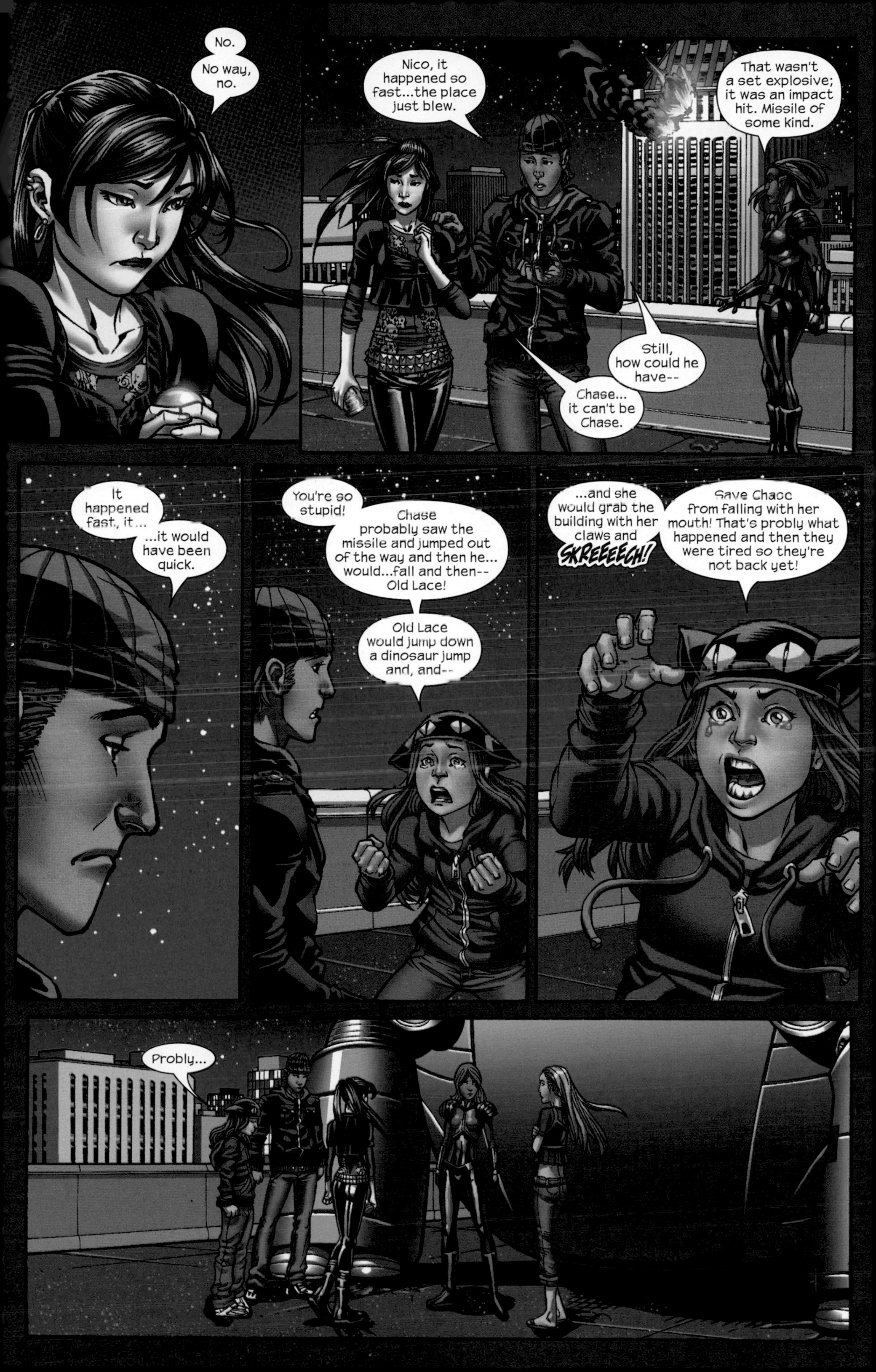
No.
No way, no.
Nico, it happened so fast...the place just blew.
That wasn't a set explosive; it was an impact hit. Missile of some kind.
Still, how could he have--
Chase... it can't be Chase.
It happened fast, it...
...it would have been quick.
You're so stupid!
Chase probably saw the missile and jumped out of the way and then he... would...fall and then-- Old Lace!
Old Lace would jump down a dinosaur jump and, and--
...and she would grab the building with her claws and
SKREEEEGH!
Save Chase from falling with her mouth! That's probly what happened and then they were tired so they're not back yet!
Probly...

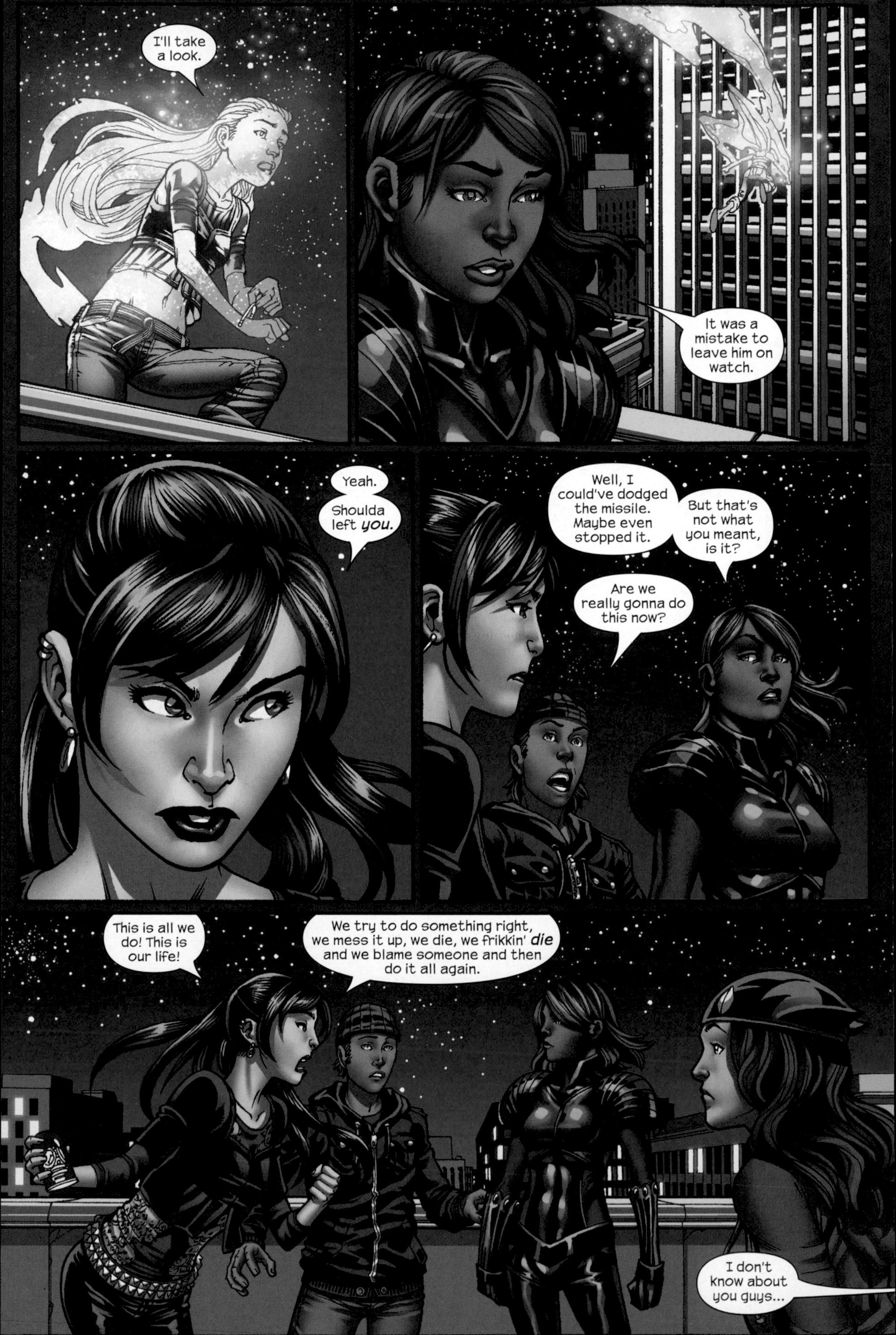
I'll take a look.
It was a mistake to leave him on watch.
Yeah.
Shoulda left *you.*
Well, I could've dodged the missile. Maybe even stopped it.
But that's not what you meant, is it?
Are we really gonna do this now?
This is all we do! This is our life!
We try to do something right, we mess it up, we die, we frikkin' *die* and we blame someone and then do it all again.
I don't know about you guys...

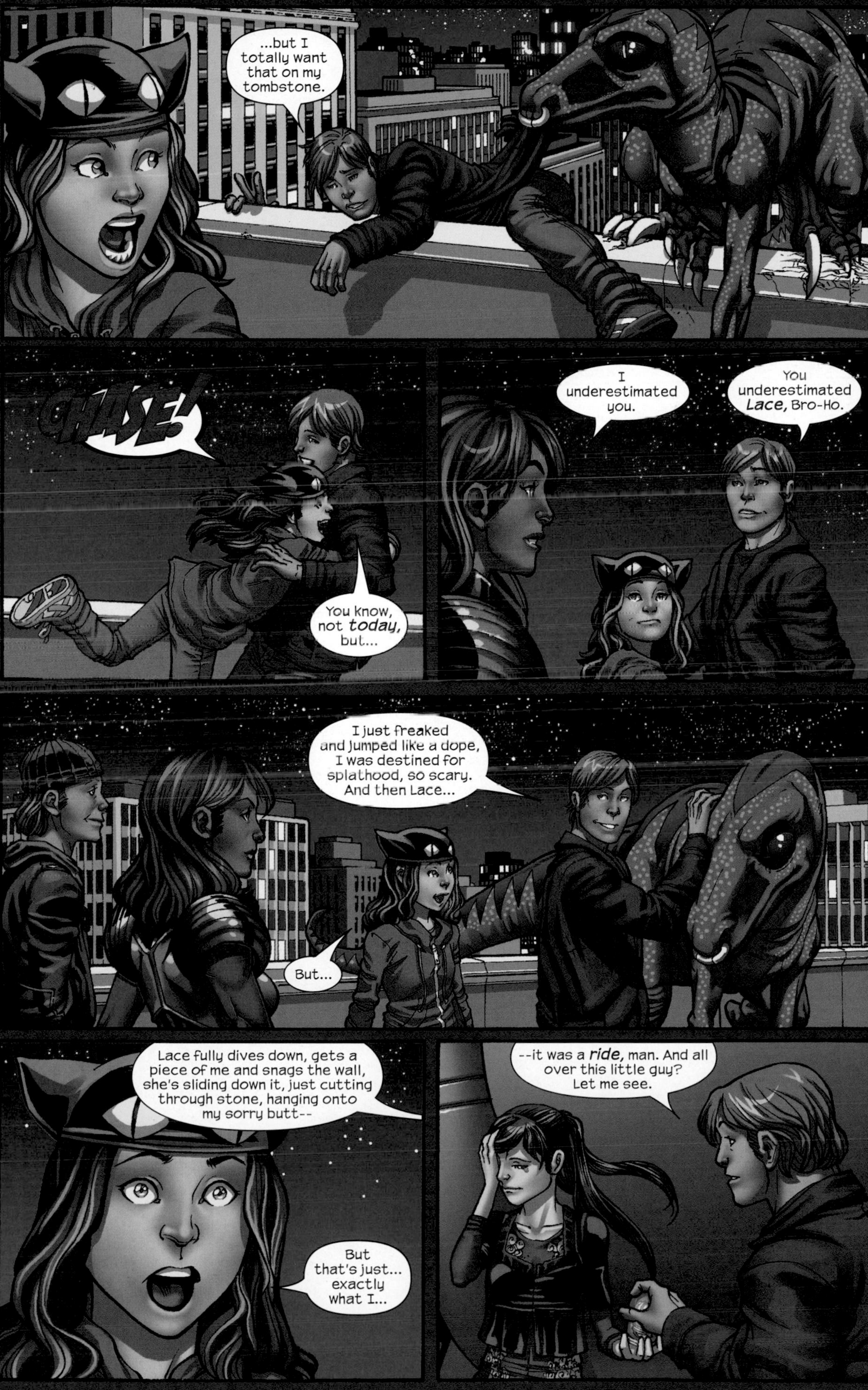
...but I totally want that on my tombstone.
CHASE!
You know, not today, but...
I underestimated you.
You underestimated Lace, Bro-Ho.
I just freaked and jumped like a dope, I was destined for splathood, so scary. And then Lace...
But...
Lace fully dives down, gets a piece of me and snags the wall, she's sliding down it, just cutting through stone, hanging onto my sorry butt--
But that's just... exactly what I...
--it was a ride, man. And all over this little guy? Let me see.

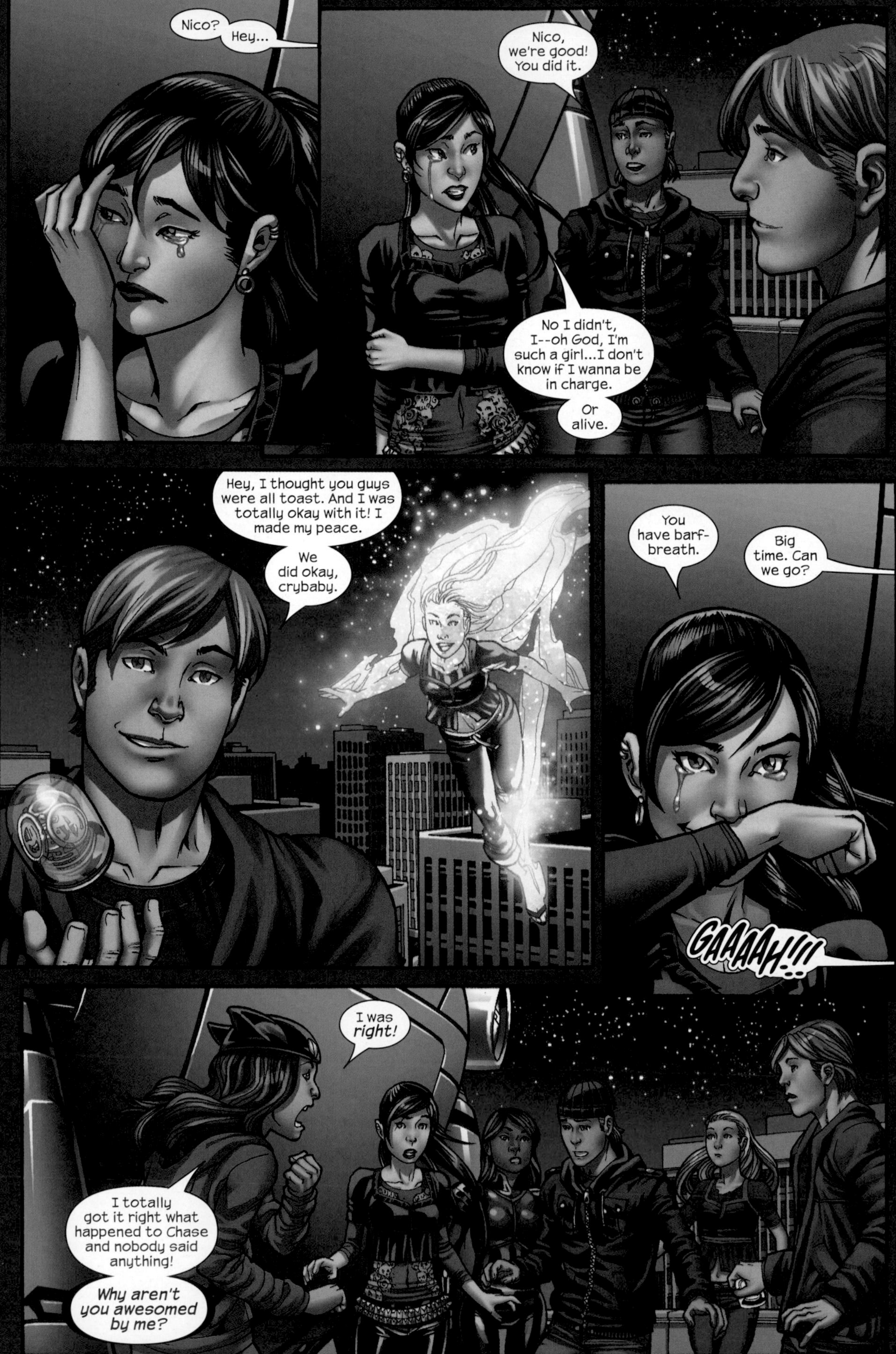
Nico? Hey...
Nico, we're good! You did it.
No I didn't, I--oh God, I'm such a girl...I don't know if I wanna be in charge.
Or alive.
Hey, I thought you guys were all toast. And I was totally okay with it! I made my peace.
We did okay, crybaby.
You have barf-breath.
Big time. Can we go?
GAAAAH!!!
I was *right*!
I totally got it right what happened to Chase and nobody said anything!
Why aren't you awesomed by me?

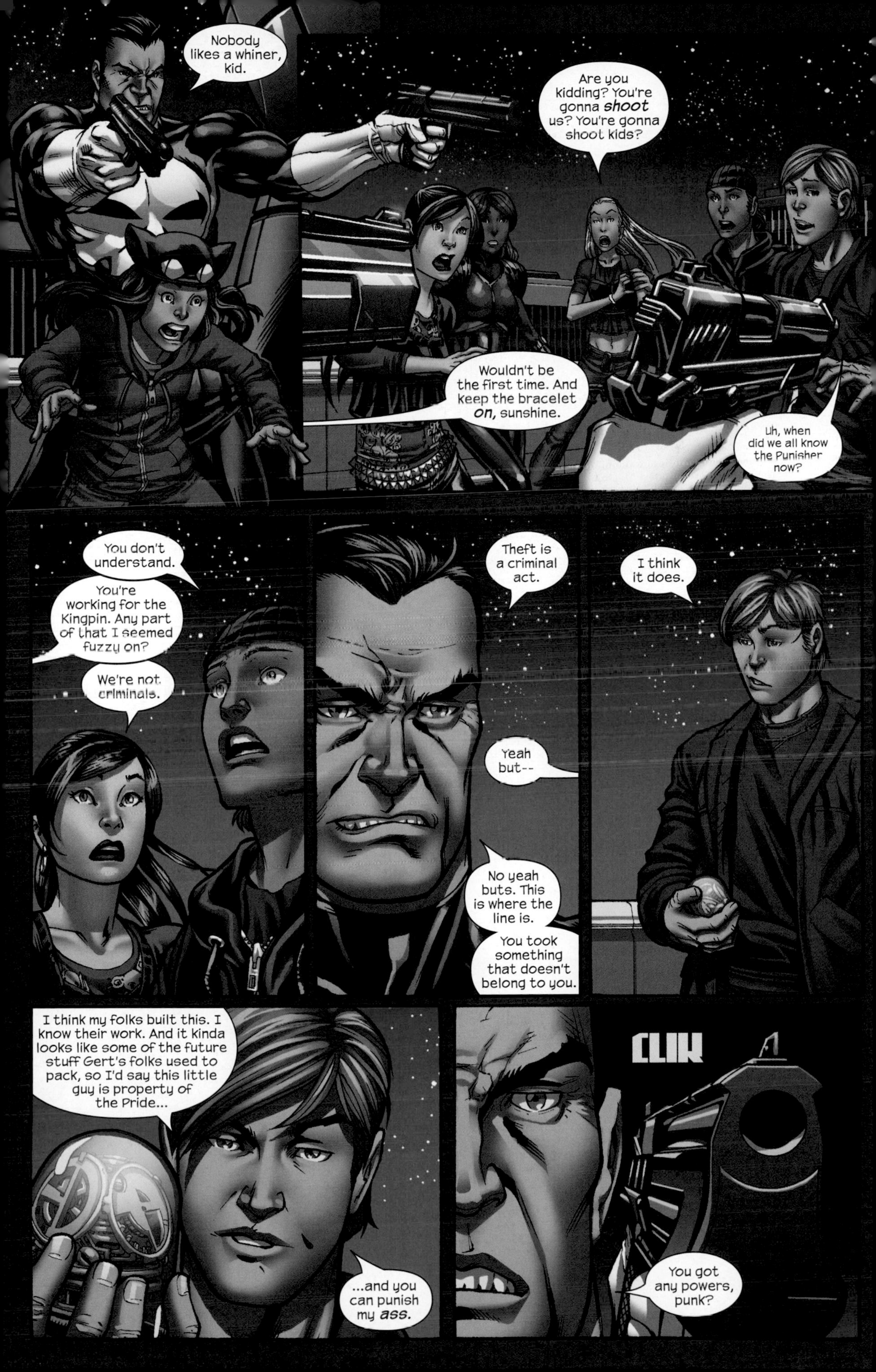
Nobody likes a whiner, kid.
Are you kidding? You're gonna shoot us? You're gonna shoot kids?
Wouldn't be the first time. And keep the bracelet on, sunshine.
Uh, when did we all know the Punisher now?
You don't understand.
You're working for the Kingpin. Any part of that I seemed fuzzy on?
We're not criminals.
Theft is a criminal act.
Yeah but--
No yeah buts. This is where the line is.
You took something that doesn't belong to you.
I think it does.
I think my folks built this. I know their work. And it kinda looks like some of the future stuff Gert's folks used to pack, so I'd say this little guy is property of the Pride...
...and you can punish my ass.
CLIK
You got any powers, punk?

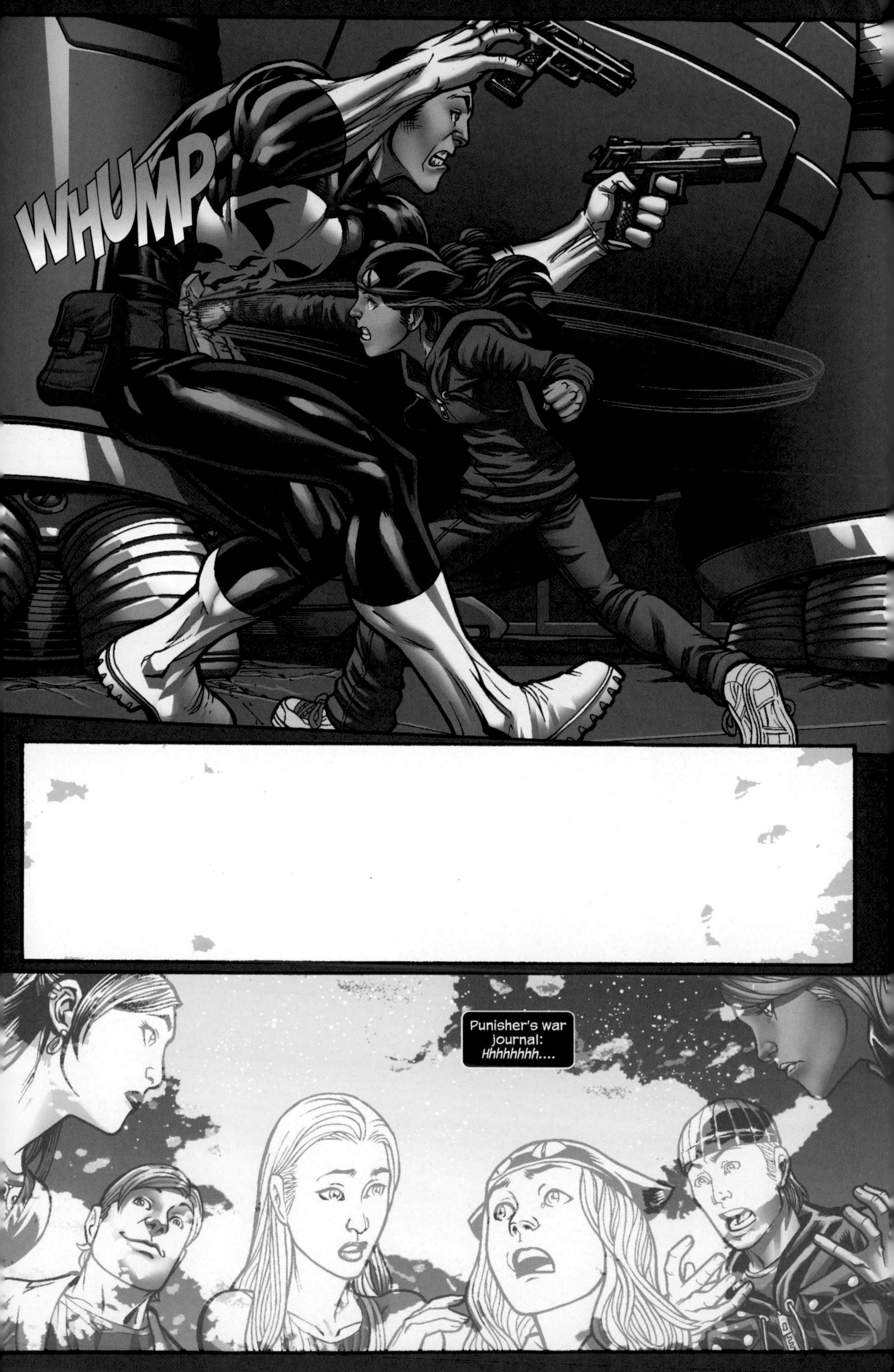
WHUMP
Punisher's war journal: *Hhhhhhhh....*

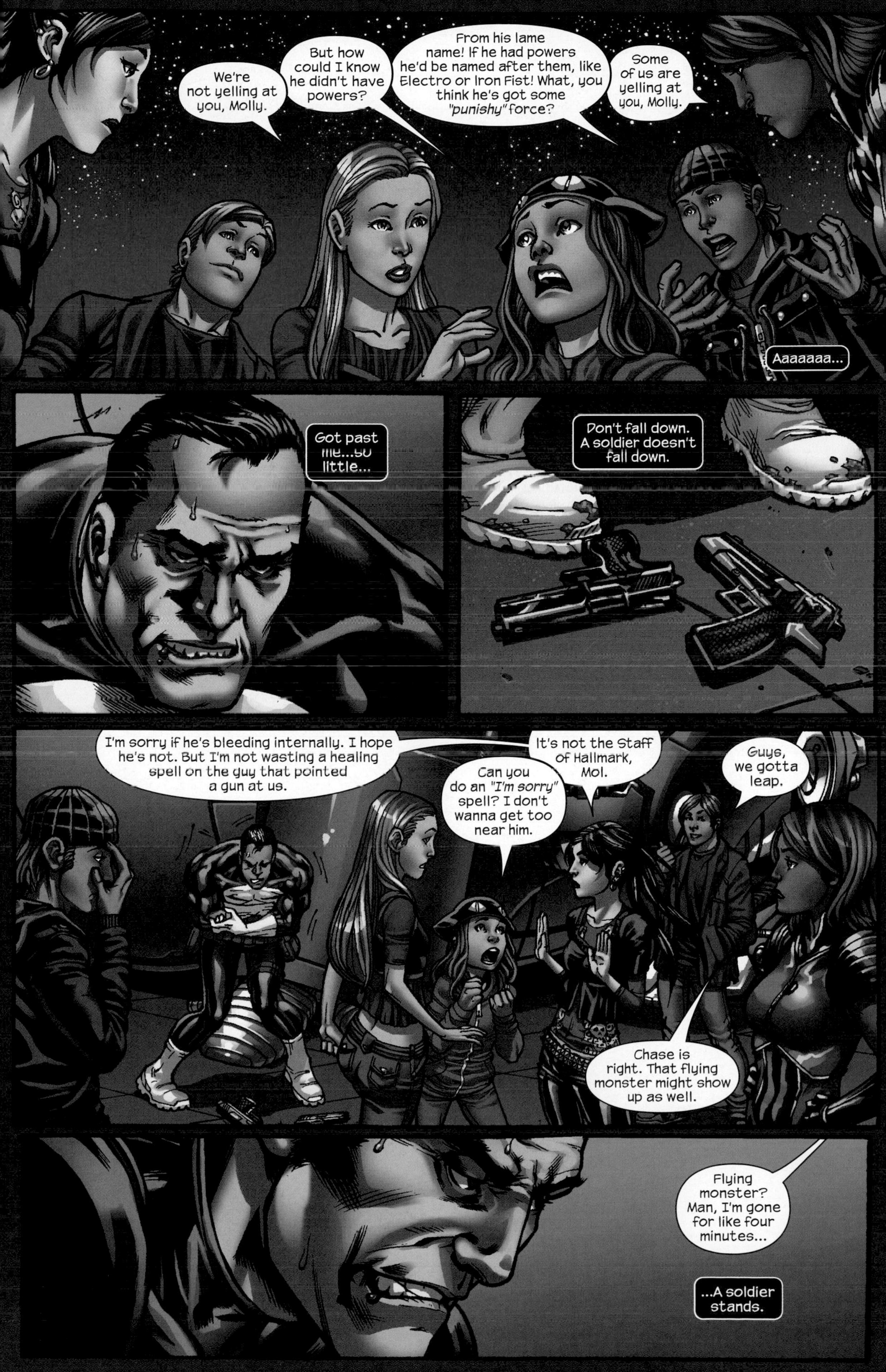
We're not yelling at you, Molly.
But how could I know he didn't have powers?
From his lame name! If he had powers he'd be named after them, like Electro or Iron Fist! What, you think he's got some "punishy" force?
Some of us are yelling at you, Molly.
Aaaaaaa...
Got past me...so little...
Don't fall down. A soldier doesn't fall down.
I'm sorry if he's bleeding internally. I hope he's not. But I'm not wasting a healing spell on the guy that pointed a gun at us.
It's not the Staff of Hallmark, Mol.
Can you do an "I'm sorry" spell? I don't wanna get too near him.
Guys, we gotta leap.
Chase is right. That flying monster might show up as well.
Flying monster? Man, I'm gone for like four minutes...
...A soldier stands.

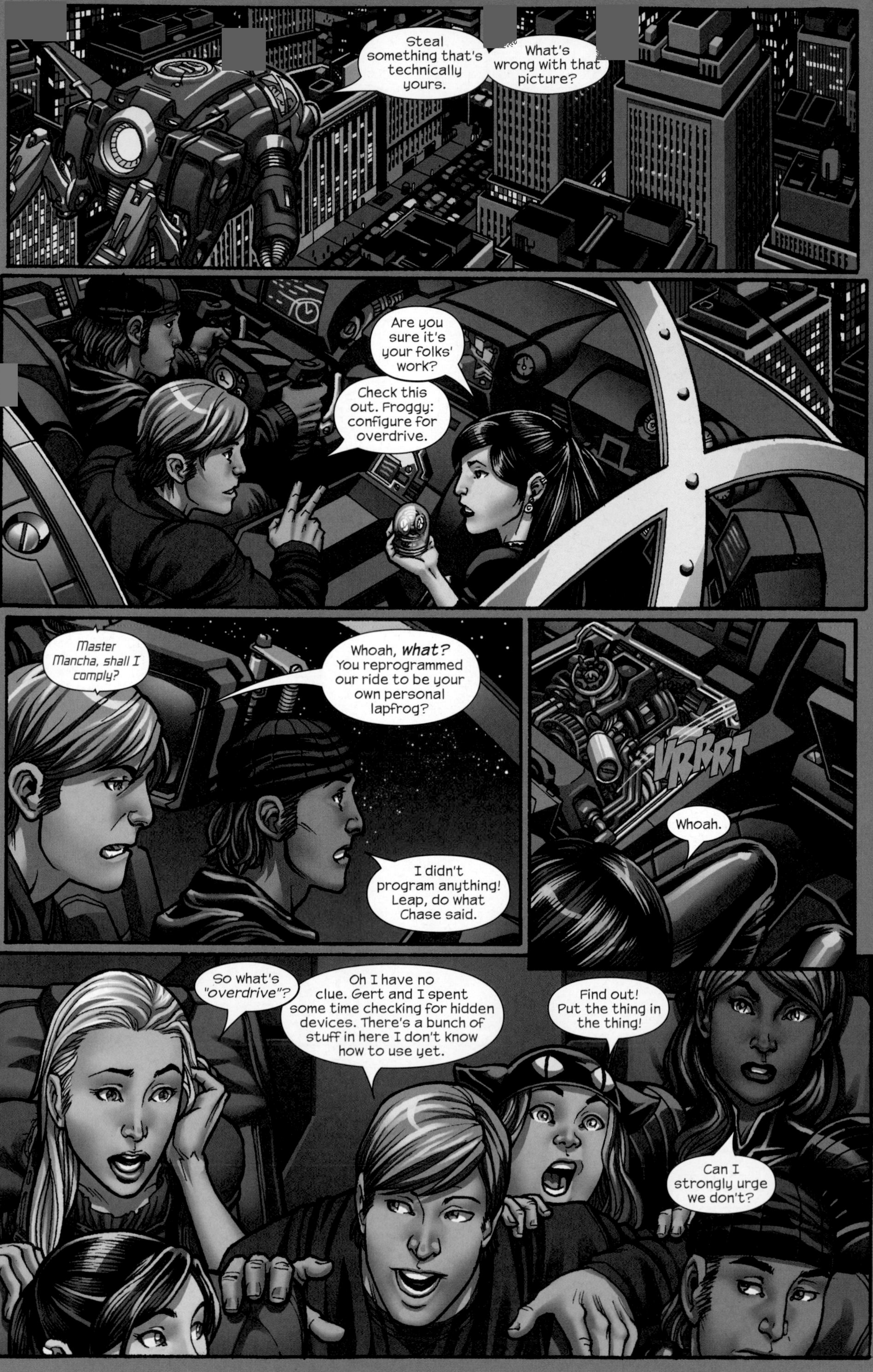

Steal something that's technically yours.
What's wrong with that picture?
Are you sure it's your folks' work?
Check this out. Froggy: configure for overdrive.
Master Mancha, shall I comply?
Whoah, **what?** You reprogrammed our ride to be your own personal lapfrog?
I didn't program anything! Leap, do what Chase said.
VRRRT
Whoah.
So what's *"overdrive"*?
Oh I have no clue. Gert and I spent some time checking for hidden devices. There's a bunch of stuff in here I don't know how to use yet.
Find out! Put the thing in the thing!
Can I strongly urge we don't?

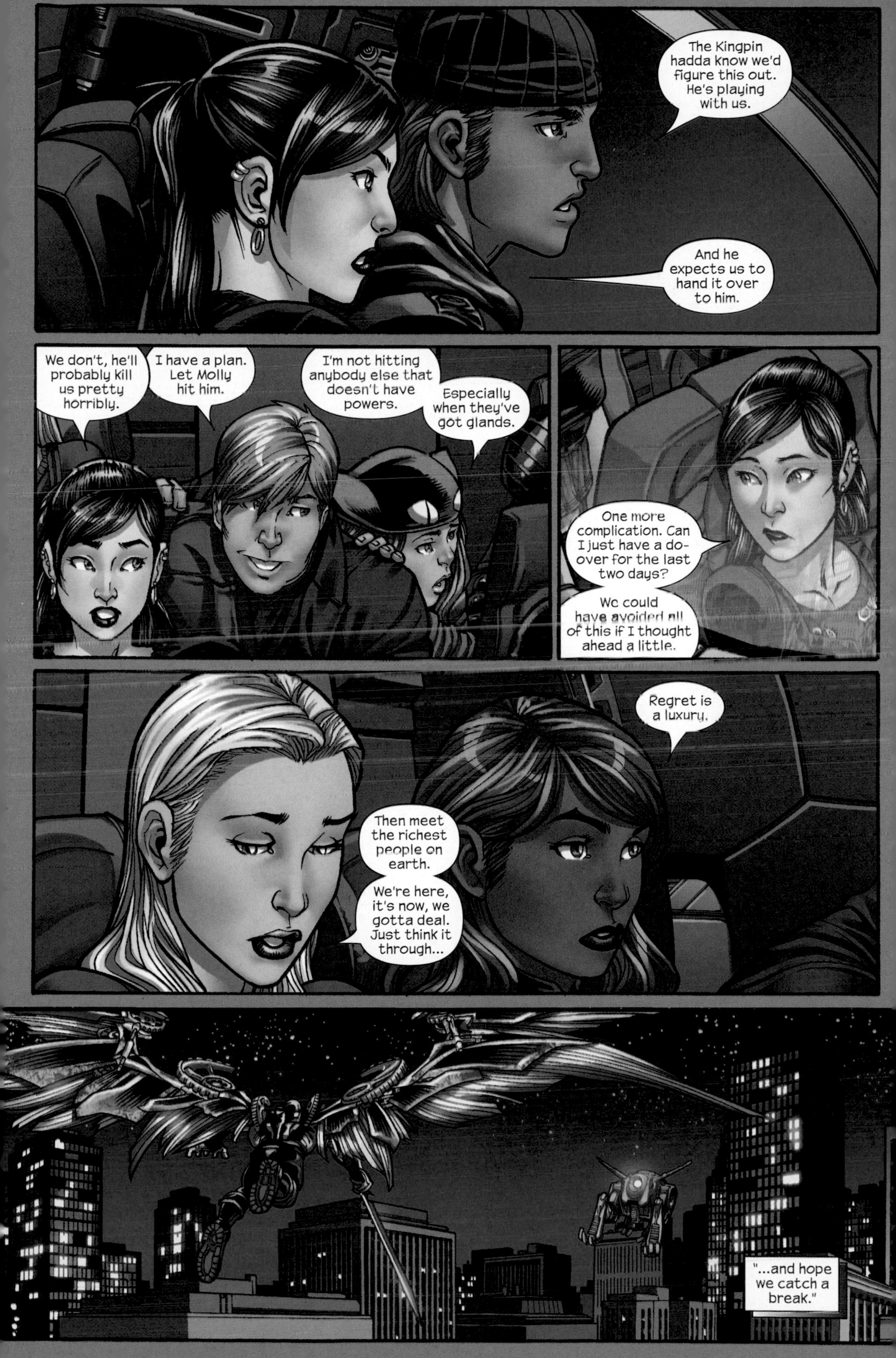
The Kingpin hadda know we'd figure this out. He's playing with us.
And he expects us to hand it over to him.
We don't, he'll probably kill us pretty horribly.
I have a plan. Let Molly hit him.
I'm not hitting anybody else that doesn't have powers.
Especially when they've got glands.
One more complication. Can I just have a do-over for the last two days?
We could have avoided all of this if I thought ahead a little.
Regret is a luxury.
Then meet the richest people on earth.
We're here, it's now, we gotta deal. Just think it through...
"...and hope we catch a break."

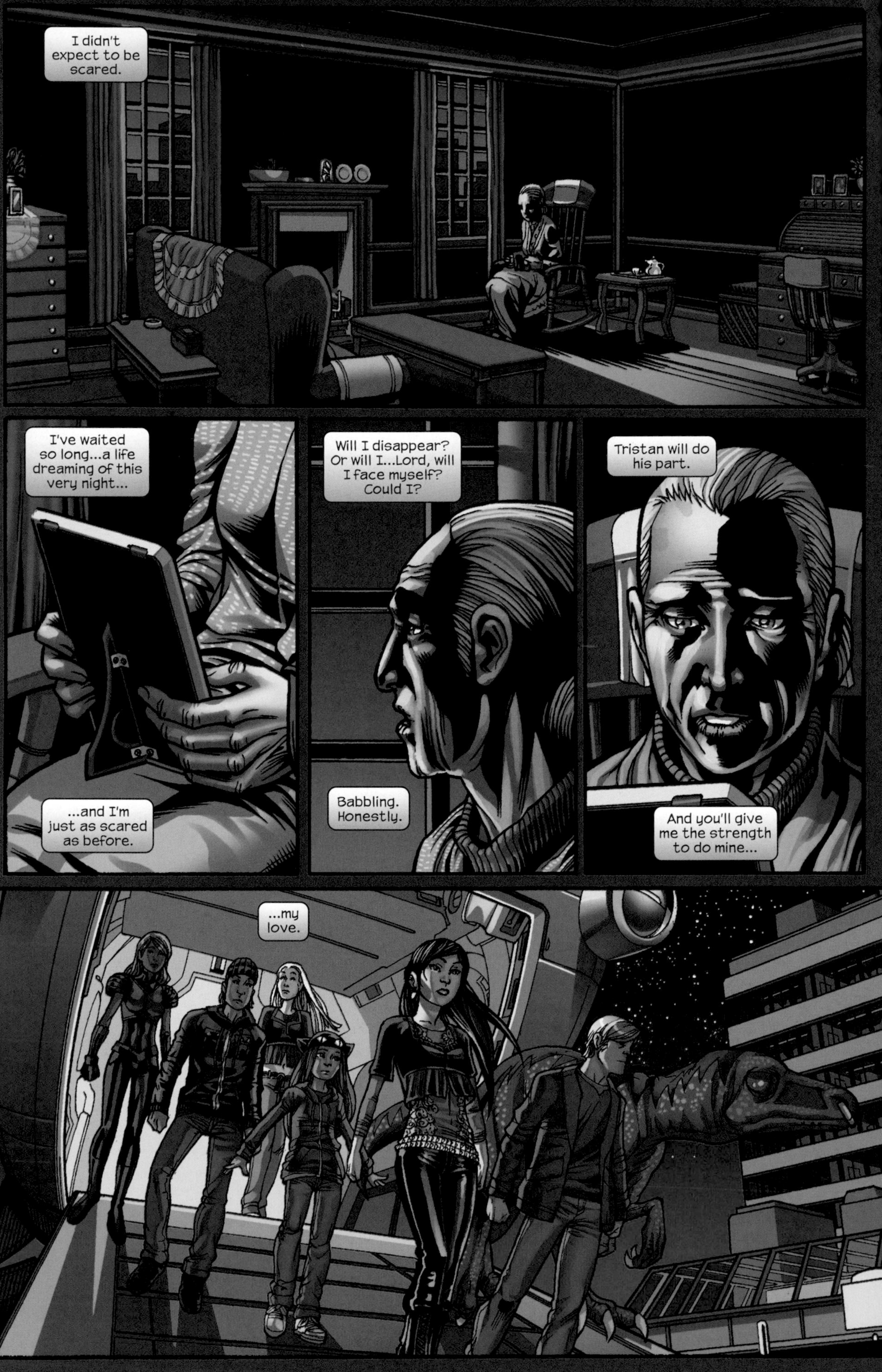
I didn't expect to be scared.
I've waited so long...a life dreaming of this very night...
...and I'm just as scared as before.
Will I disappear? Or will I...Lord, will I face myself? Could I?
Babbling. Honestly.
Tristan will do his part.
And you'll give me the strength to do mine...
...my love.

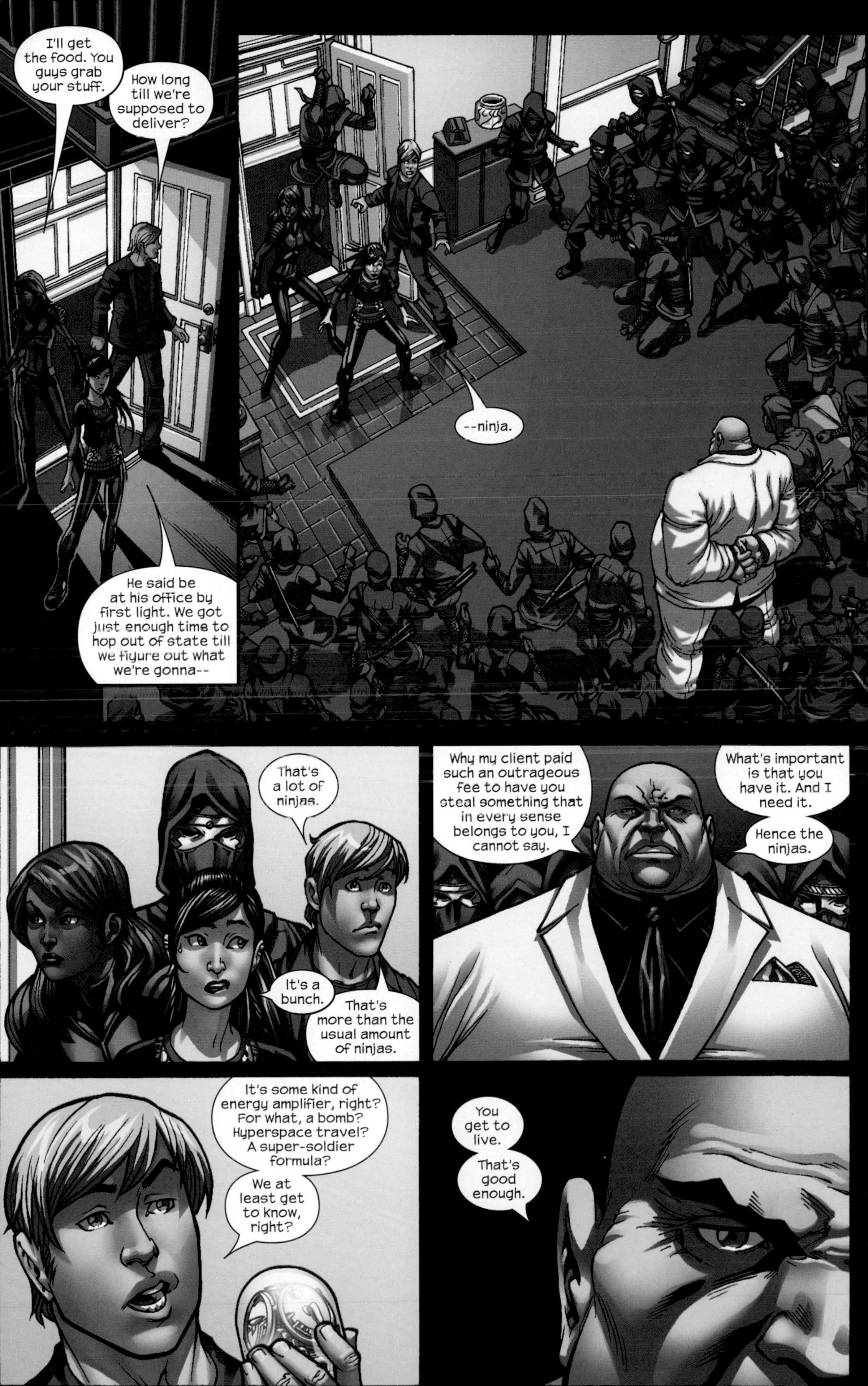
I'll get the food. You guys grab your stuff.
How long till we're supposed to deliver?
He said be at his office by first light. We got just enough time to hop out of state till we figure out what we're gonna--
--ninja.
That's a lot of ninjas.
It's a bunch.
That's more than the usual amount of ninjas.
Why my client paid such an outrageous fee to have you steal something that in every sense belongs to you, I cannot say.
What's important is that you have it. And I need it.
Hence the ninjas.
It's some kind of energy amplifier, right? For what, a bomb? Hyperspace travel? A super-soldier formula?
We at least get to know, right?
You get to live.
That's good enough.

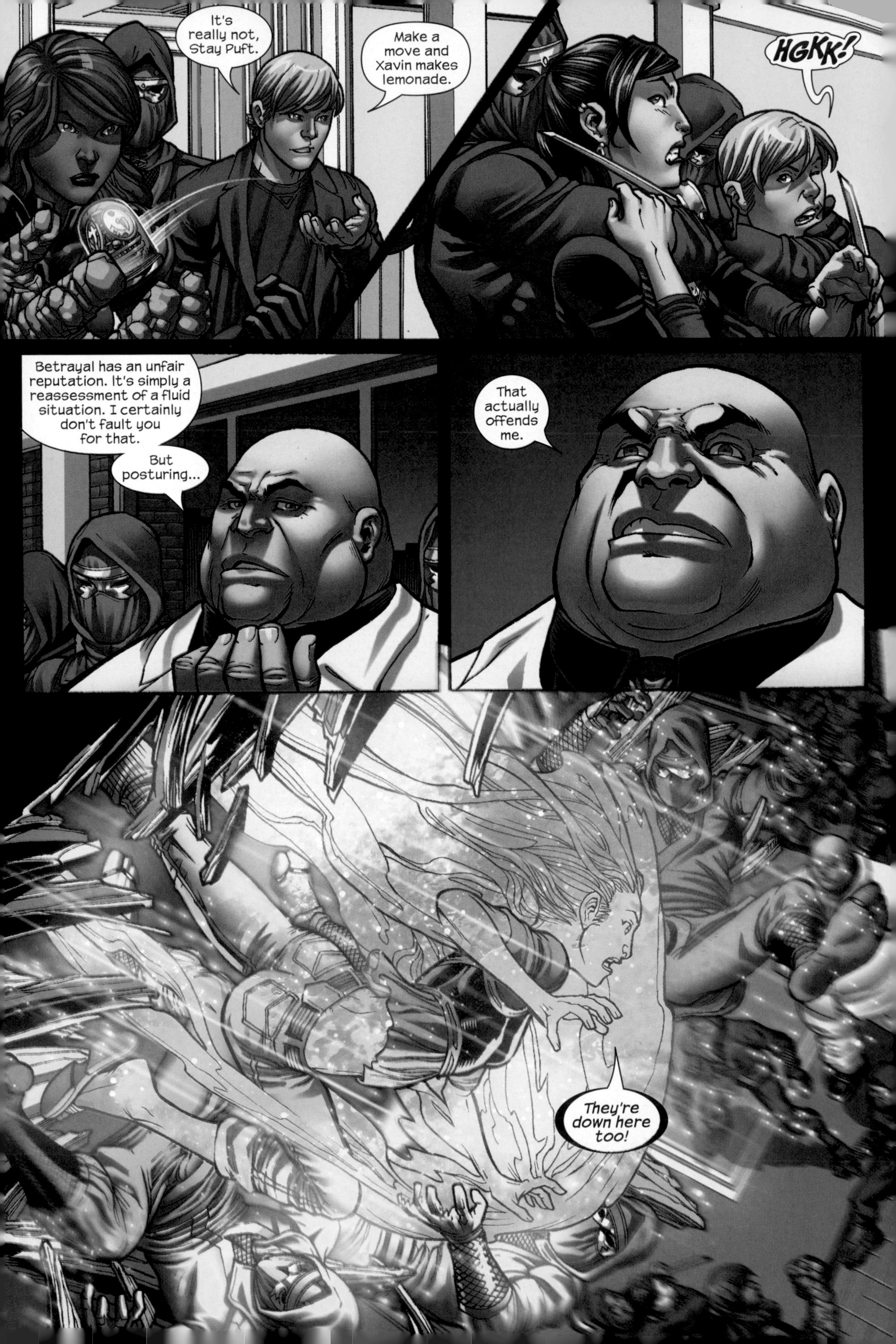

It's really not, Stay Puft.
Make a move and Xavin makes lemonade.
HGKK!
Betrayal has an unfair reputation. It's simply a reassessment of a fluid situation. I certainly don't fault you for that.
But posturing...
That actually offends me.
They're down here too!

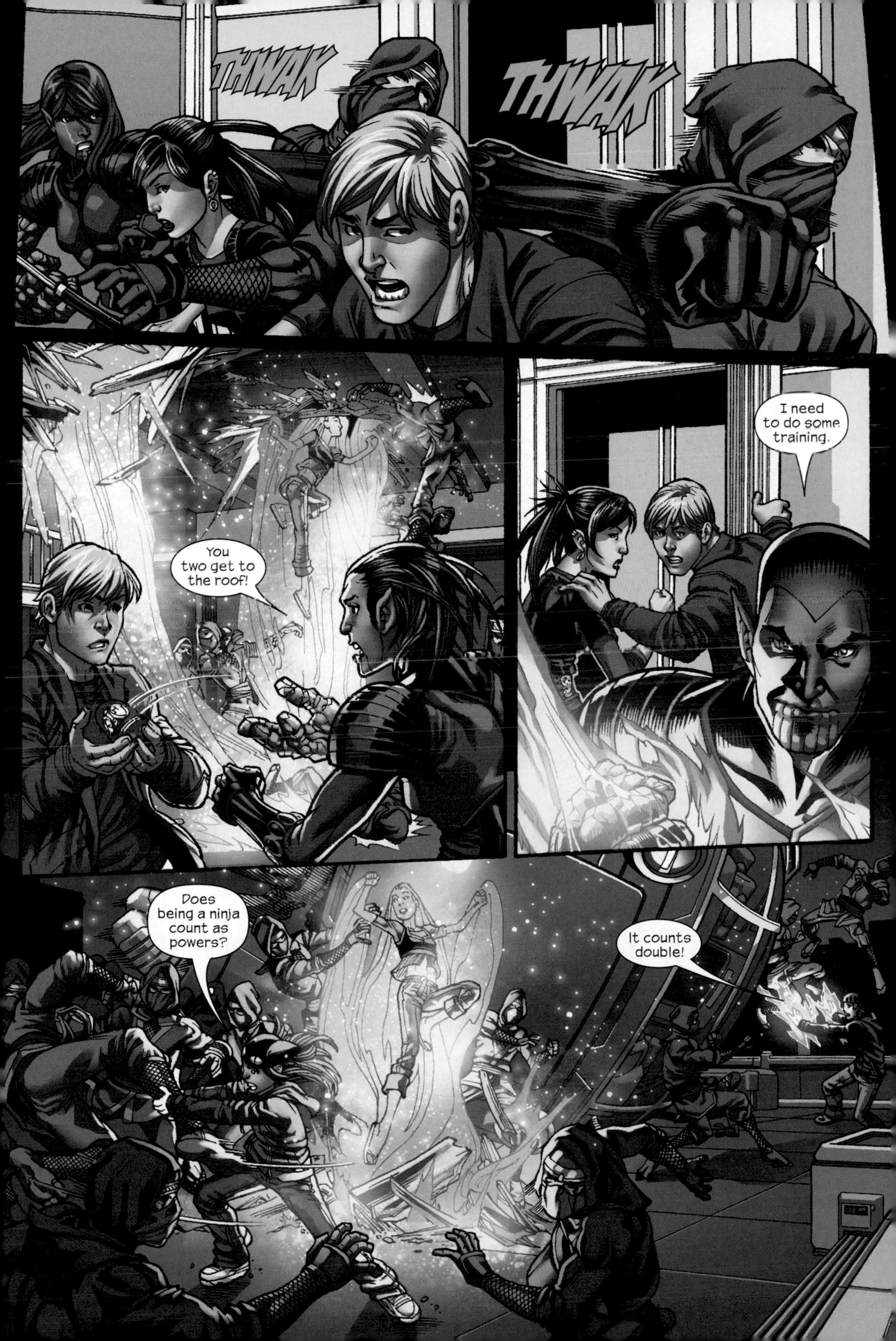
THWAK
THWAK
You two get to the roof!
I need to do some training.
Does being a ninja count as powers?
It counts double!

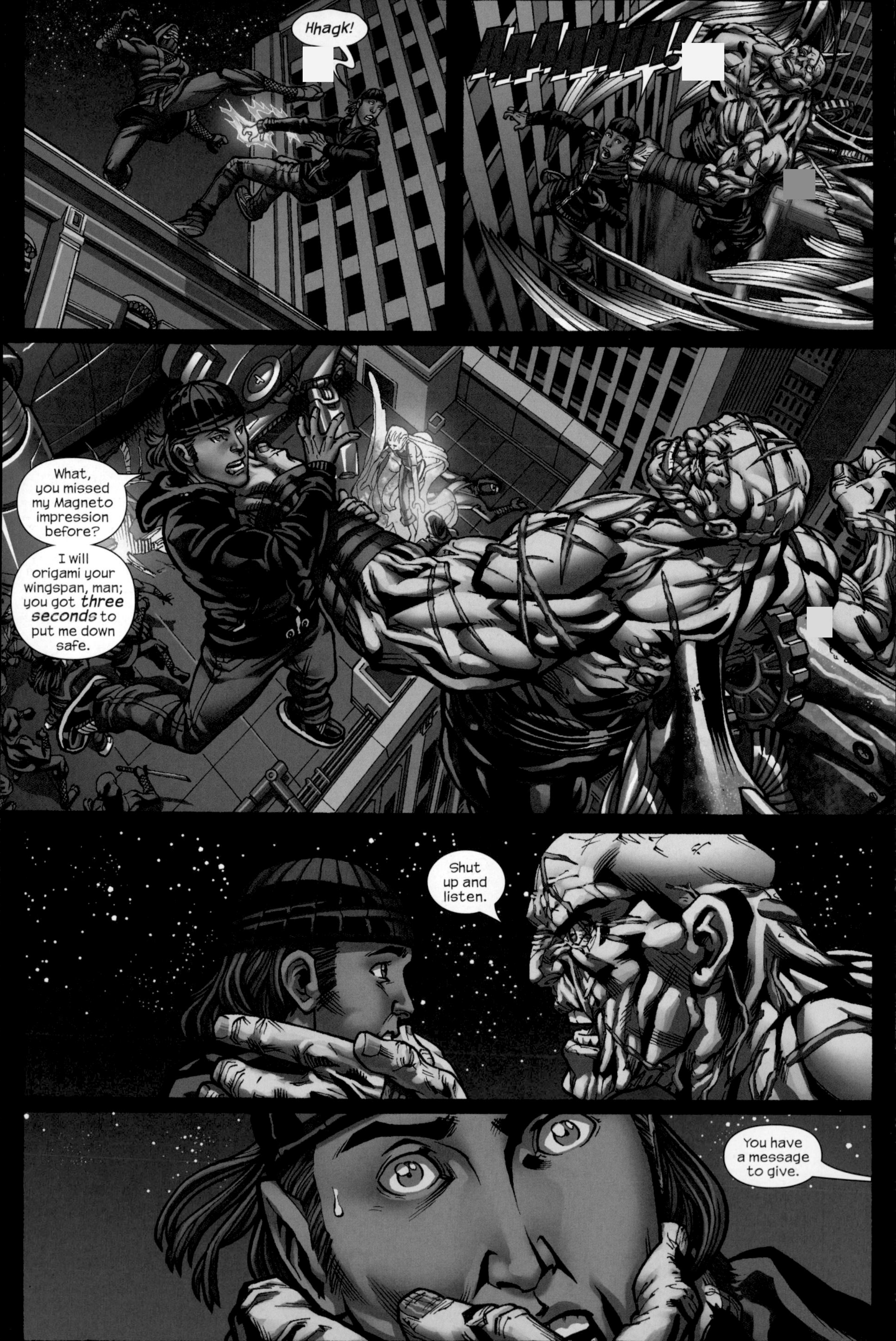

Hhagk!
What, you missed my Magneto impression before?
I will origami your wingspan, man; you got *three seconds* to put me down safe.
Shut up and listen.
You have a message to give.

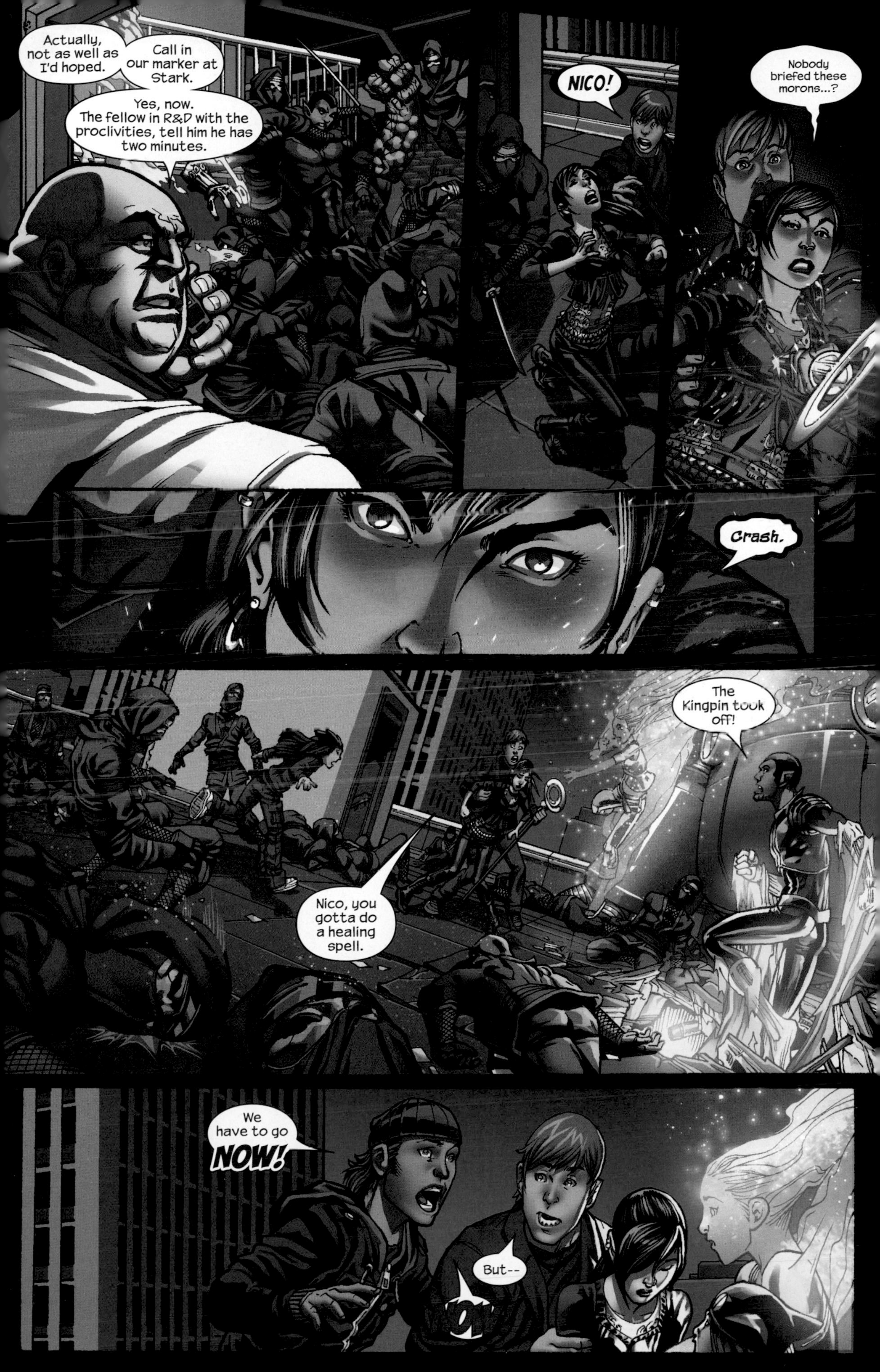
Actually, not as well as I'd hoped.
Call in our marker at Stark.
Yes, now. The fellow in R&D with the proclivities, tell him he has two minutes.
NICO!
Nobody briefed these morons...?
Crash.
The Kingpin took off!
Nico, you gotta do a healing spell.
We have to go NOW!
But--

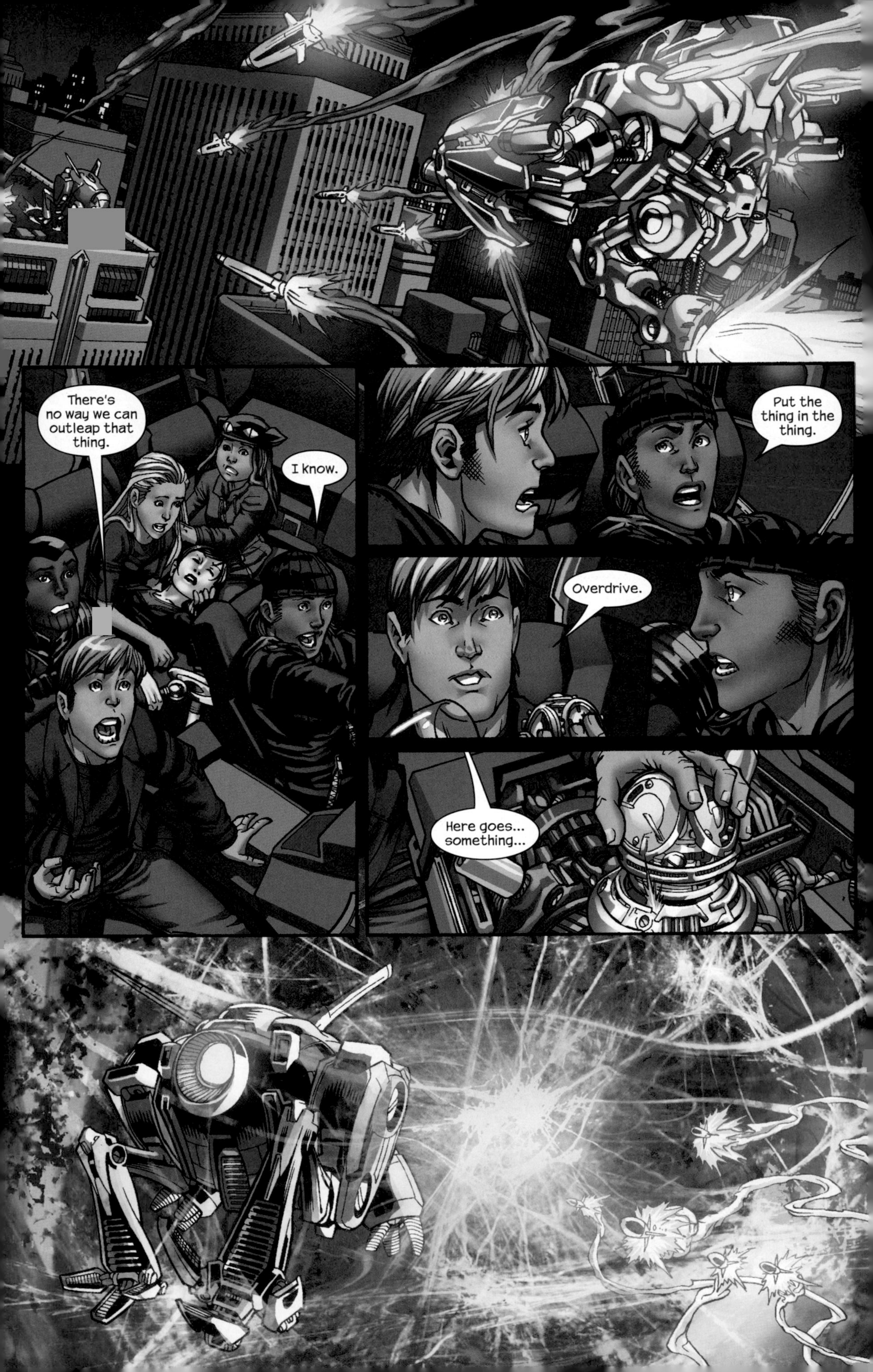
There's no way we can outleap that thing.
I know.
Put the thing in the thing.
Overdrive.
Here goes... something...

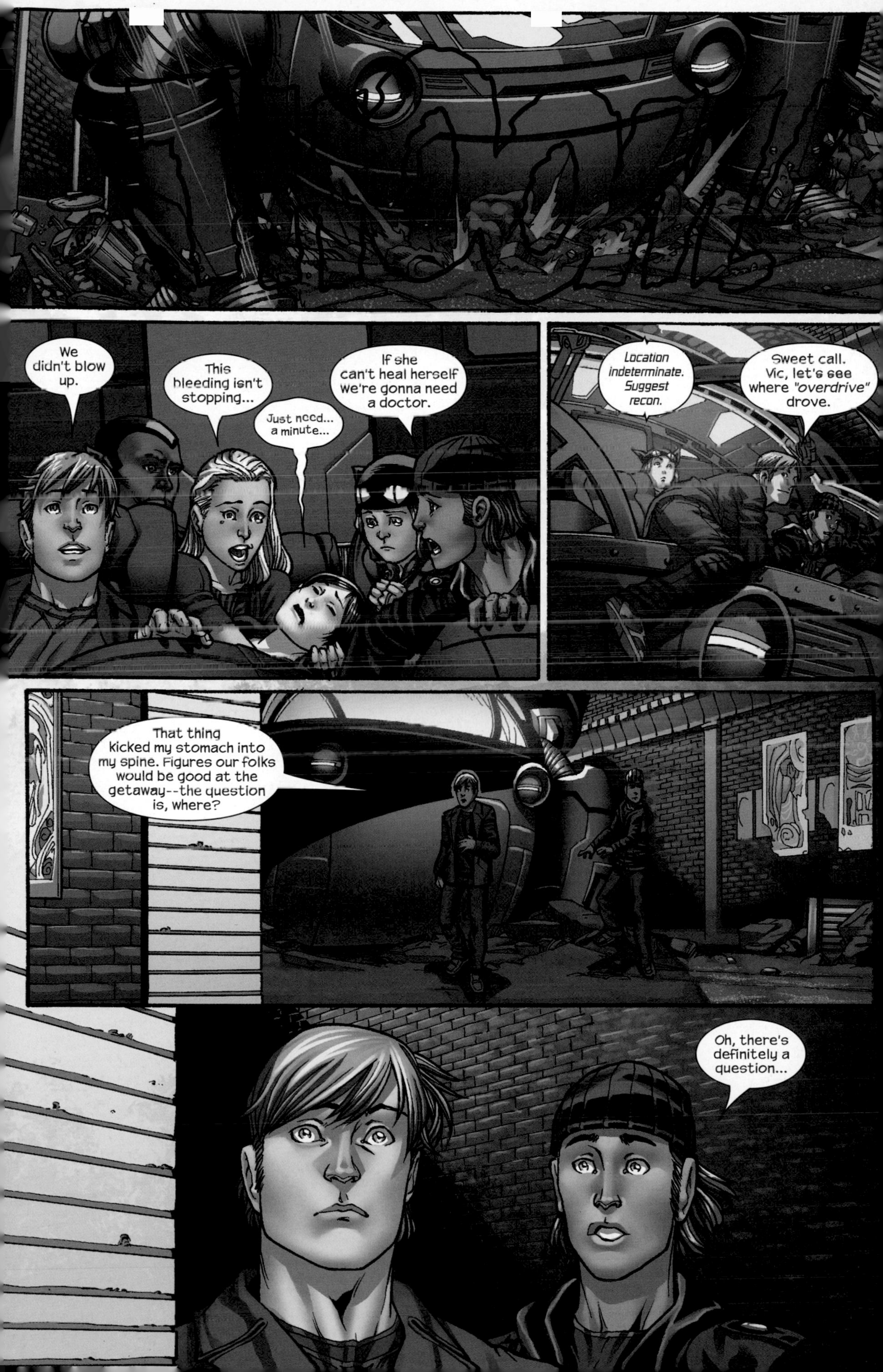

We didn't blow up.
This bleeding isn't stopping...
Just need... a minute...
If she can't heal herself we're gonna need a doctor.
Location indeterminate. Suggest recon.
Sweet call. Vic, let's see where "overdrive" drove.
That thing kicked my stomach into my spine. Figures our folks would be good at the getaway--the question is, where?
Oh, there's definitely a question...

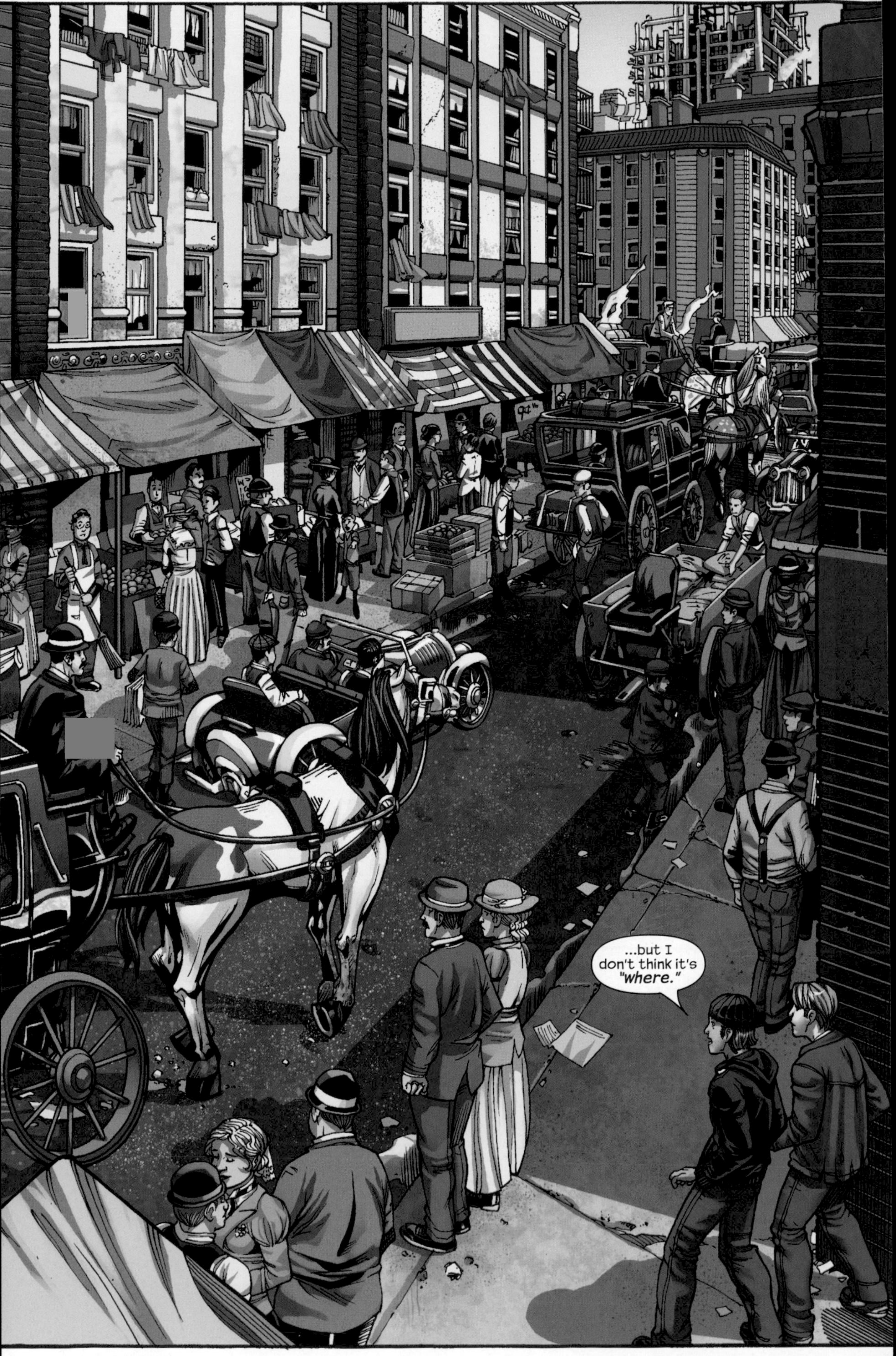
...but I don't think it's "where."

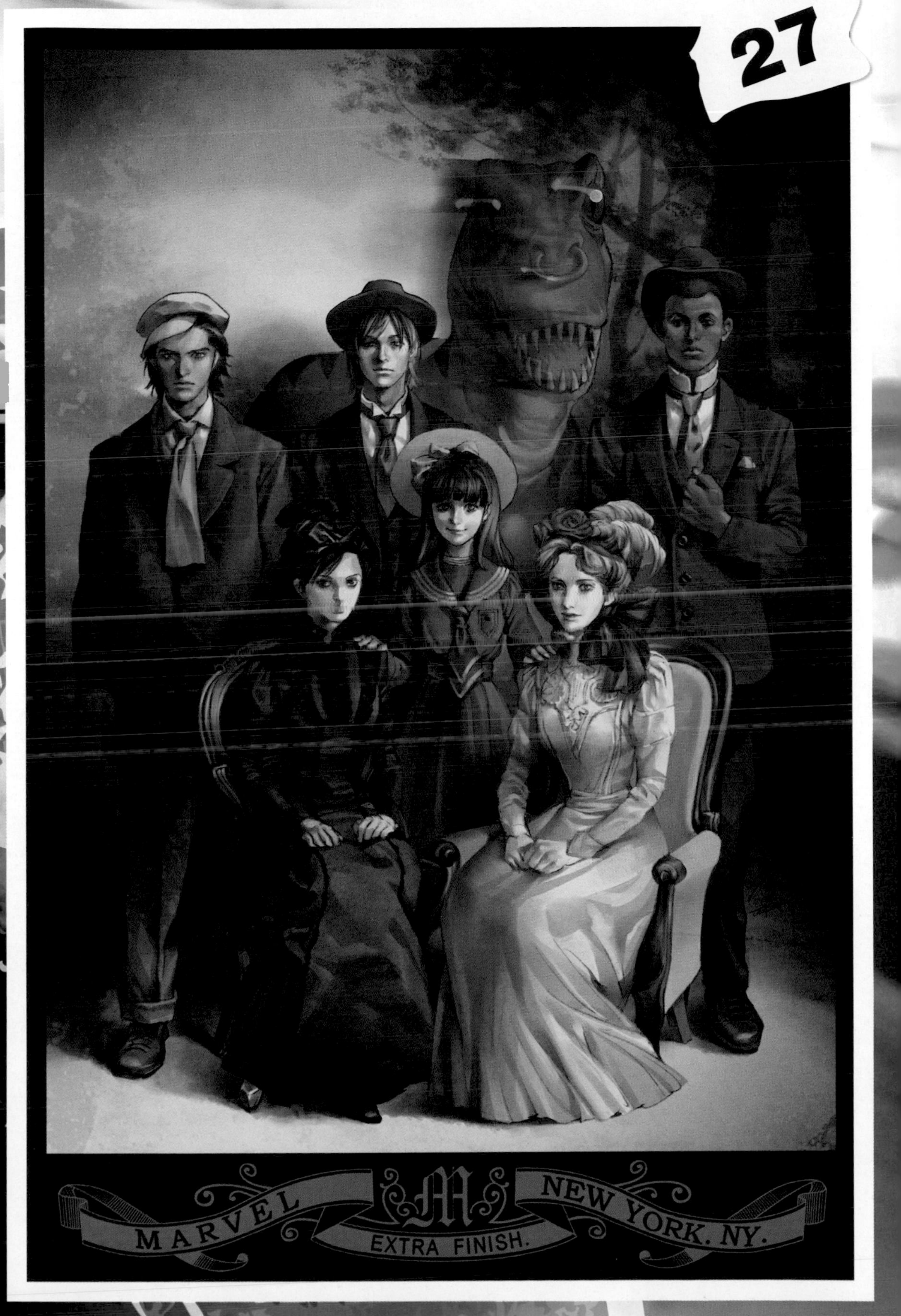
27
MARVEL
NEW YORK, NY.
EXTRA FINISH.

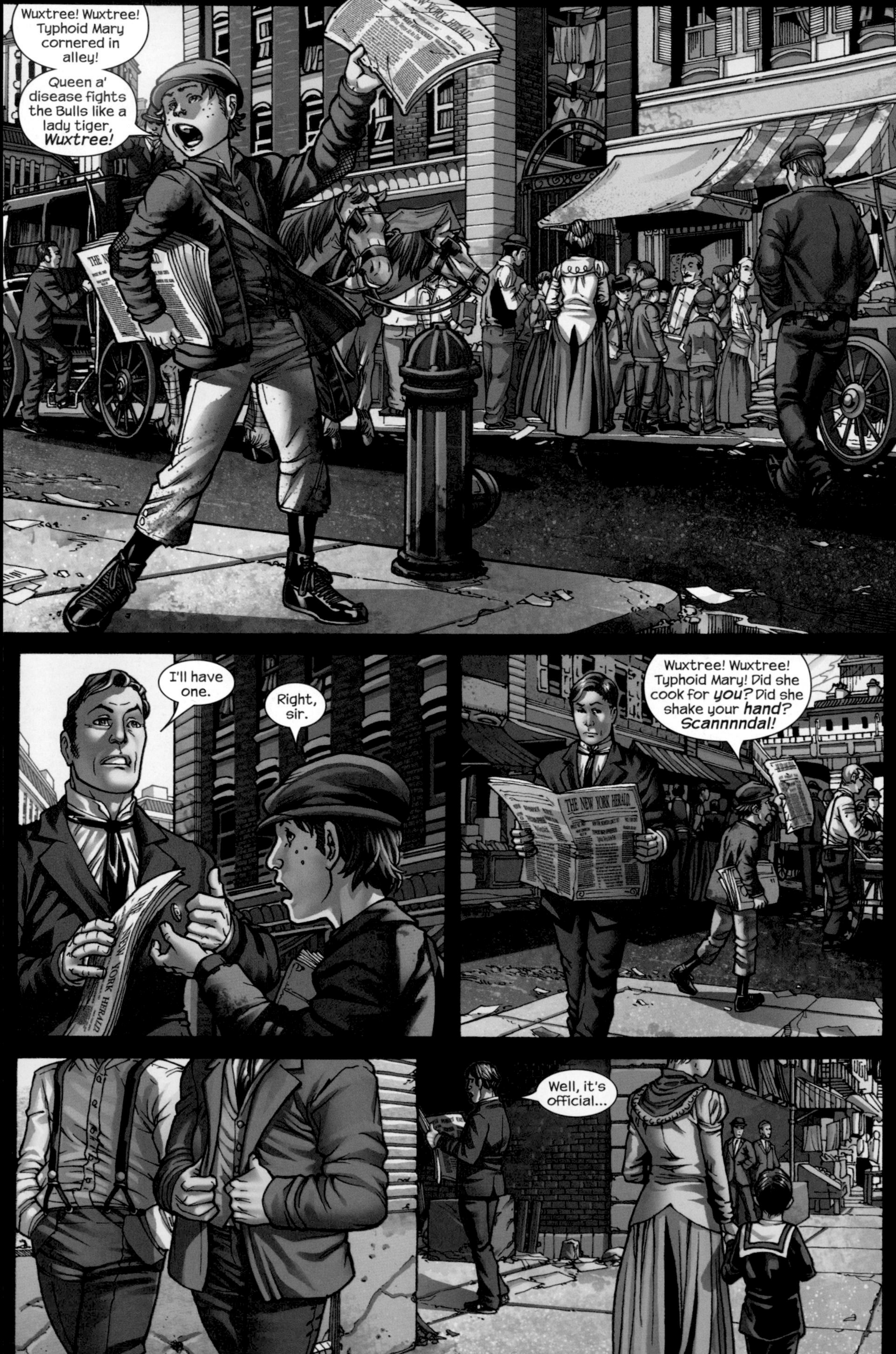
Wuxtree! Wuxtree! Typhoid Mary cornered in alley!
Queen a' disease fights the Bulls like a lady tiger, Wuxtree!
THE NEW YORK HERALD
I'll have one.
Right, sir.
Wuxtree! Wuxtree! Typhoid Mary! Did she cook for you? Did she shake your hand? Scannnndal!
THE NEW YORK HERALD
Well, it's official...

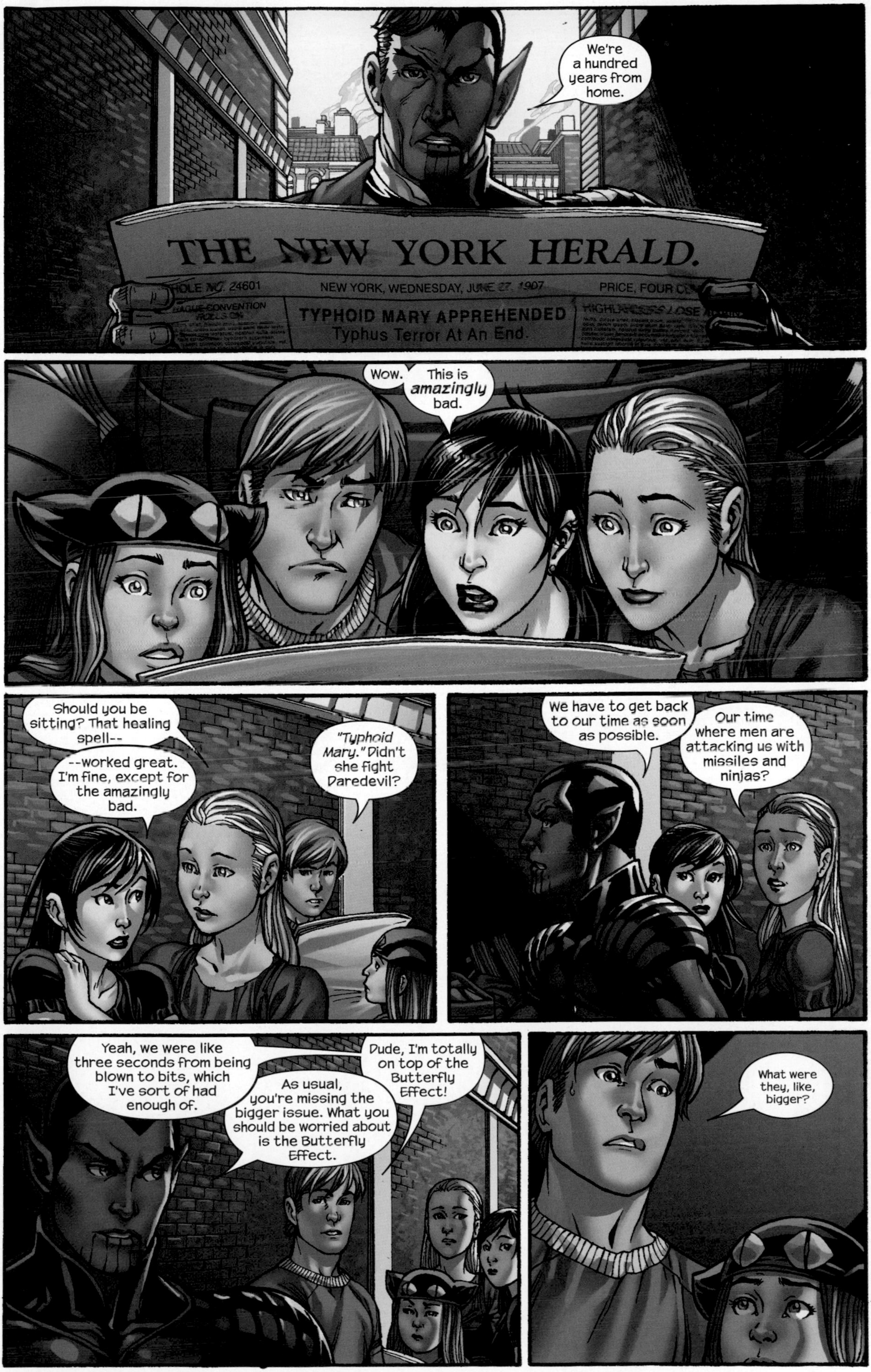
We're a hundred years from home.
THE NEW YORK HERALD.
NEW YORK, WEDNESDAY, JUNE 27, 1907
TYPHOID MARY APPREHENDED
Typhus Terror At An End.
Wow.
This is *amazingly* bad.
Should you be sitting? That healing spell--
--worked great. I'm fine, except for the amazingly bad.
"Typhoid Mary." Didn't she fight Daredevil?
We have to get back to our time as soon as possible.
Our time where men are attacking us with missiles and ninjas?
Yeah, we were like three seconds from being blown to bits, which I've sort of had enough of.
As usual, you're missing the bigger issue. What you should be worried about is the Butterfly Effect.
Dude, I'm totally on top of the Butterfly Effect!
What were they, like, bigger?

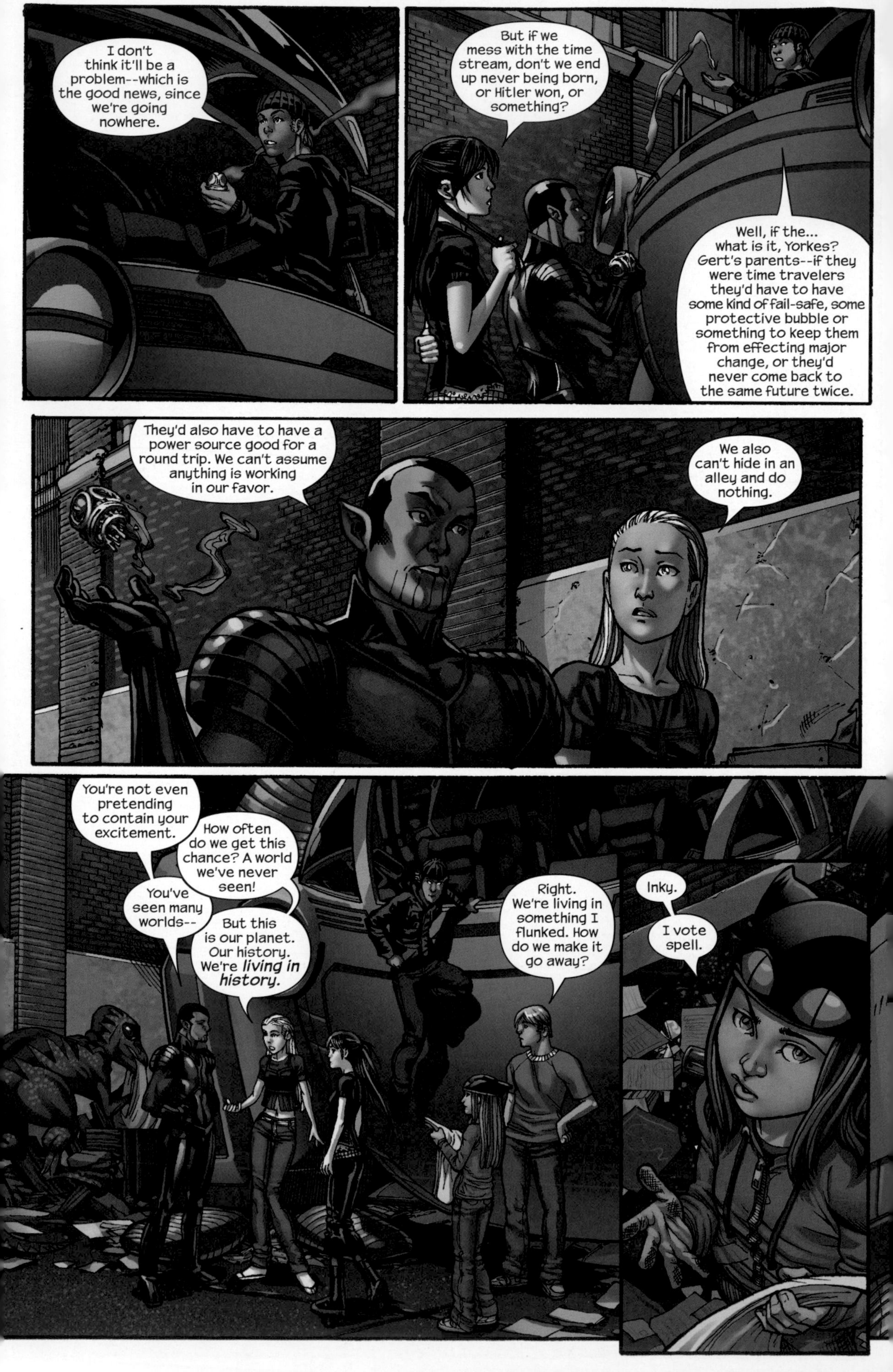
I don't think it'll be a problem--which is the good news, since we're going nowhere.
But if we mess with the time stream, don't we end up never being born, or Hitler won, or something?
Well, if the... what is it, Yorkes? Gert's parents--if they were time travelers they'd have to have some kind of fail-safe, some protective bubble or something to keep them from effecting major change, or they'd never come back to the same future twice.
They'd also have to have a power source good for a round trip. We can't assume anything is working in our favor.
We also can't hide in an alley and do nothing.
You're not even pretending to contain your excitement.
How often do we get this chance? A world we've never seen!
You've seen many worlds--
But this is our planet. Our history. We're *living in history.*
Right. We're living in something I flunked. How do we make it go away?
Inky.
I vote spell.

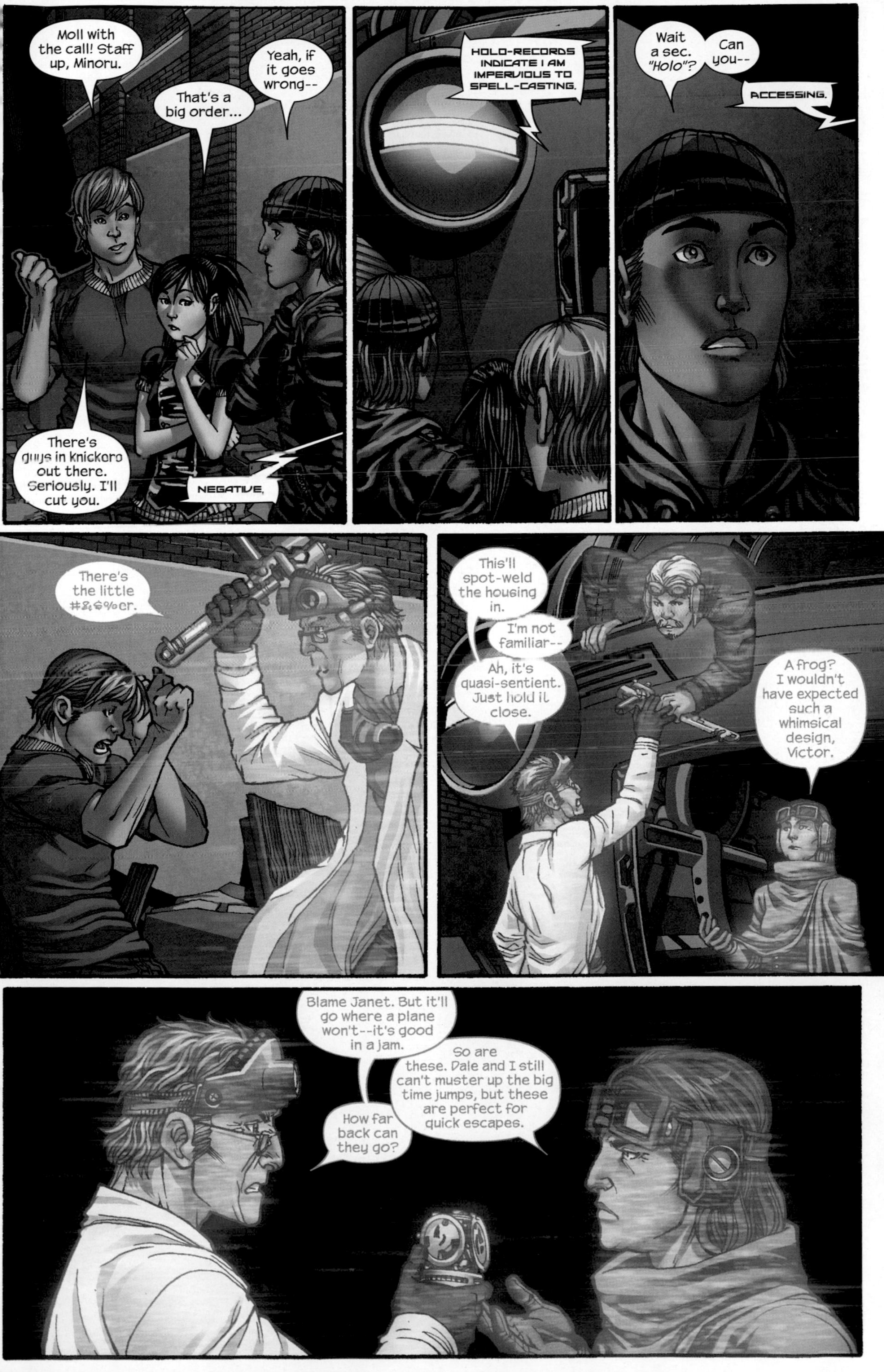
Moll with the call! Staff up, Minoru.
That's a big order...
Yeah, if it goes wrong--
There's guys in knickers out there. Seriously. I'll cut you.
NEGATIVE.
HOLO-RECORDS INDICATE I AM IMPERVIOUS TO SPELL-CASTING.
Wait a sec. "Holo"?
Can you--
ACCESSING.
There's the little #&$%er.
This'll spot-weld the housing in.
I'm not familiar--
Ah, it's quasi-sentient. Just hold it close.
A frog? I wouldn't have expected such a whimsical design, Victor.
Blame Janet. But it'll go where a plane won't--it's good in a jam.
So are these. Dale and I still can't muster up the big time jumps, but these are perfect for quick escapes.
How far back can they go?

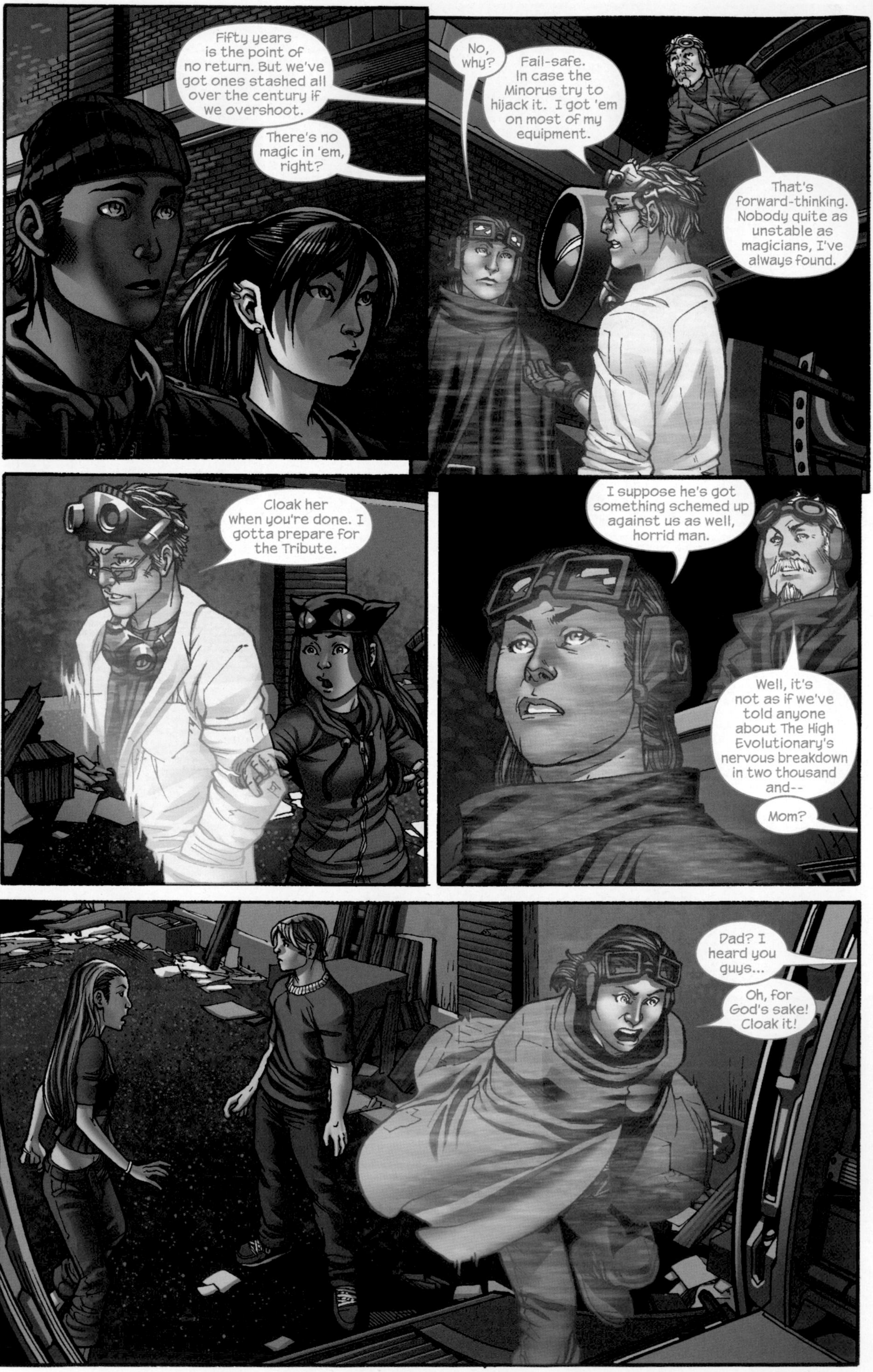
Fifty years is the point of no return. But we've got ones stashed all over the century if we overshoot.
There's no magic in 'em, right?
No, why?
Fail-safe. In case the Minorus try to hijack it. I got 'em on most of my equipment.
That's forward-thinking. Nobody quite as unstable as magicians, I've always found.
Cloak her when you're done. I gotta prepare for the Tribute.
I suppose he's got something schemed up against us as well, horrid man.
Well, it's not as if we've told anyone about The High Evolutionary's nervous breakdown in two thousand and--
Mom?
Dad? I heard you guys...
Oh, for God's sake! Cloak it!

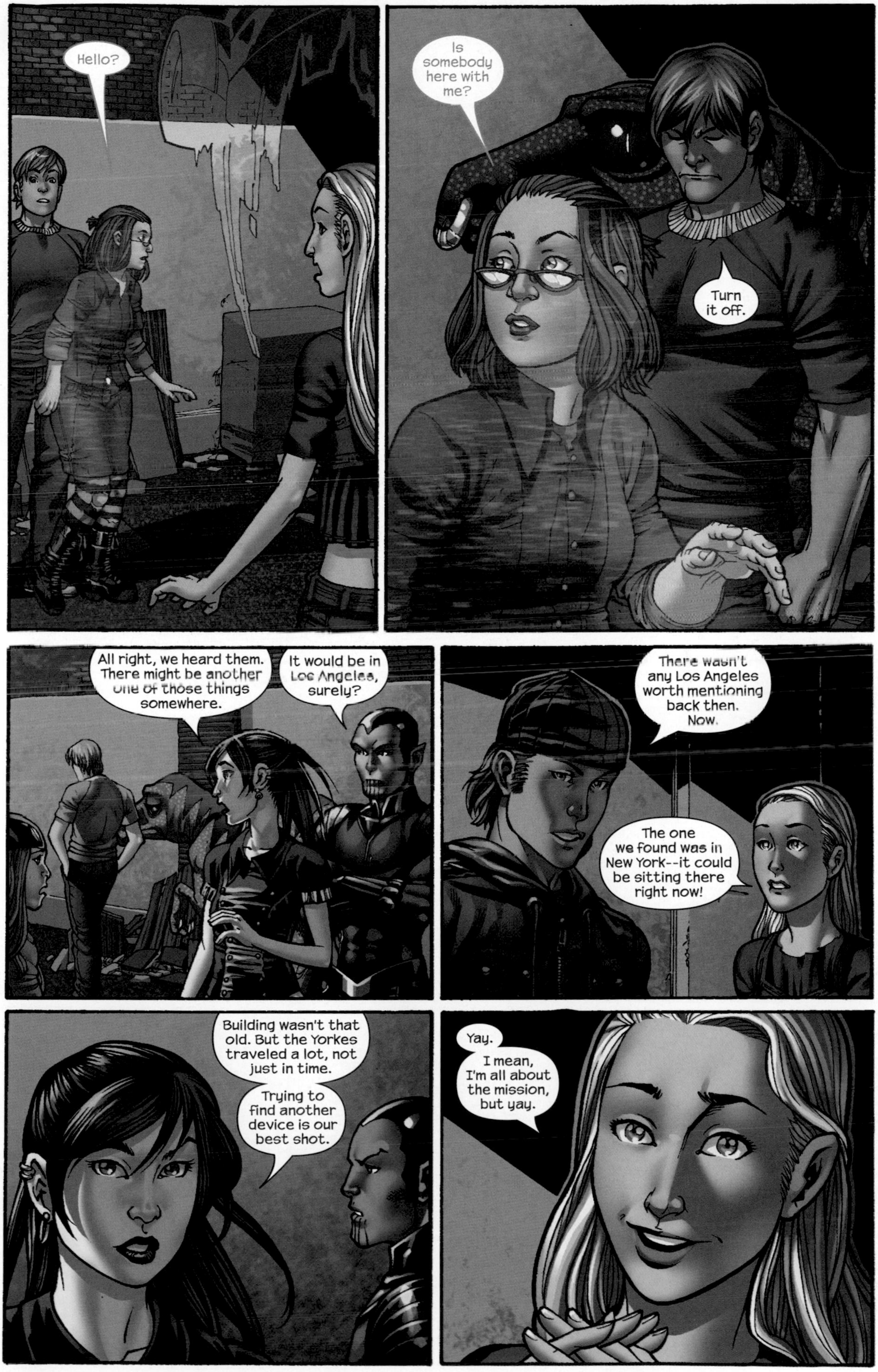
Hello?
Is somebody here with me?
Turn it off.
All right, we heard them. There might be another one of those things somewhere.
It would be in Los Angeles, surely?
There wasn't any Los Angeles worth mentioning back then. Now.
The one we found was in New York--it could be sitting there right now!
Building wasn't that old. But the Yorkes traveled a lot, not just in time.
Trying to find another device is our best shot.
Yay.
I mean, I'm all about the mission, but yay.

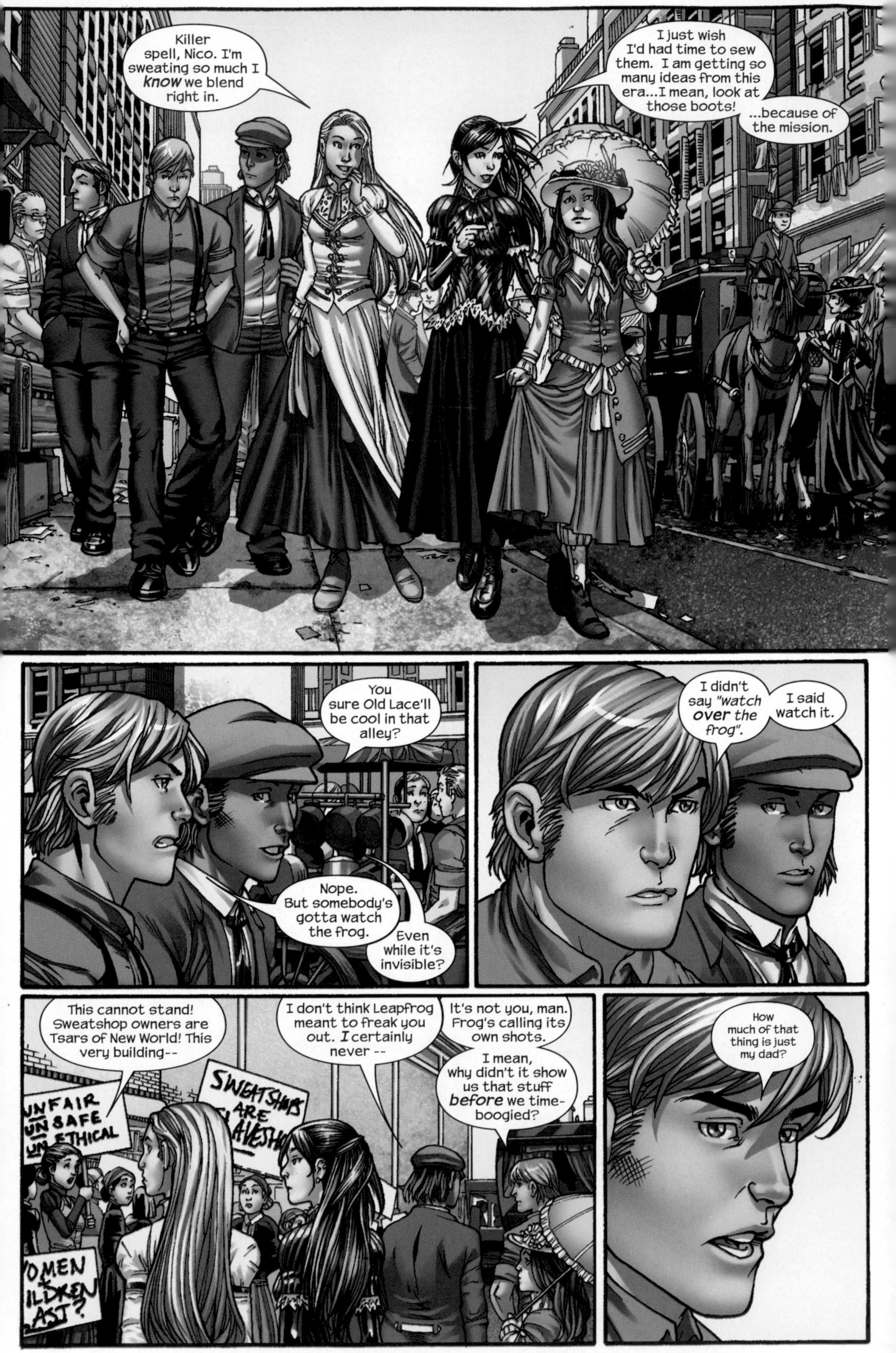

Killer spell, Nico. I'm sweating so much I *know* we blend right in.
I just wish I'd had time to sew them. I am getting so many ideas from this era...I mean, look at those boots!
...because of the mission.
You sure Old Lace'll be cool in that alley?
Nope. But somebody's gotta watch the frog.
Even while it's invisible?
I didn't say *"watch* **over** *the frog"*.
I said watch it.
This cannot stand! Sweatshop owners are Tsars of New World! This very building--
UNFAIR UNSAFE UNETHICAL
SWEATSHOPS ARE SLAVESHOPS
I don't think Leapfrog meant to freak you out. *I* certainly never --
It's not you, man. Frog's calling its own shots.
I mean, why didn't it show us that stuff *before* we time-boogied?
How much of that thing is just my dad?

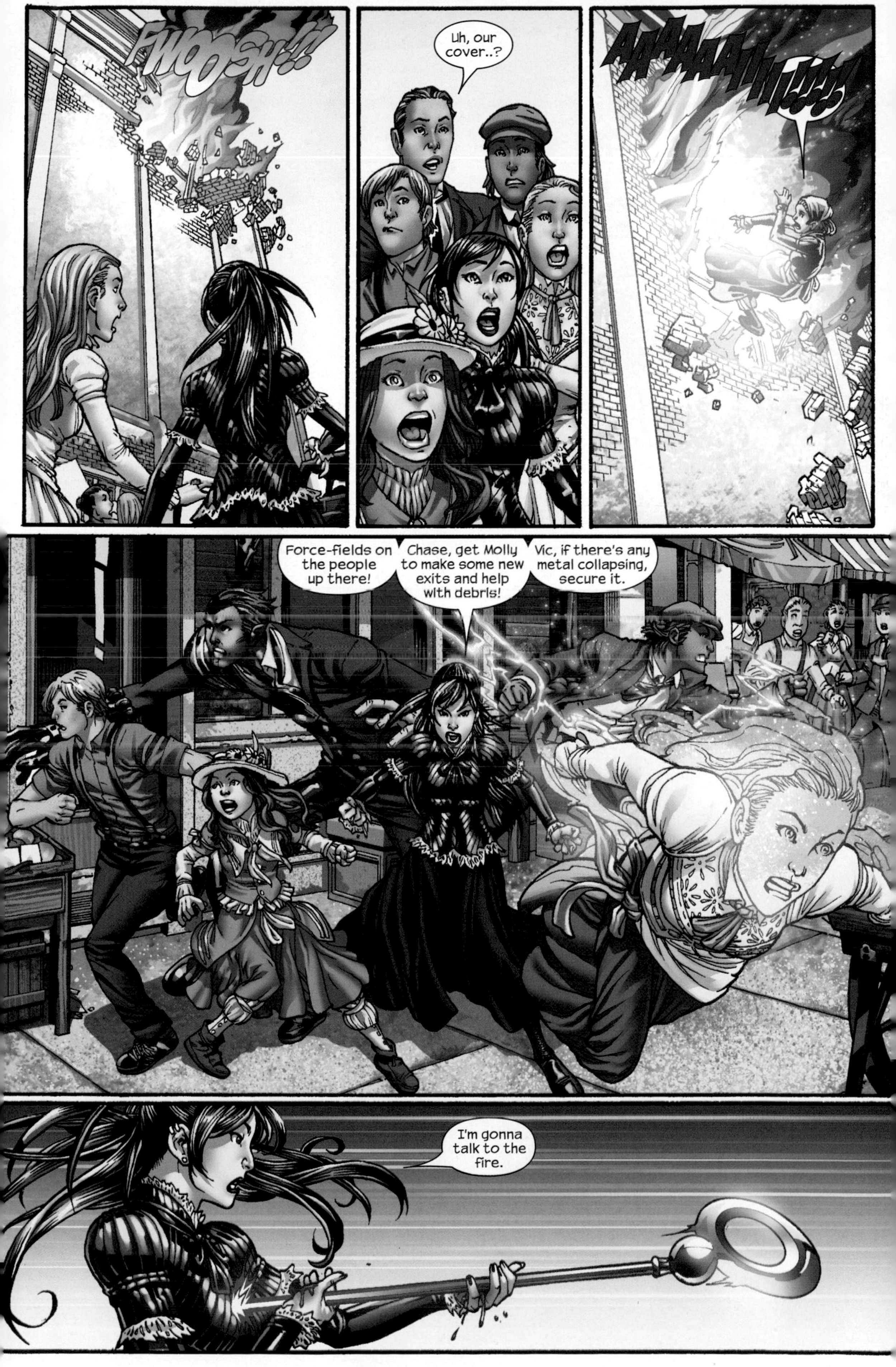
FWOOSH!!!
Uh, our cover..?
AAAAAAIIIII!!!!!
Force-fields on the people up there!
Chase, get Molly to make some new exits and help with debris!
Vic, if there's any metal collapsing, secure it.
I'm gonna talk to the fire.

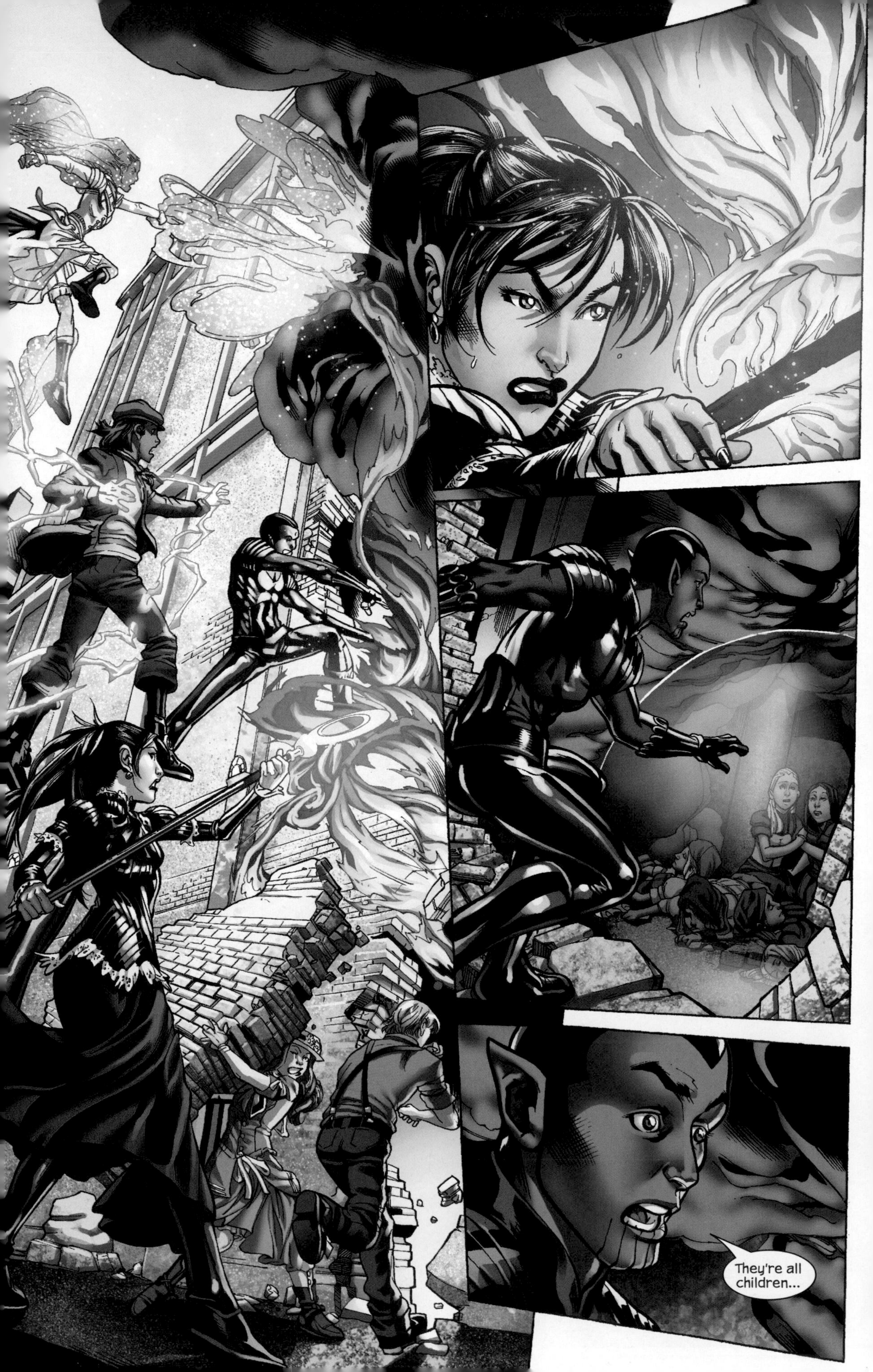
They're all children...

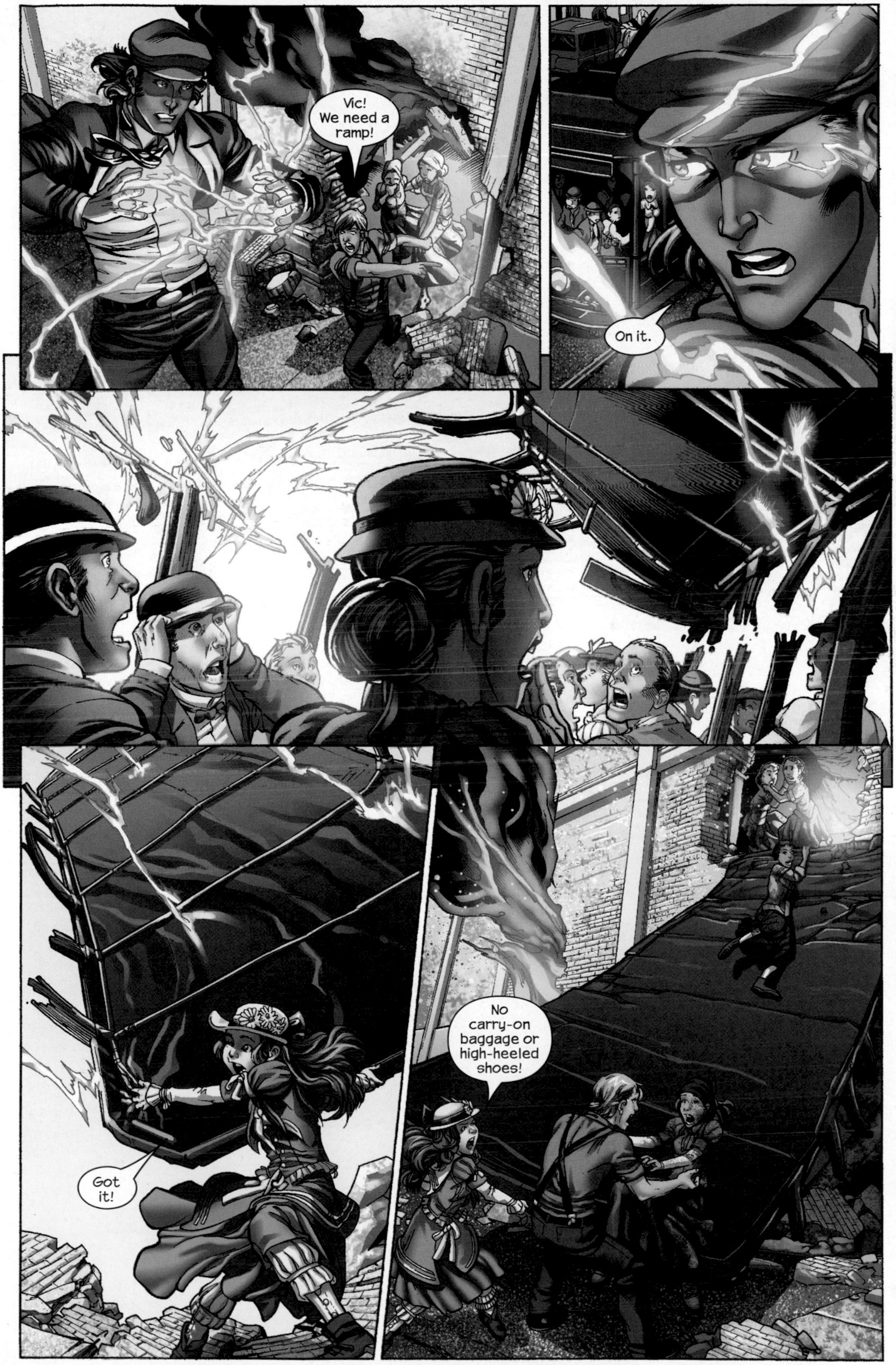
Vic! We need a ramp!
On it.
Got it!
No carry-on baggage or high-heeled shoes!

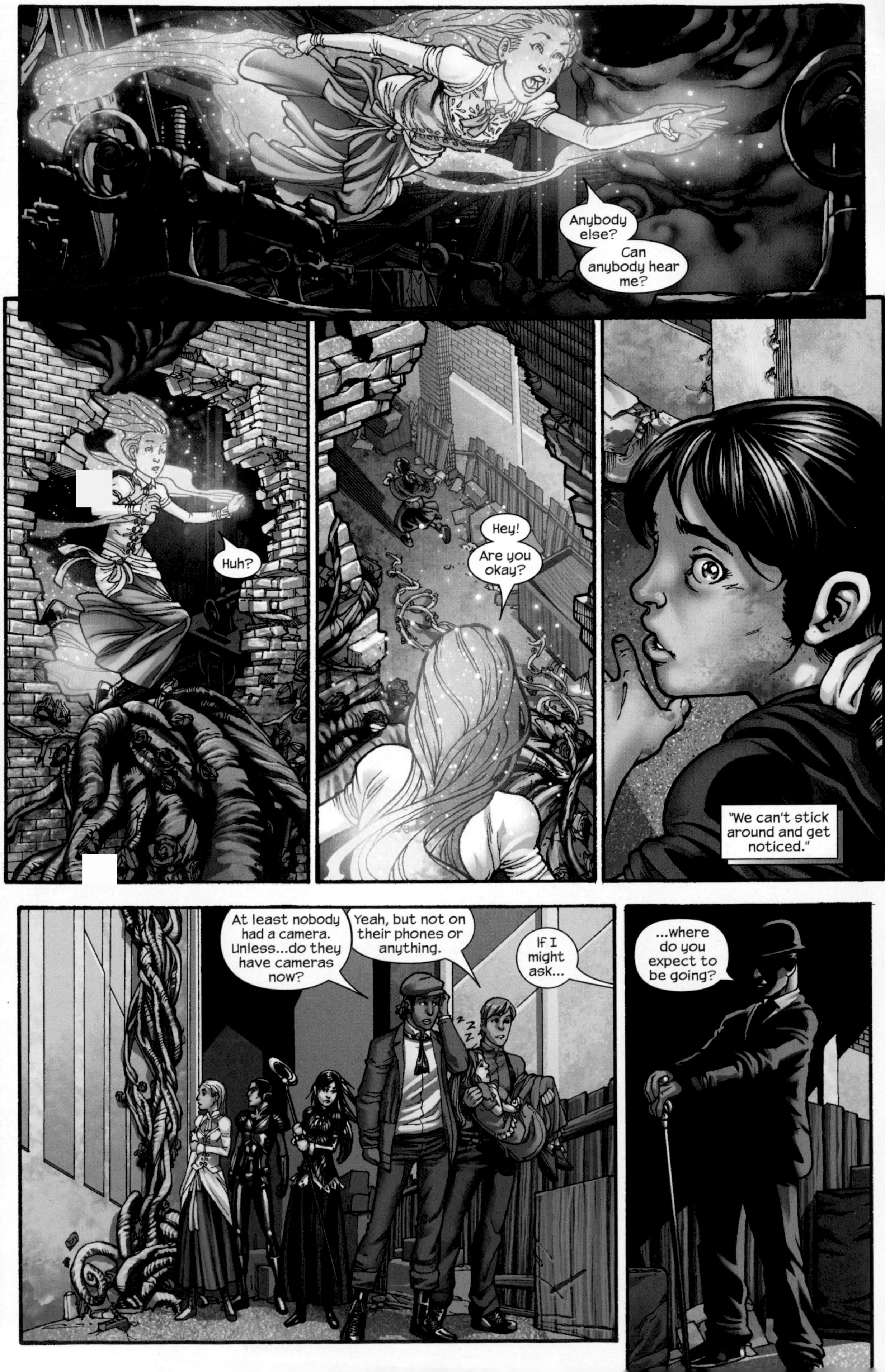
Anybody else?
Can anybody hear me?
Huh?
Hey!
Are you okay?
"We can't stick around and get noticed."
At least nobody had a camera. Unless...do they have cameras now?
Yeah, but not on their phones or anything.
If I might ask...
...where do you expect to be going?

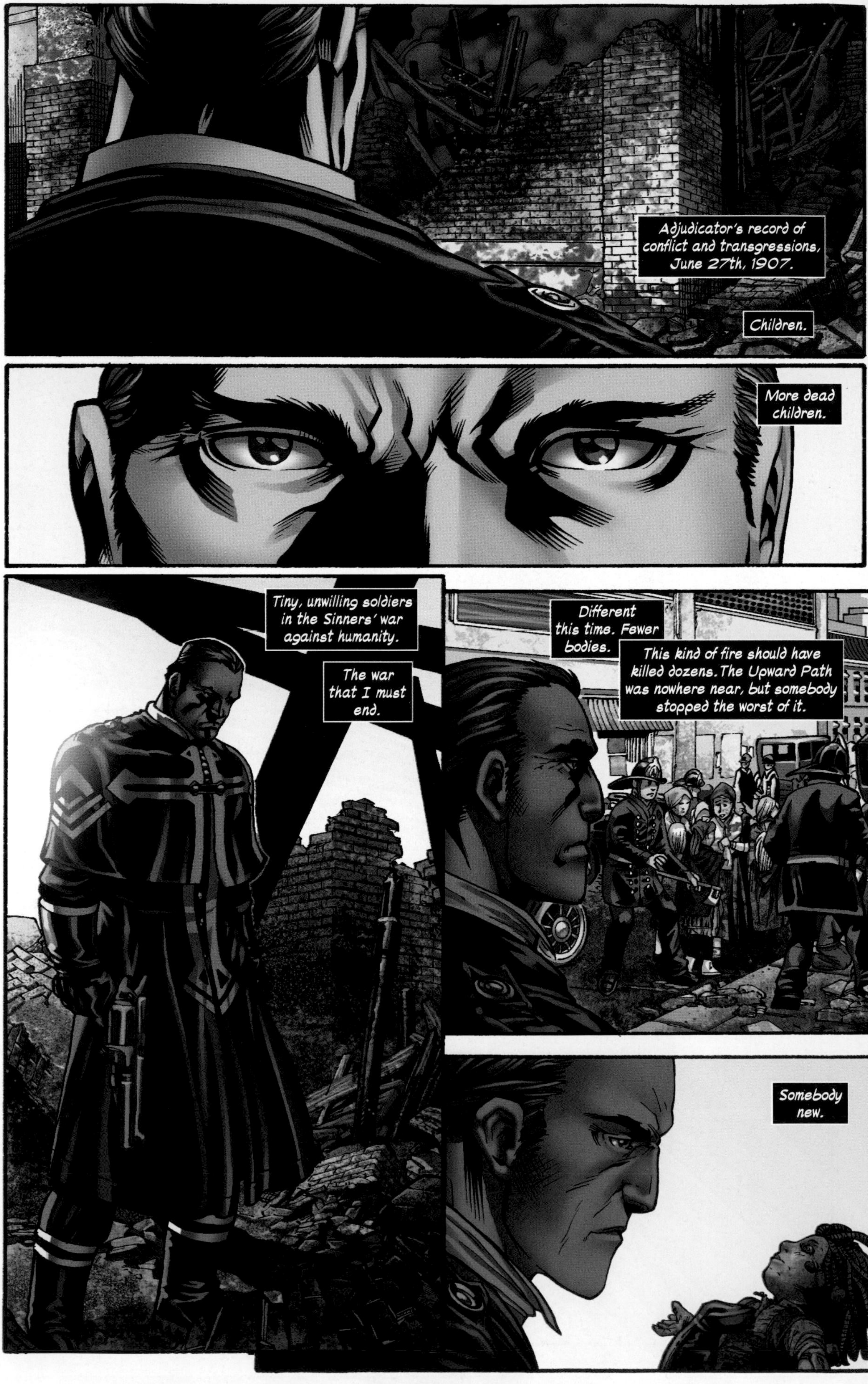

Adjudicator's record of conflict and transgressions, June 27th, 1907.
Children.
More dead children.
Tiny, unwilling soldiers in the Sinners' war against humanity.
The war that I must end.
Different this time. Fewer bodies.
This kind of fire should have killed dozens. The Upward Path was nowhere near, but somebody stopped the worst of it.
Somebody new.

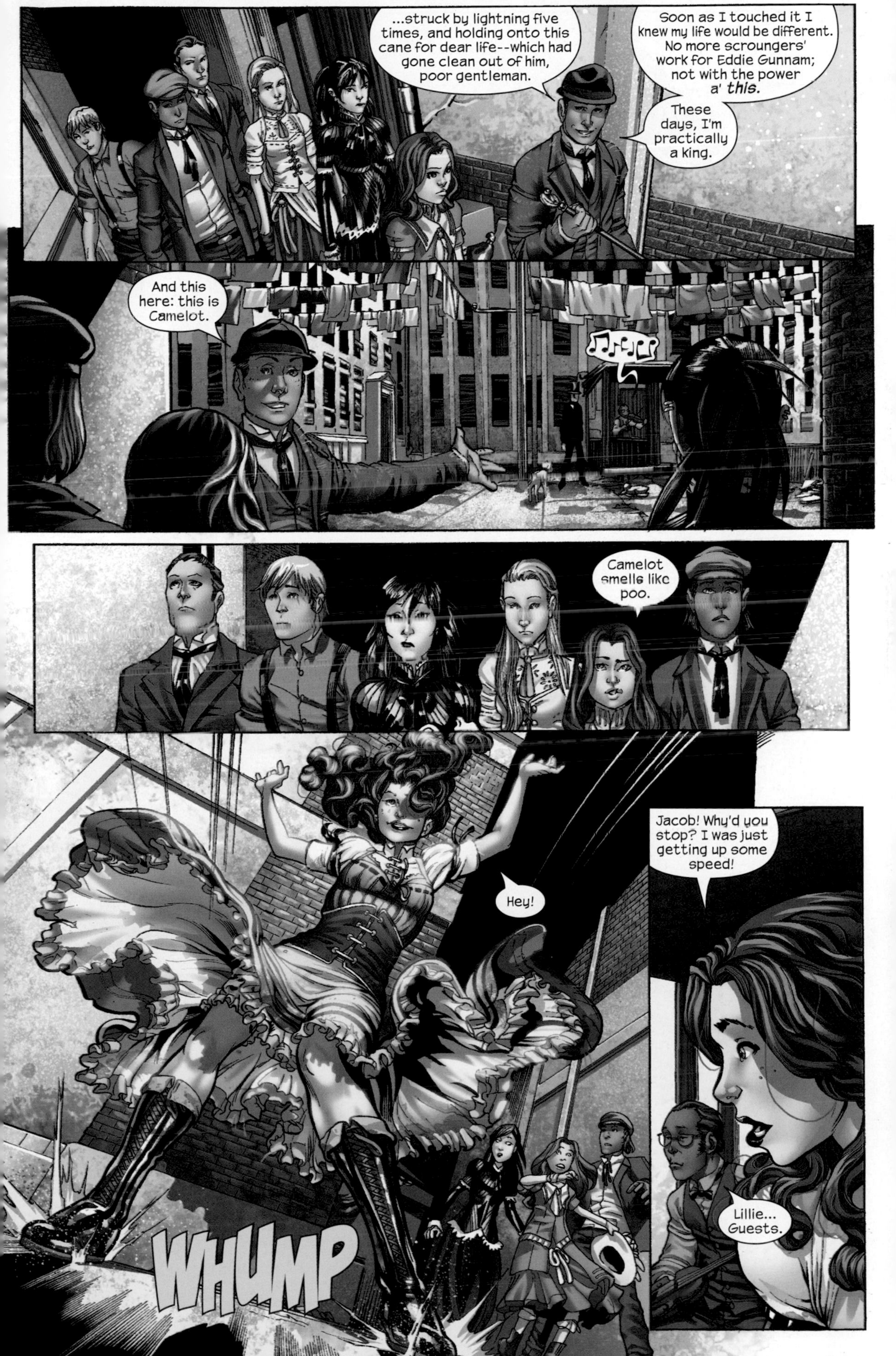
...struck by lightning five times, and holding onto this cane for dear life--which had gone clean out of him, poor gentleman.
Soon as I touched it I knew my life would be different. No more scroungers' work for Eddie Gunnam; not with the power a' *this.*
These days, I'm practically a king.
And this here: this is Camelot.
Camelot smells like poo.
Hey!
Jacob! Why'd you stop? I was just getting up some speed!
Lillie... Guests.
WHUMP

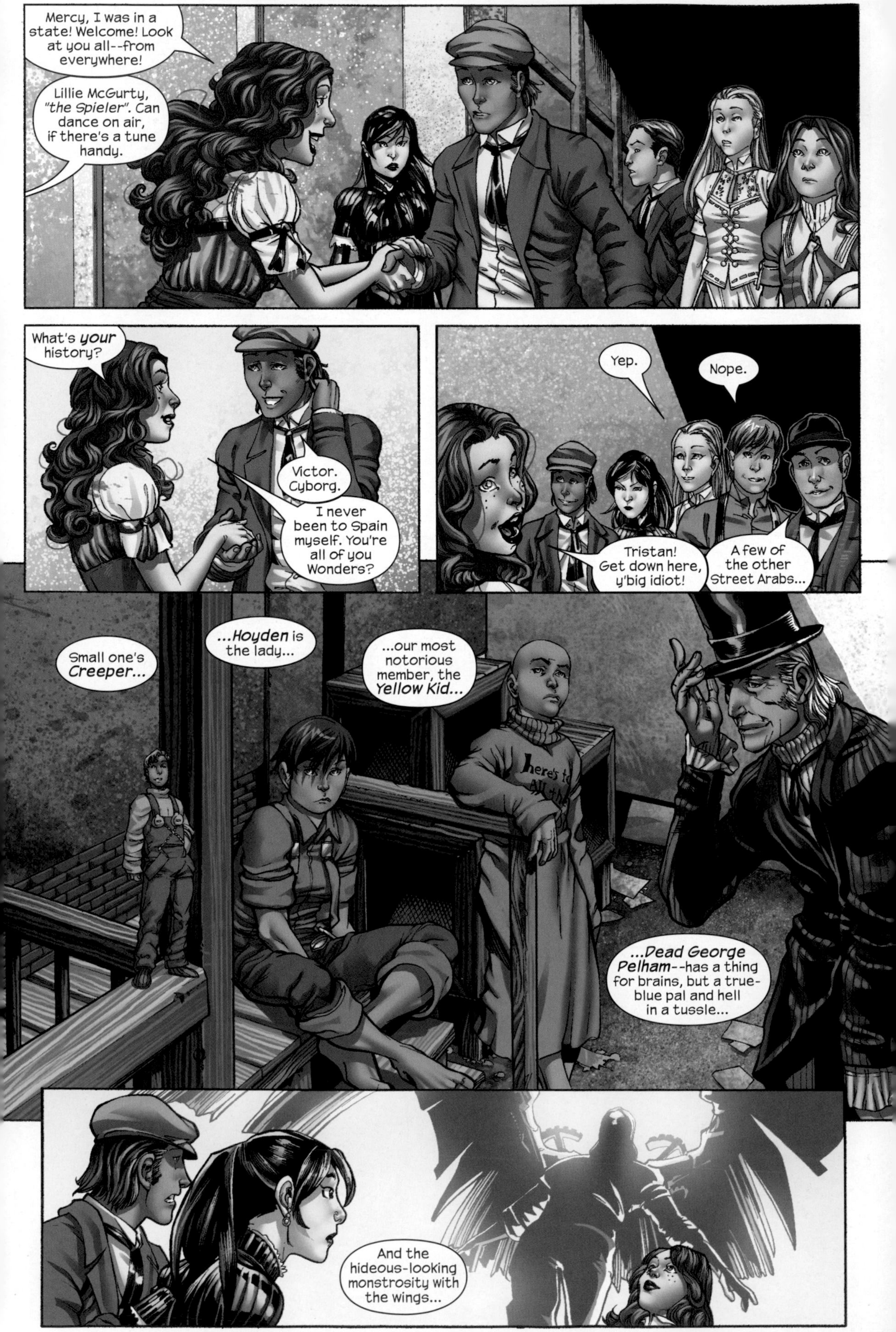

Mercy, I was in a state! Welcome! Look at you all--from everywhere!
Lillie McGurty, "the Spieler". Can dance on air, if there's a tune handy.
What's your history?
Victor. Cyborg.
I never been to Spain myself. You're all of you Wonders?
Yep.
Nope.
Tristan! Get down here, y'big idiot!
A few of the other Street Arabs...
Small one's Creeper...
...Hoyden is the lady...
...our most notorious member, the Yellow Kid...
...Dead George Pelham--has a thing for brains, but a true-blue pal and hell in a tussle...
And the hideous-looking monstrosity with the wings...

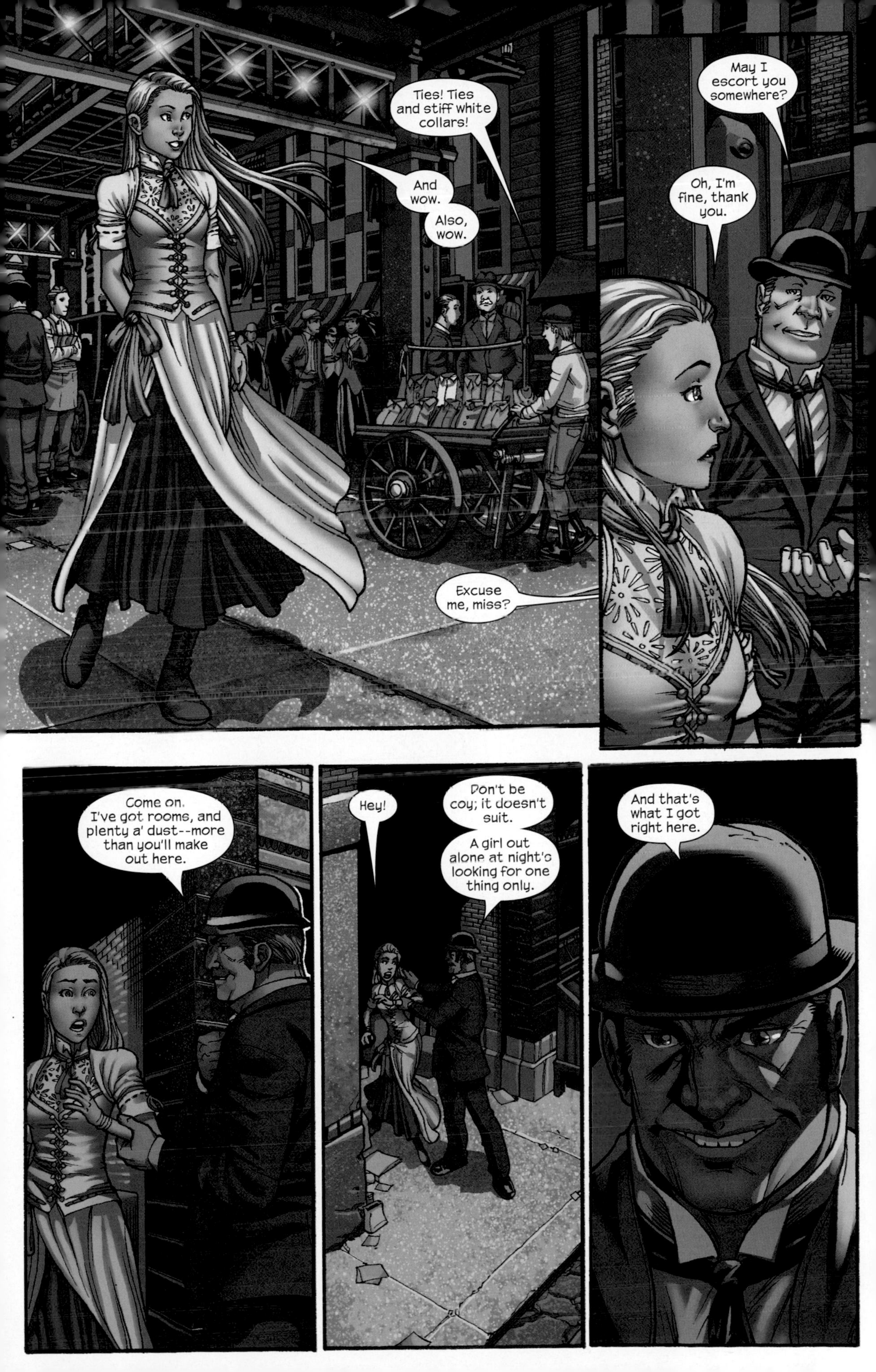
Ties! Ties and stiff white collars!
And wow.
Also, wow.
Excuse me, miss?
May I escort you somewhere?
Oh, I'm fine, thank you.
Come on. I've got rooms, and plenty a' dust--more than you'll make out here.
Hey!
Don't be coy; it doesn't suit.
A girl out alone at night's looking for one thing only.
And that's what I got right here.

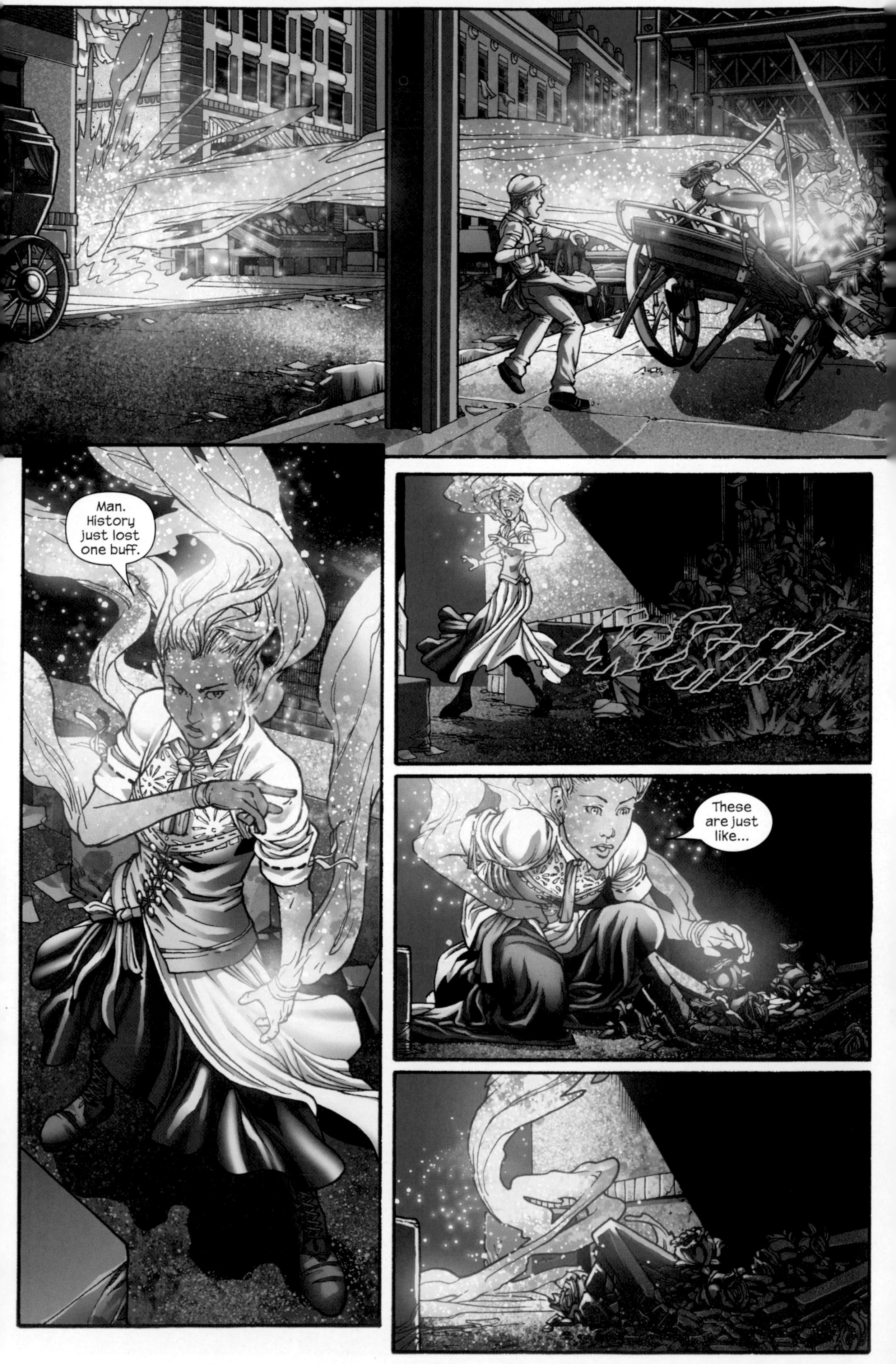
Man. History just lost one buff.
These are just like...

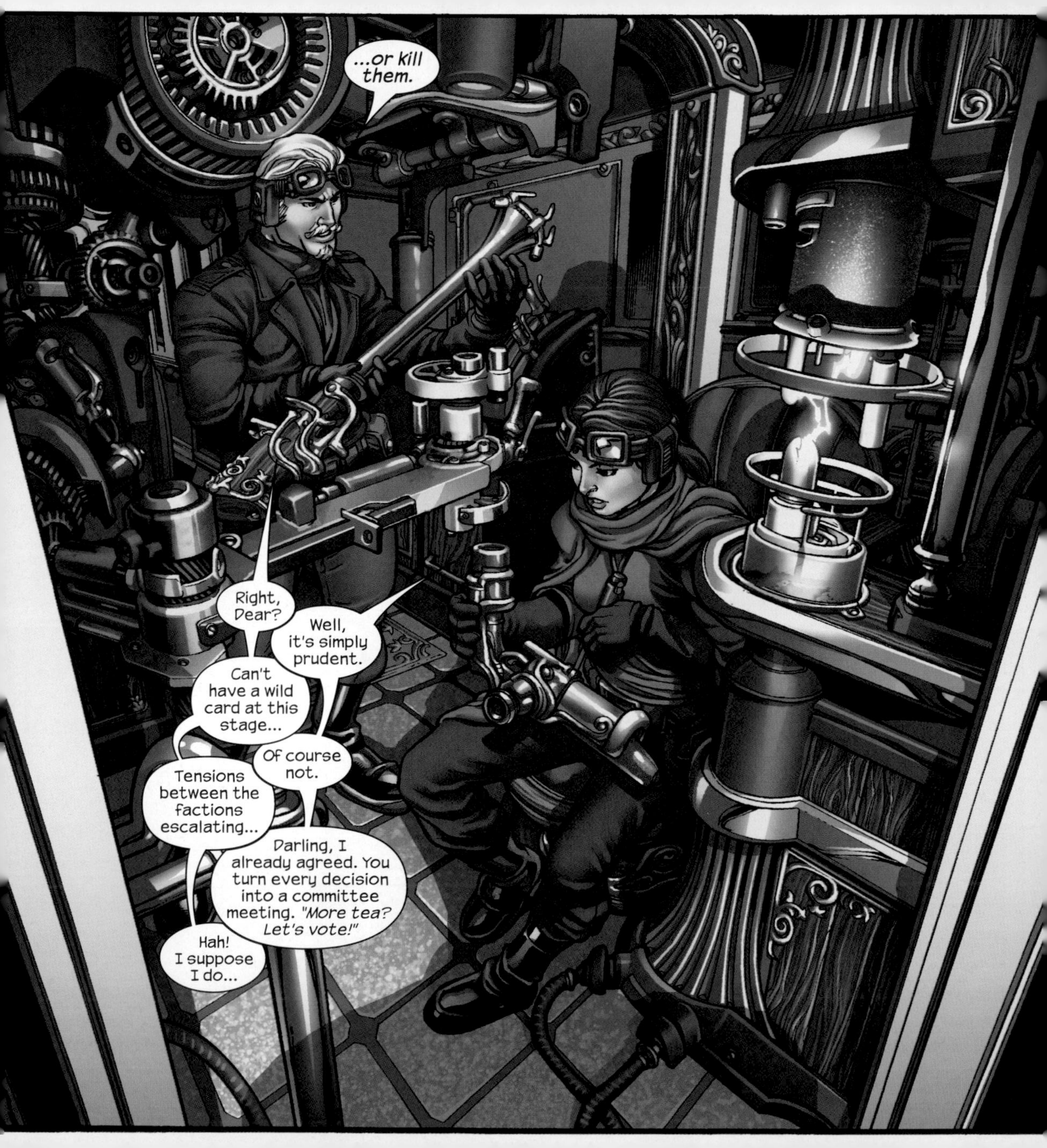
...or kill them.
Right, Dear?
Well, it's simply prudent.
Can't have a wild card at this stage...
Of course not.
Tensions between the factions escalating...
Darling, I already agreed. You turn every decision into a committee meeting. "More tea? Let's vote!"
Hah! I suppose I do...

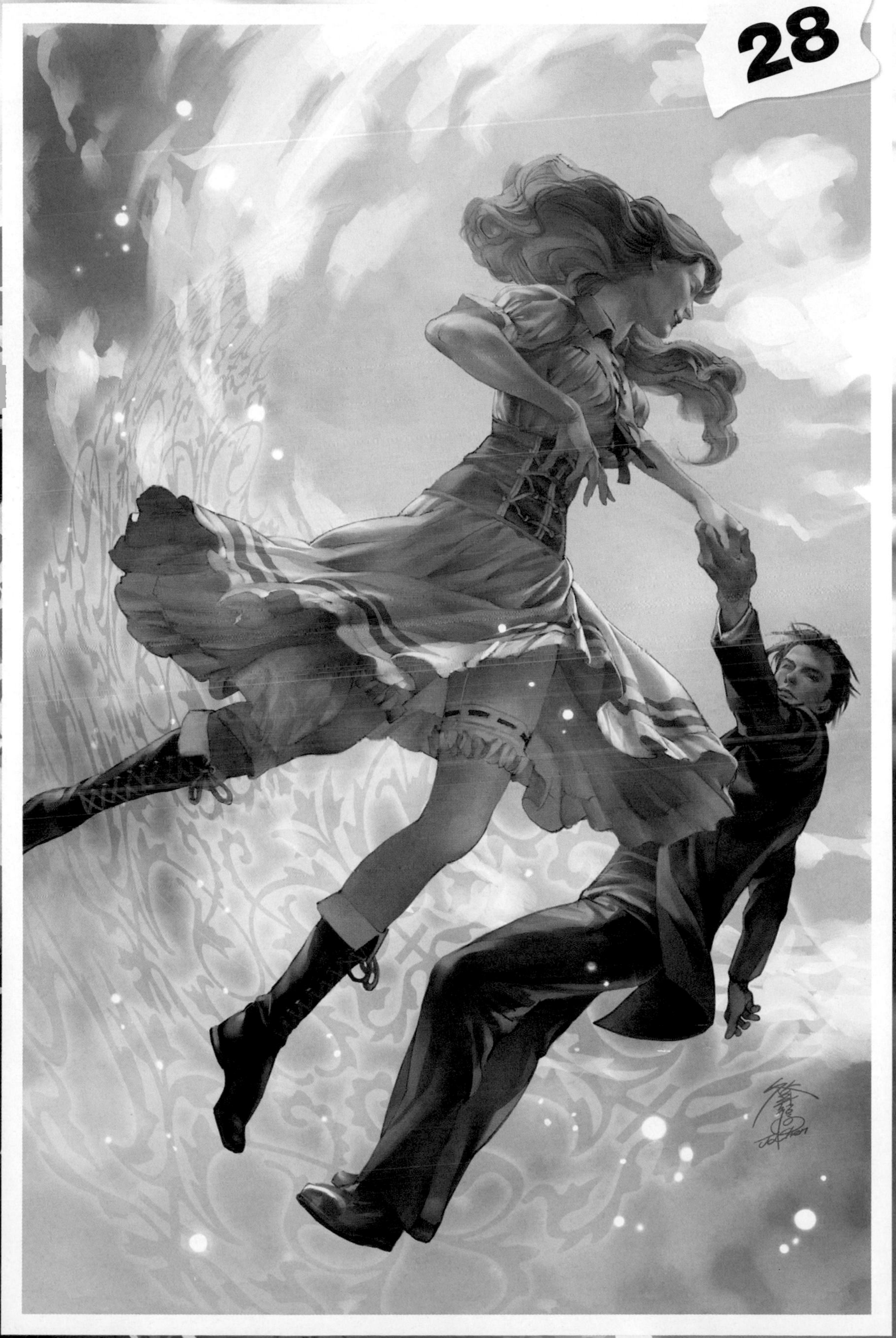
28

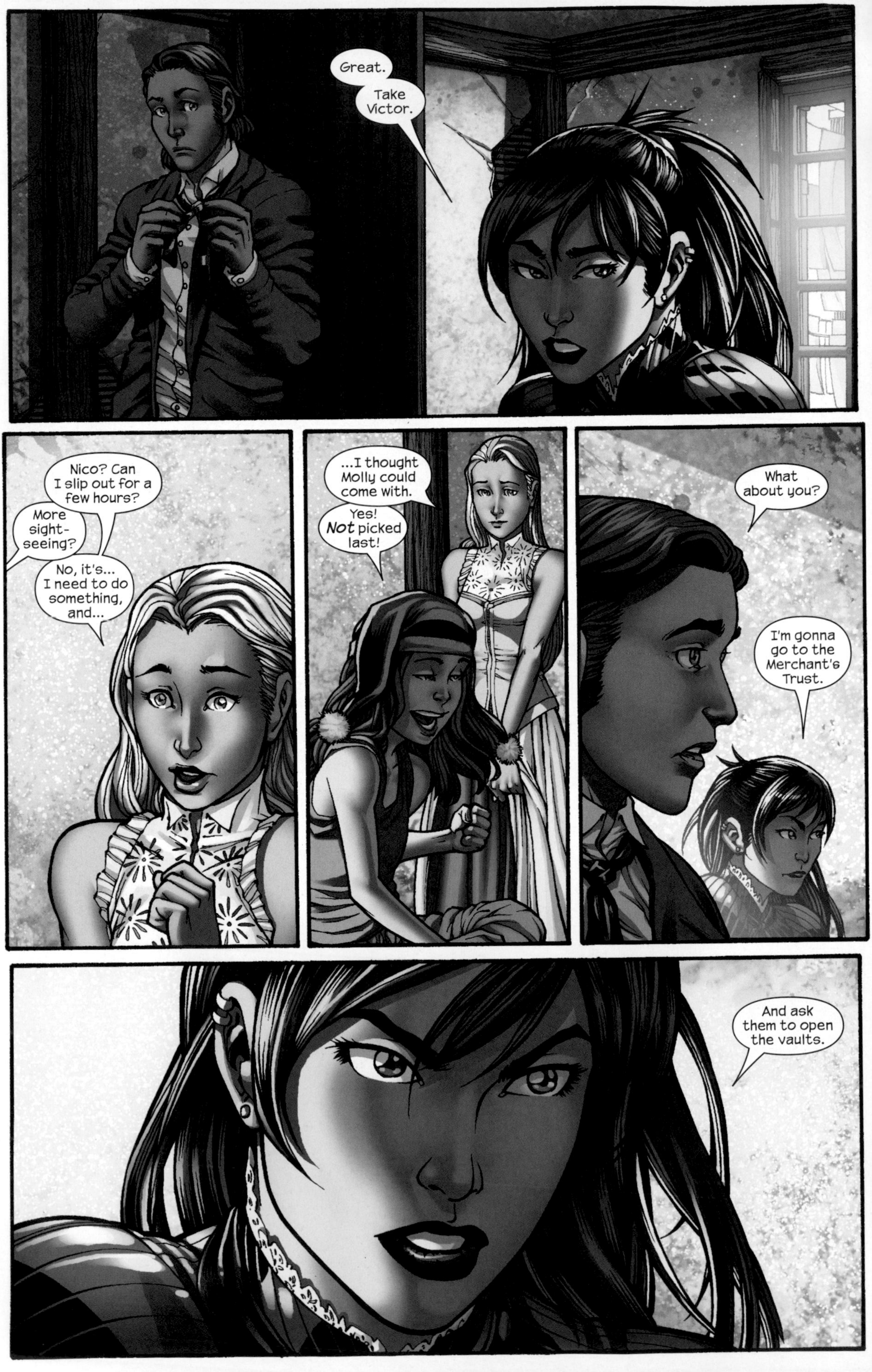
Great.
Take Victor.
Nico? Can I slip out for a few hours?
More sight-seeing?
No, it's... I need to do something, and...
...I thought Molly could come with.
Yes! *Not* picked last!
What about you?
I'm gonna go to the Merchant's Trust.
And ask them to open the vaults.

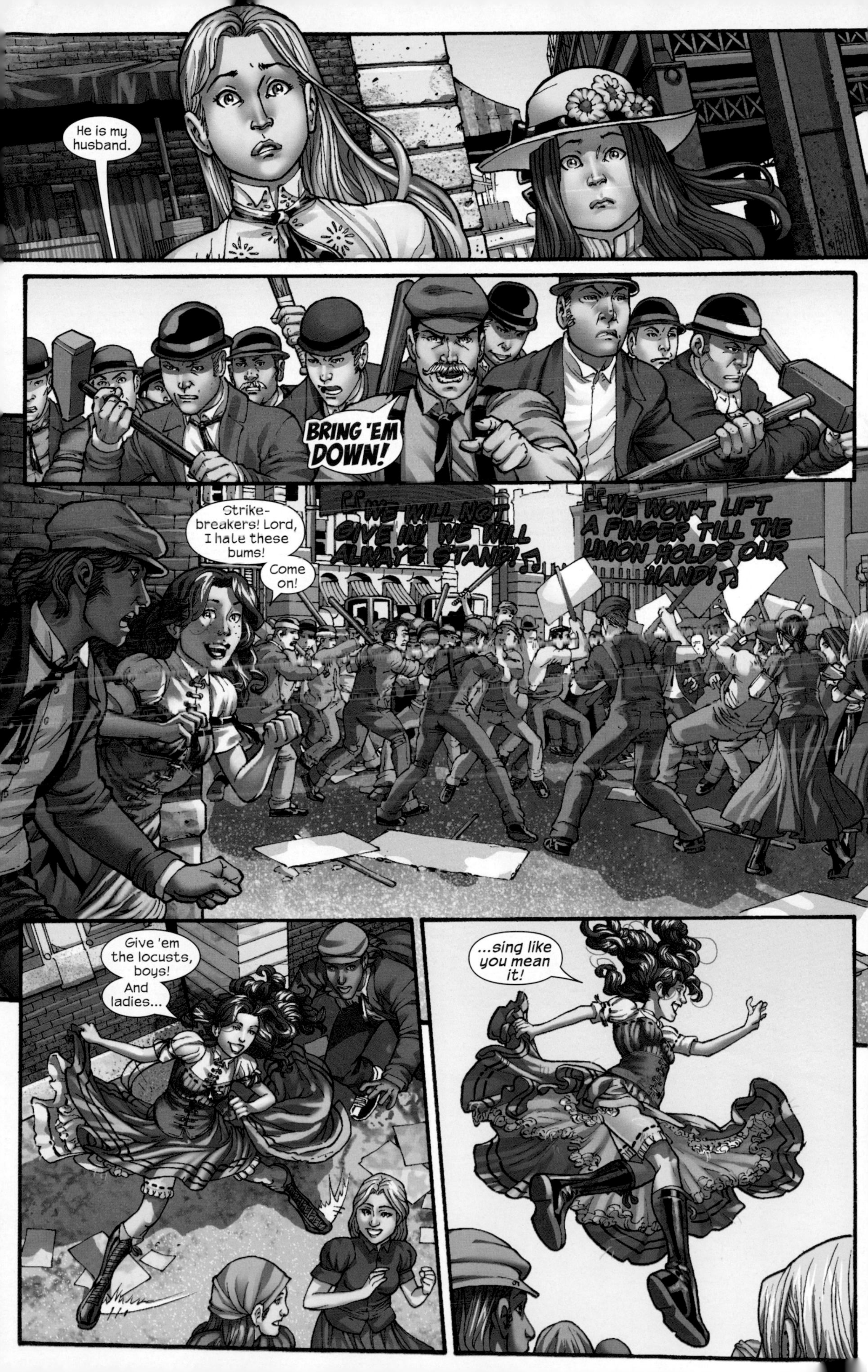
He is my husband.
BRING 'EM DOWN!
Strike-breakers! Lord, I hate these bums!
Come on!
WE WILL NOT GIVE IN! WE WILL ALWAYS STAND!
WE WON'T LIFT A FINGER TILL THE UNION HOLDS OUR HAND!
Give 'em the locusts, boys!
And ladies...
...sing like you mean it!

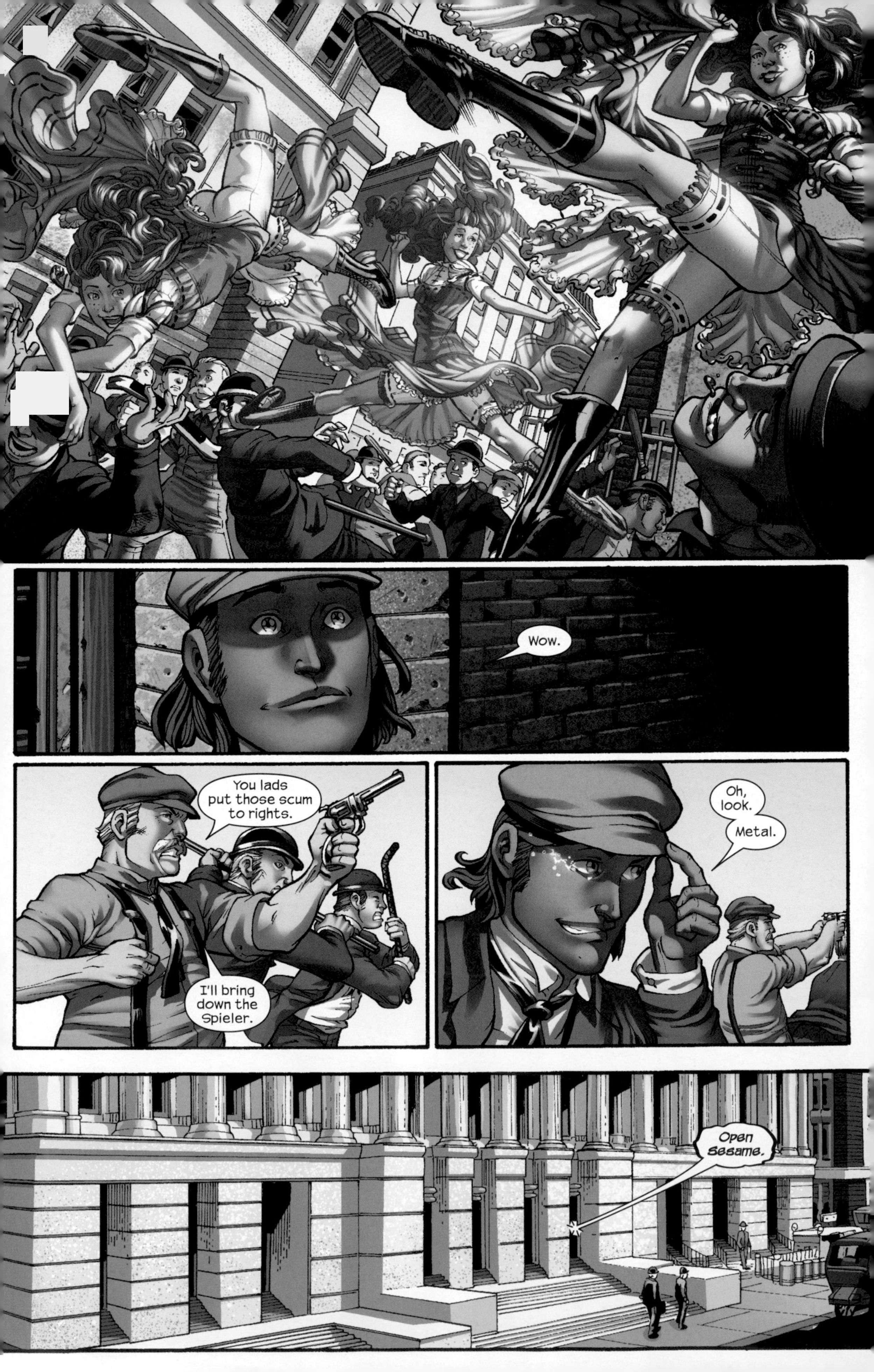
Wow.
You lads put those scum to rights.
I'll bring down the Spieler.
Oh, look.
Metal.
Open Sesame.

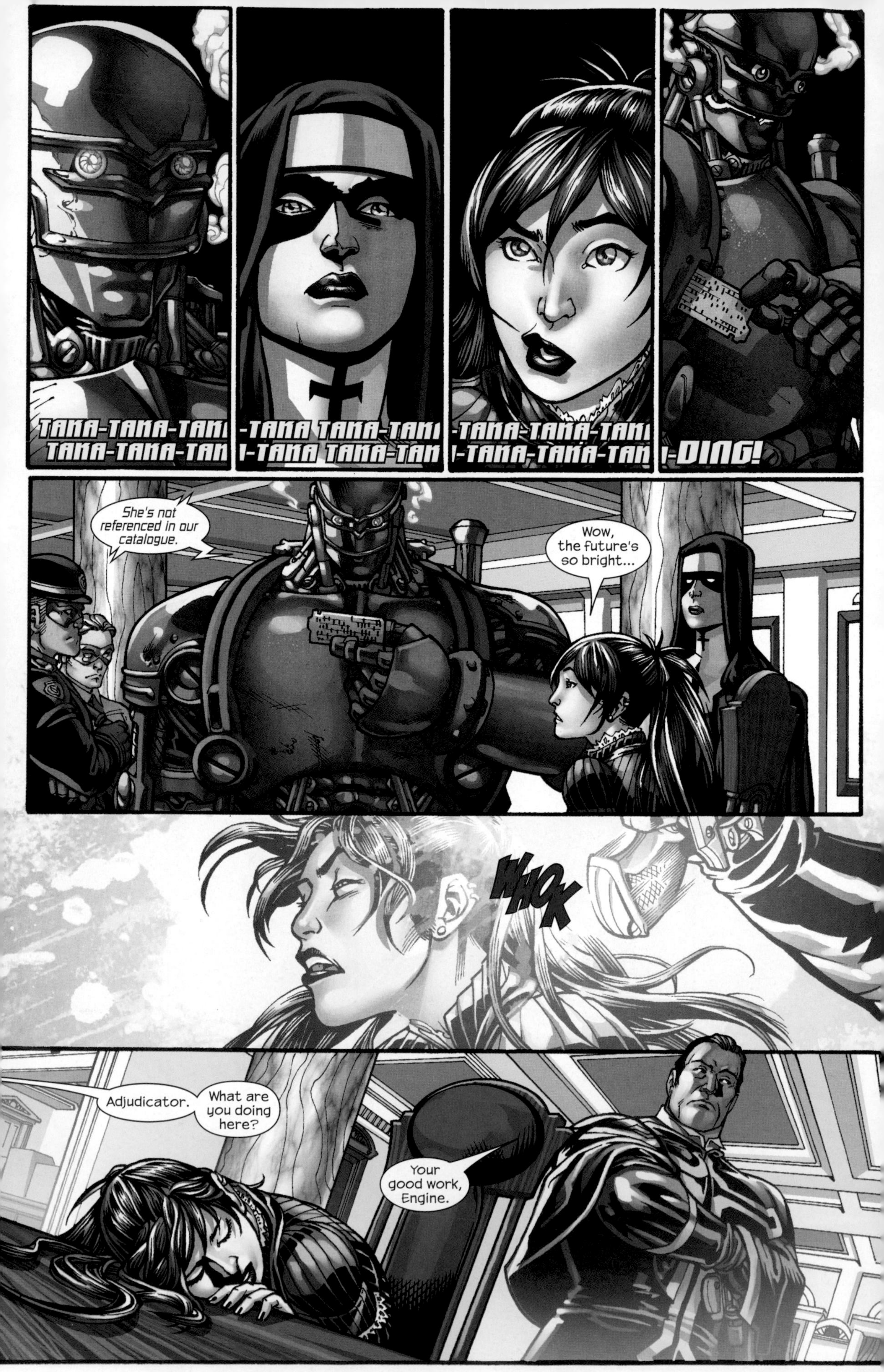
TAKA-TAKA-TAKA-TAKA TAKA-TAKA-TAKA-TAKA-TAKA-TAKA-
TAKA-TAKA-TAKA-TAKA TAKA-TAKA-TAKA-TAKA-TAKA-DING!
She's not referenced in our catalogue.
Wow, the future's so bright...
WHOK
Adjudicator.
What are you doing here?
Your good work, Engine.

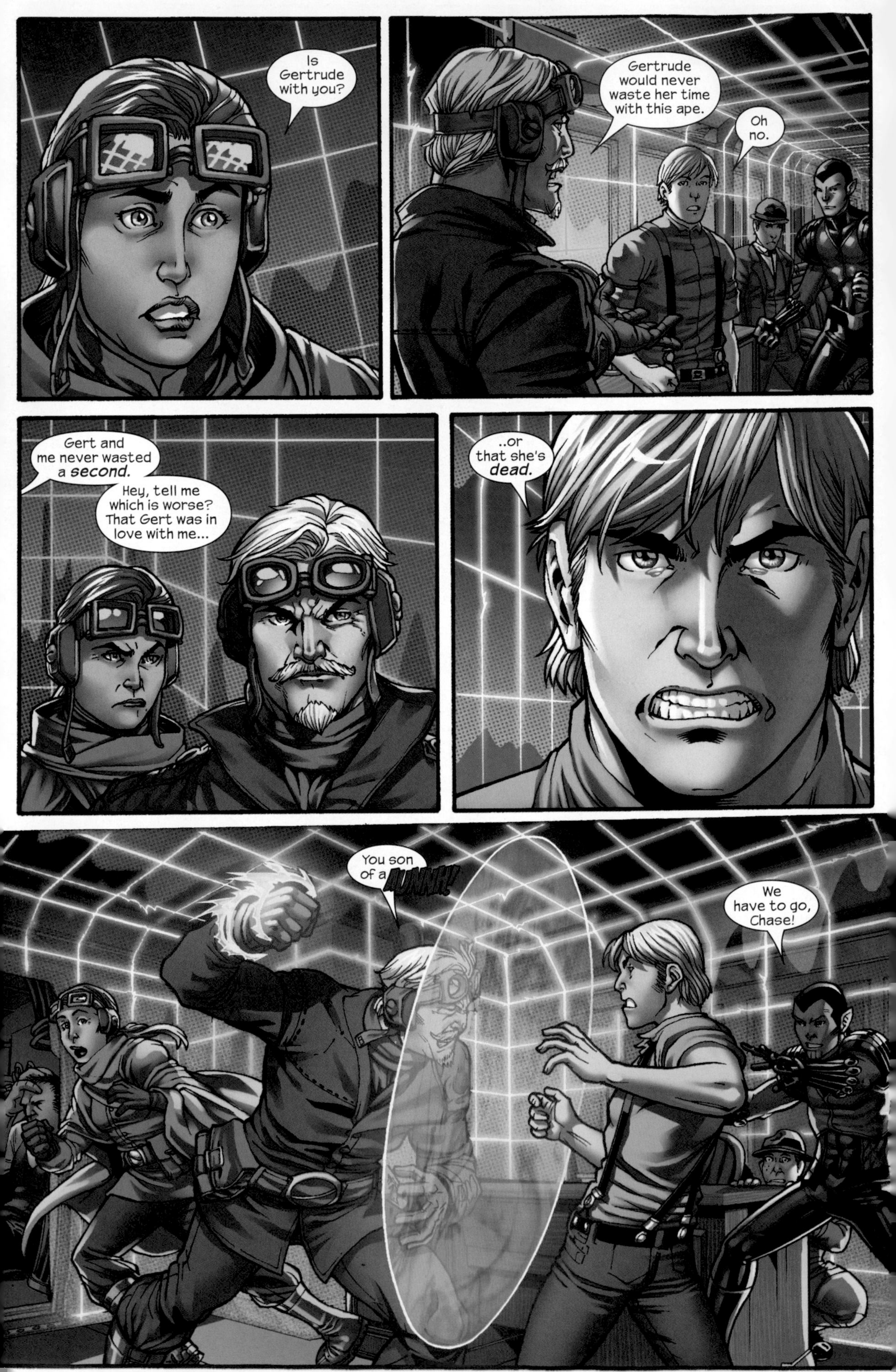
Is Gertrude with you?
Gertrude would never waste her time with this ape.
Oh no.
Gert and me never wasted a *second.*
Hey, tell me which is worse? That Gert was in love with me...
..or that she's *dead.*
You son of a AUNNH!
We have to go, Chase!

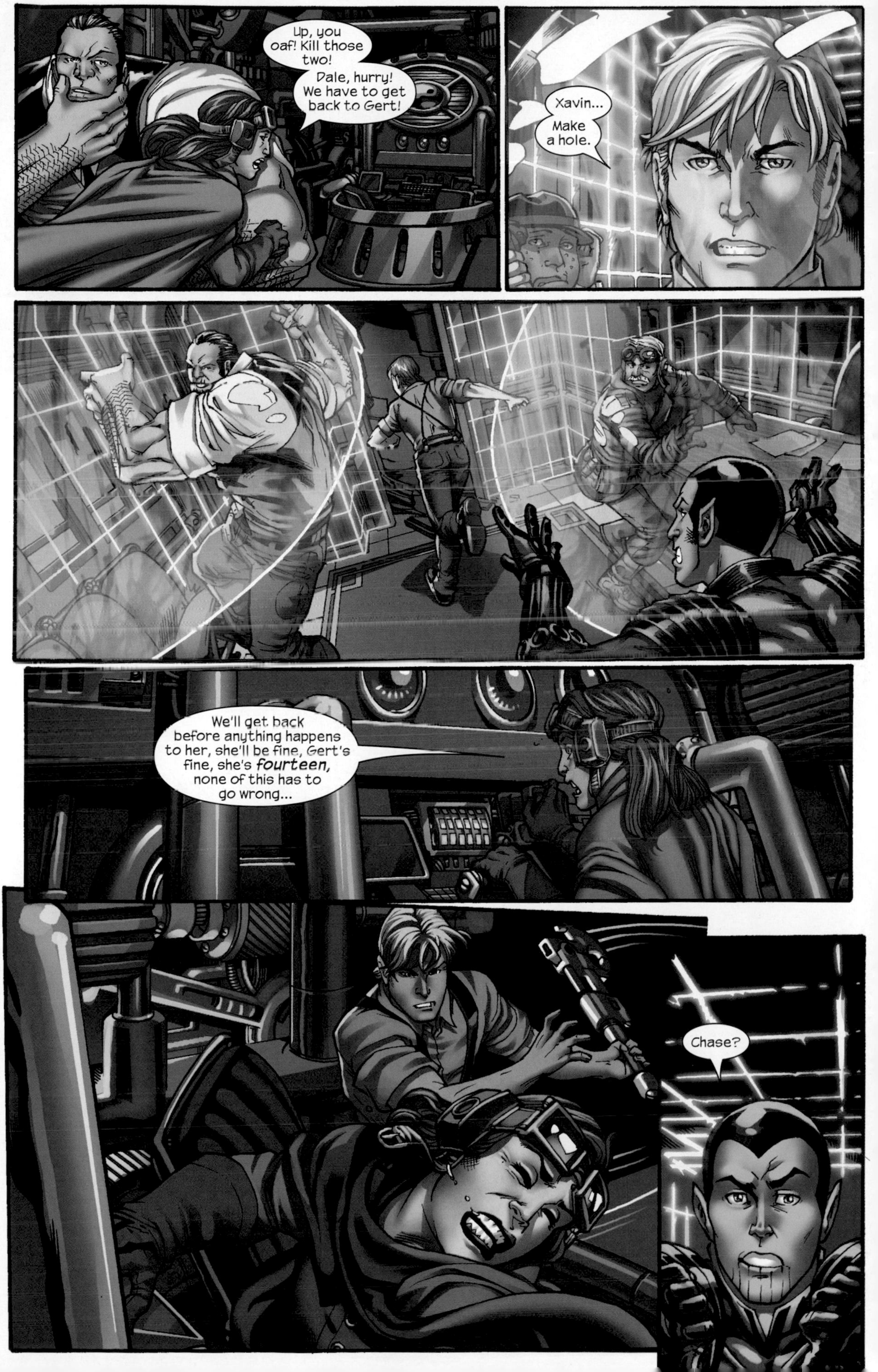
Up, you oaf! Kill those two!
Dale, hurry! We have to get back to Gert!
Xavin...
Make a hole.
We'll get back before anything happens to her, she'll be fine, Gert's fine, she's *fourteen,* none of this has to go wrong...
Chase?

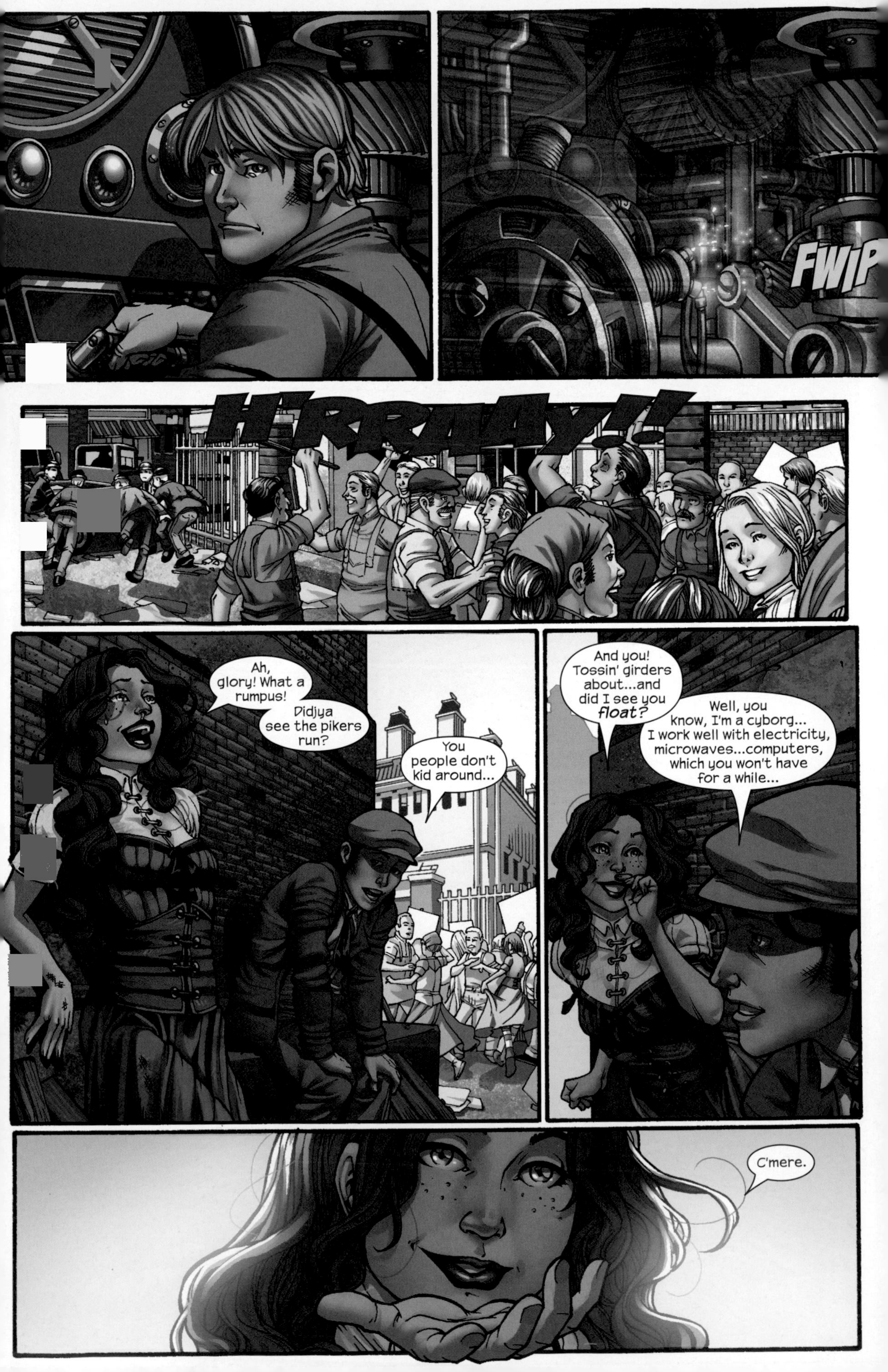
FWIP
H'RRAAY!!
Ah, glory! What a rumpus!
Didjya see the pikers run?
You people don't kid around...
And you! Tossin' girders about...and did I see you *float*?
Well, you know, I'm a cyborg... I work well with electricity, microwaves...computers, which you won't have for a while...
C'mere.

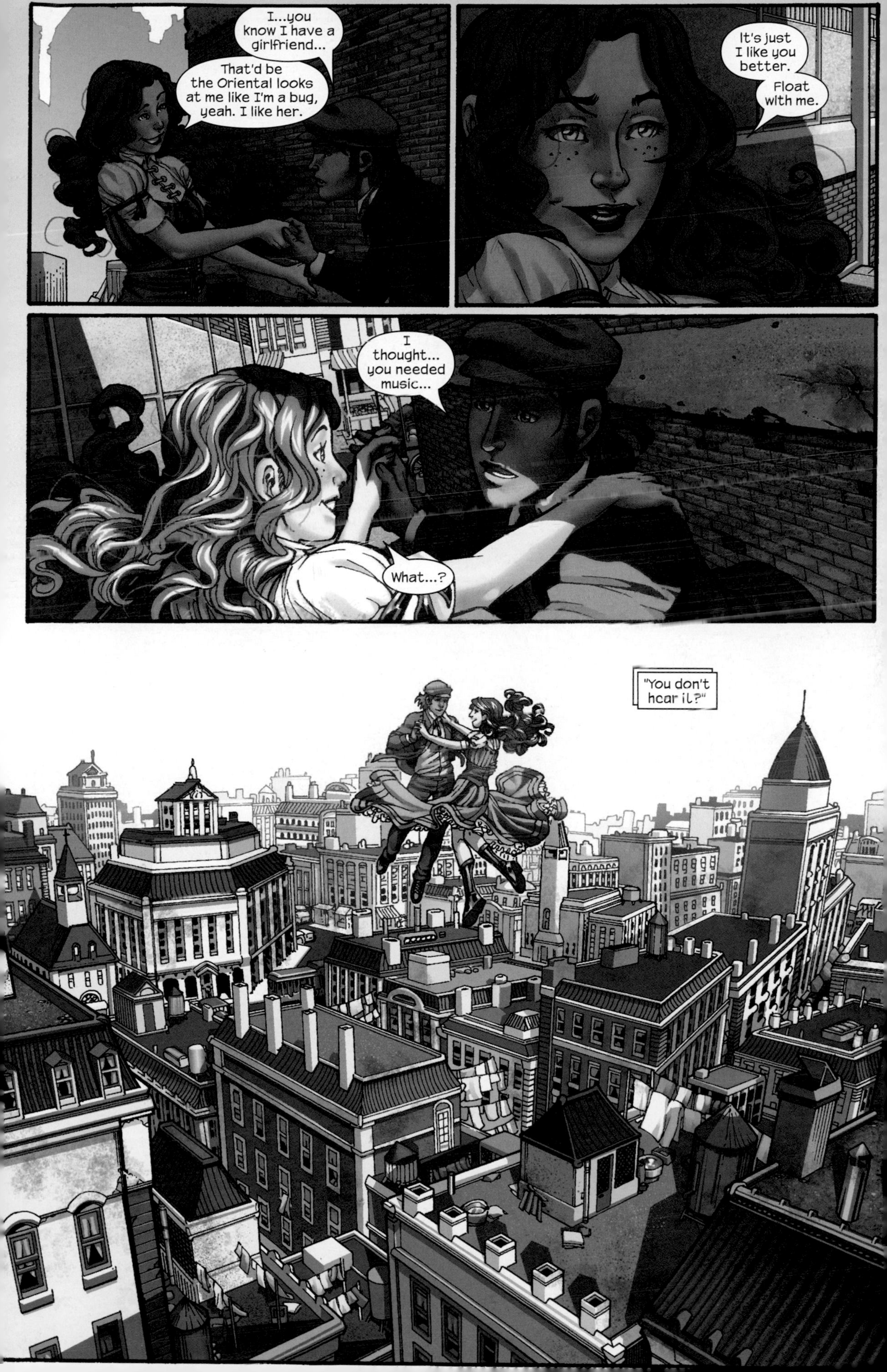

I...you know I have a girlfriend...
That'd be the Oriental looks at me like I'm a bug, yeah. I like her.
It's just I like you better.
Float with me.
I thought... you needed music...
What...?
"You don't hear it?"

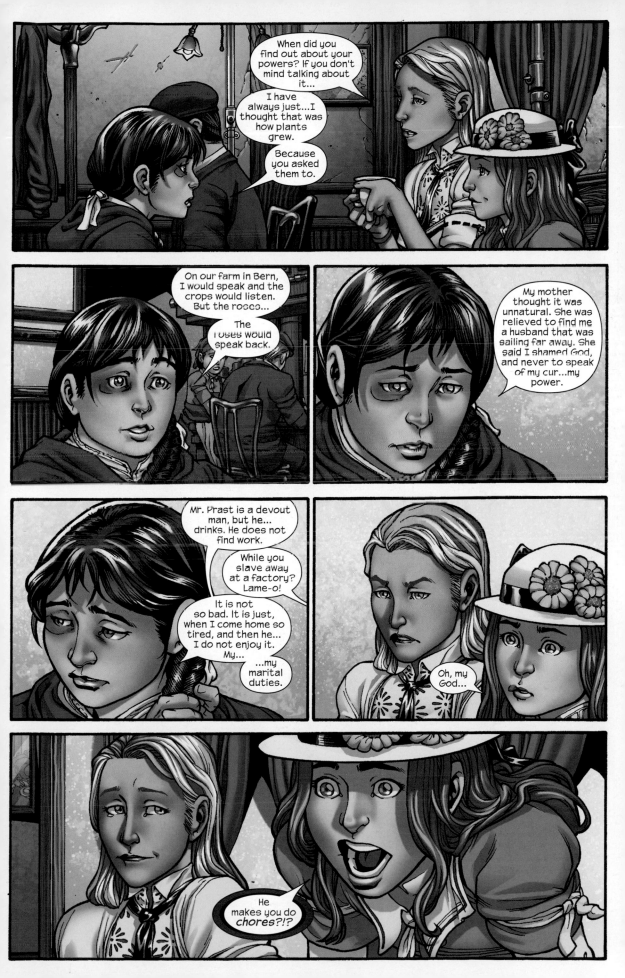

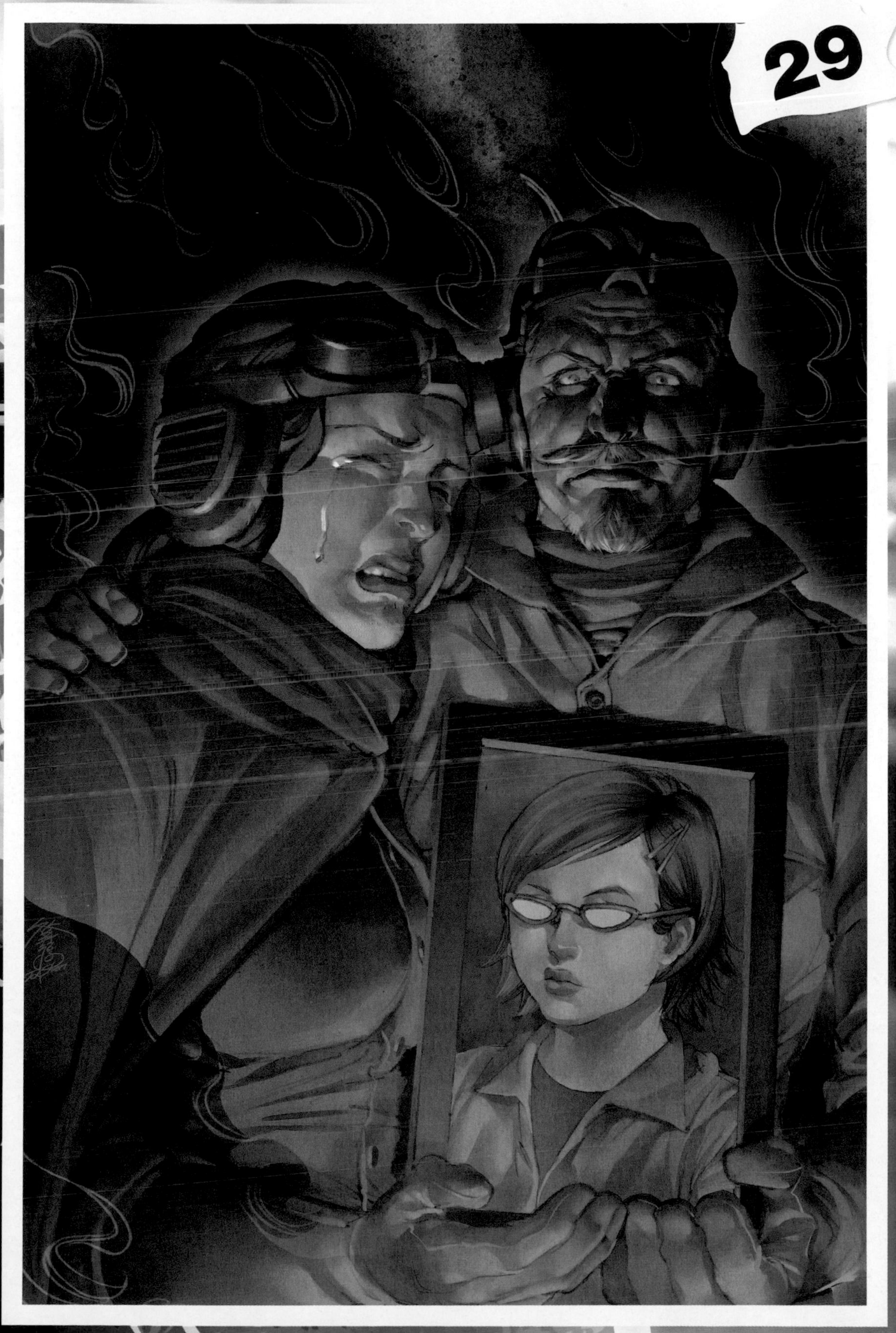
29

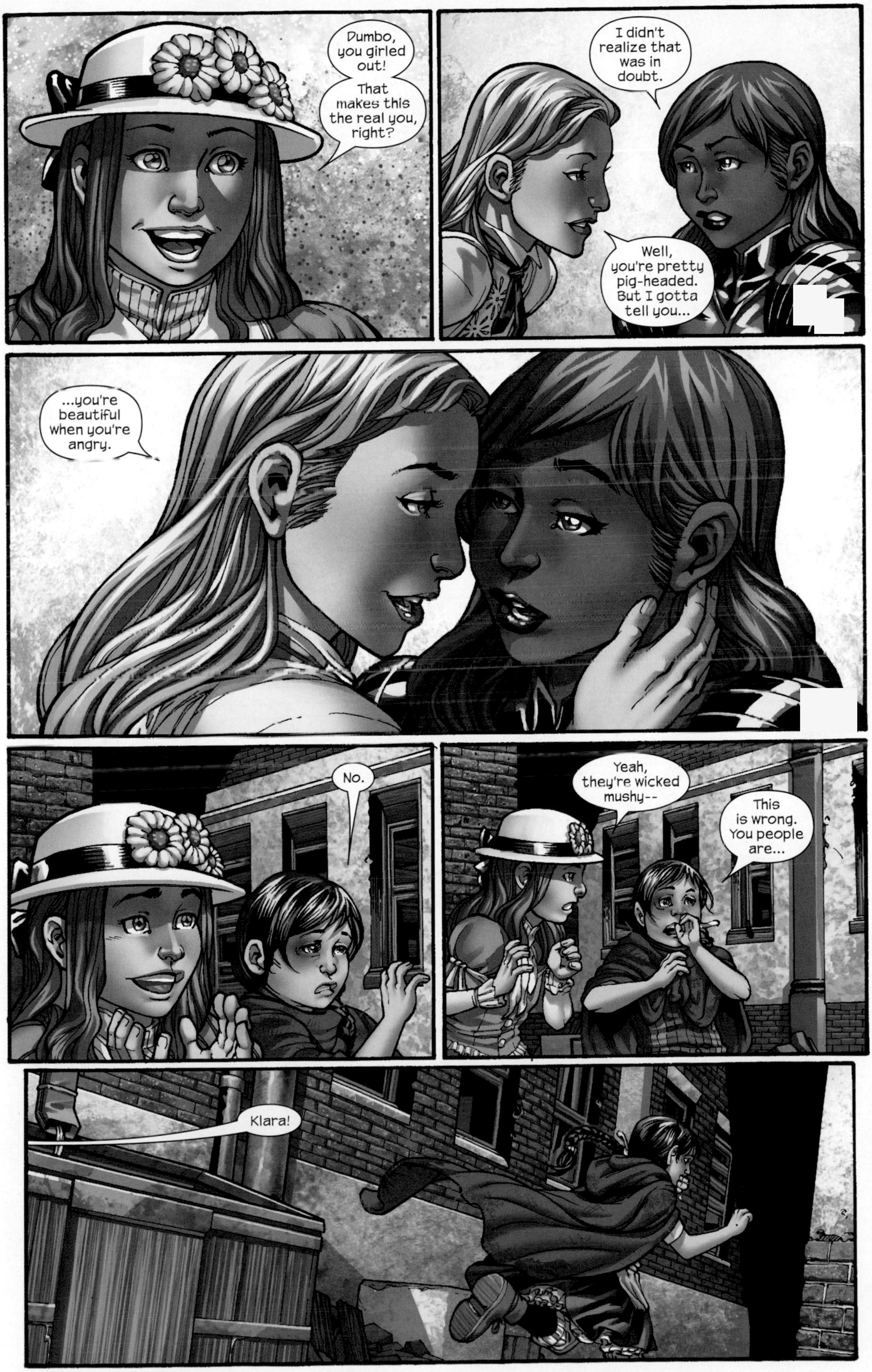

Dumbo, you girled out!
That makes this the real you, right?
I didn't realize that was in doubt.
Well, you're pretty pig-headed. But I gotta tell you...
...you're beautiful when you're angry.
No.
Yeah, they're wicked mushy--
This is wrong. You people are...
Klara!

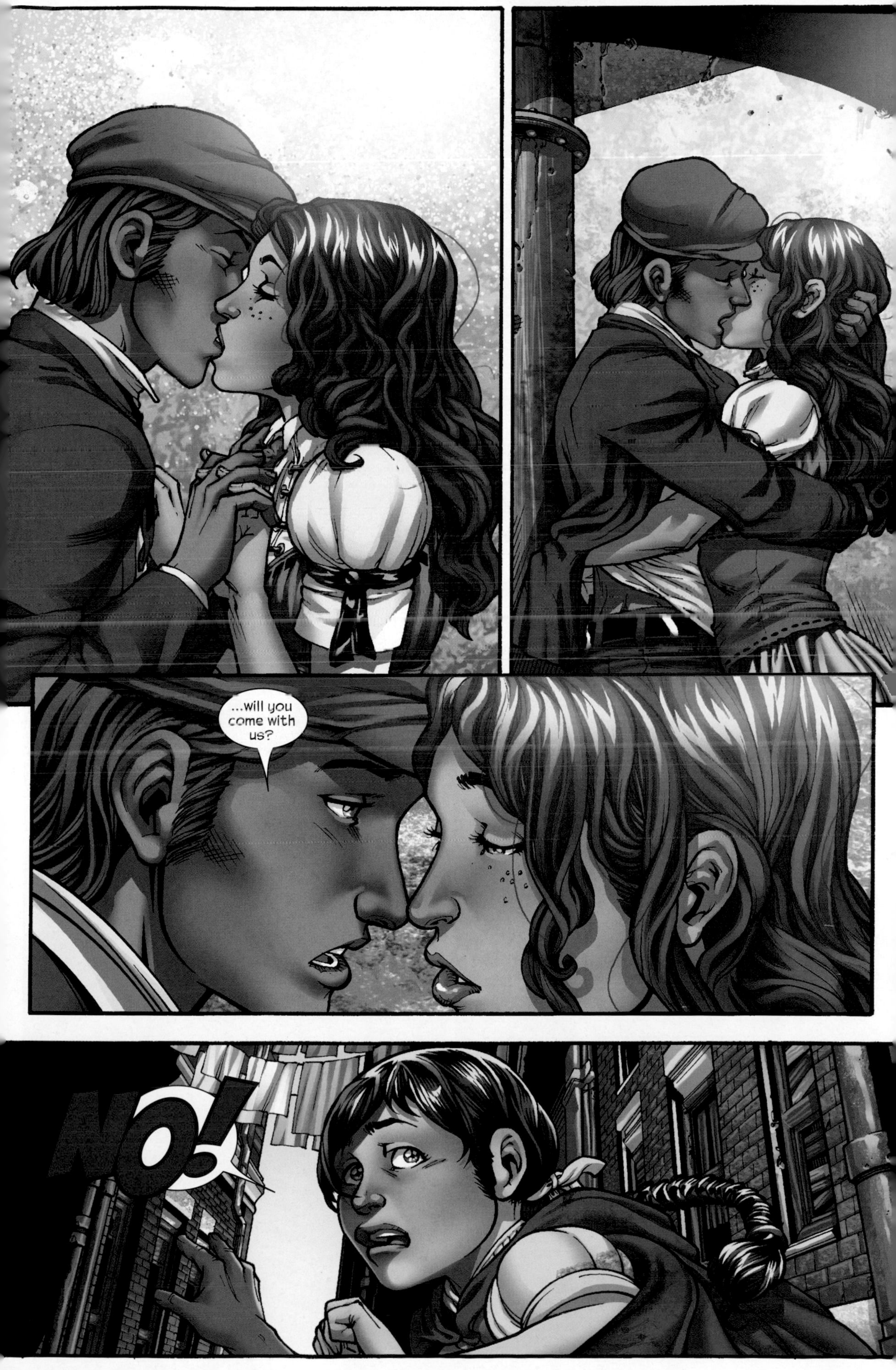

...will you come with us?
NO!

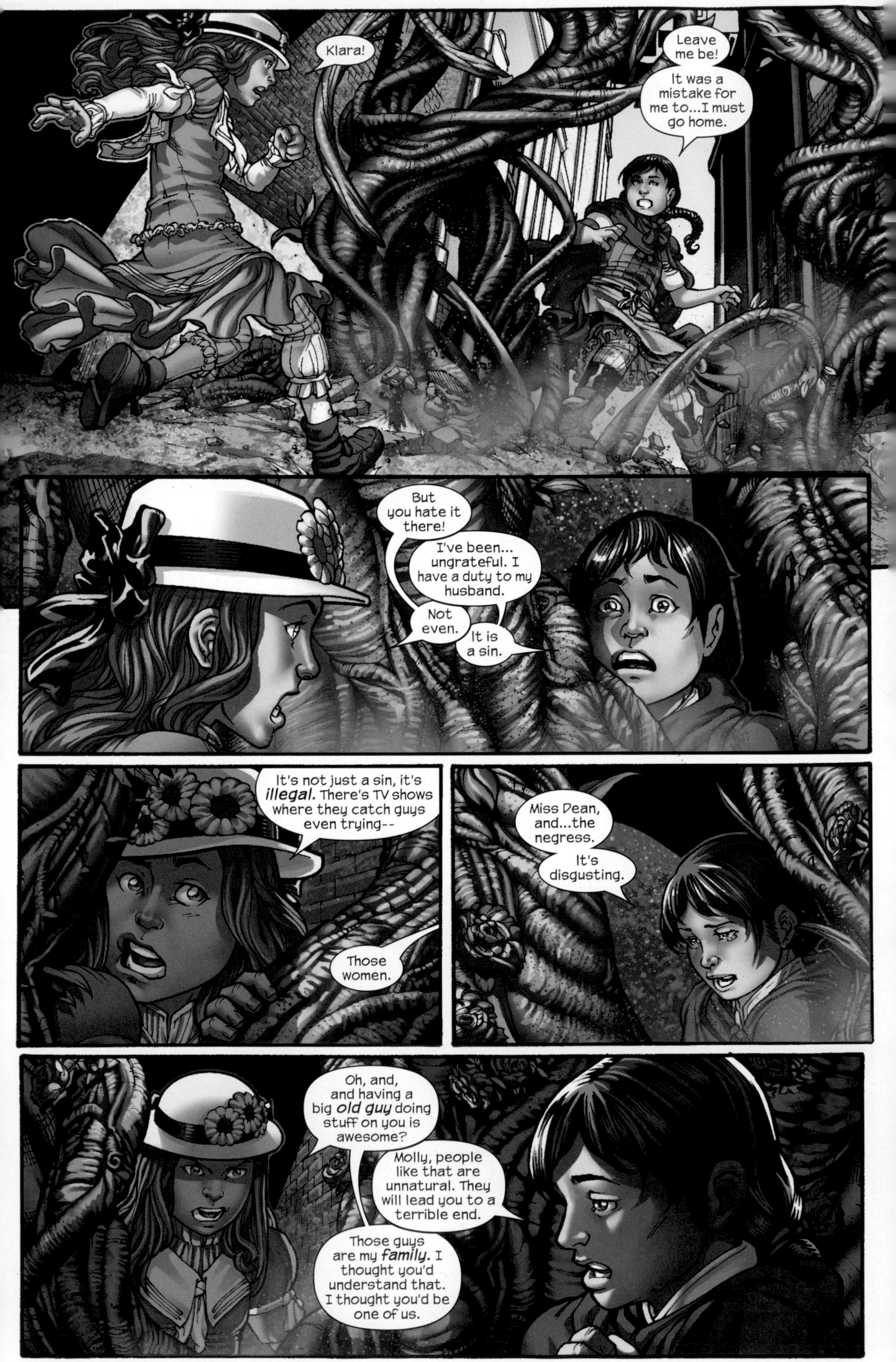

Klara!
Leave me be!
It was a mistake for me to...I must go home.
But you hate it there!
I've been... ungrateful. I have a duty to my husband.
Not even.
It is a sin.
It's not just a sin, it's *illegal.* There's TV shows where they catch guys even trying--
Those women.
Miss Dean, and...the negress.
It's disgusting.
Oh, and, and having a big *old guy* doing stuff on you is awesome?
Molly, people like that are unnatural. They will lead you to a terrible end.
Those guys are my *family.* I thought you'd understand that. I thought you'd be one of us.

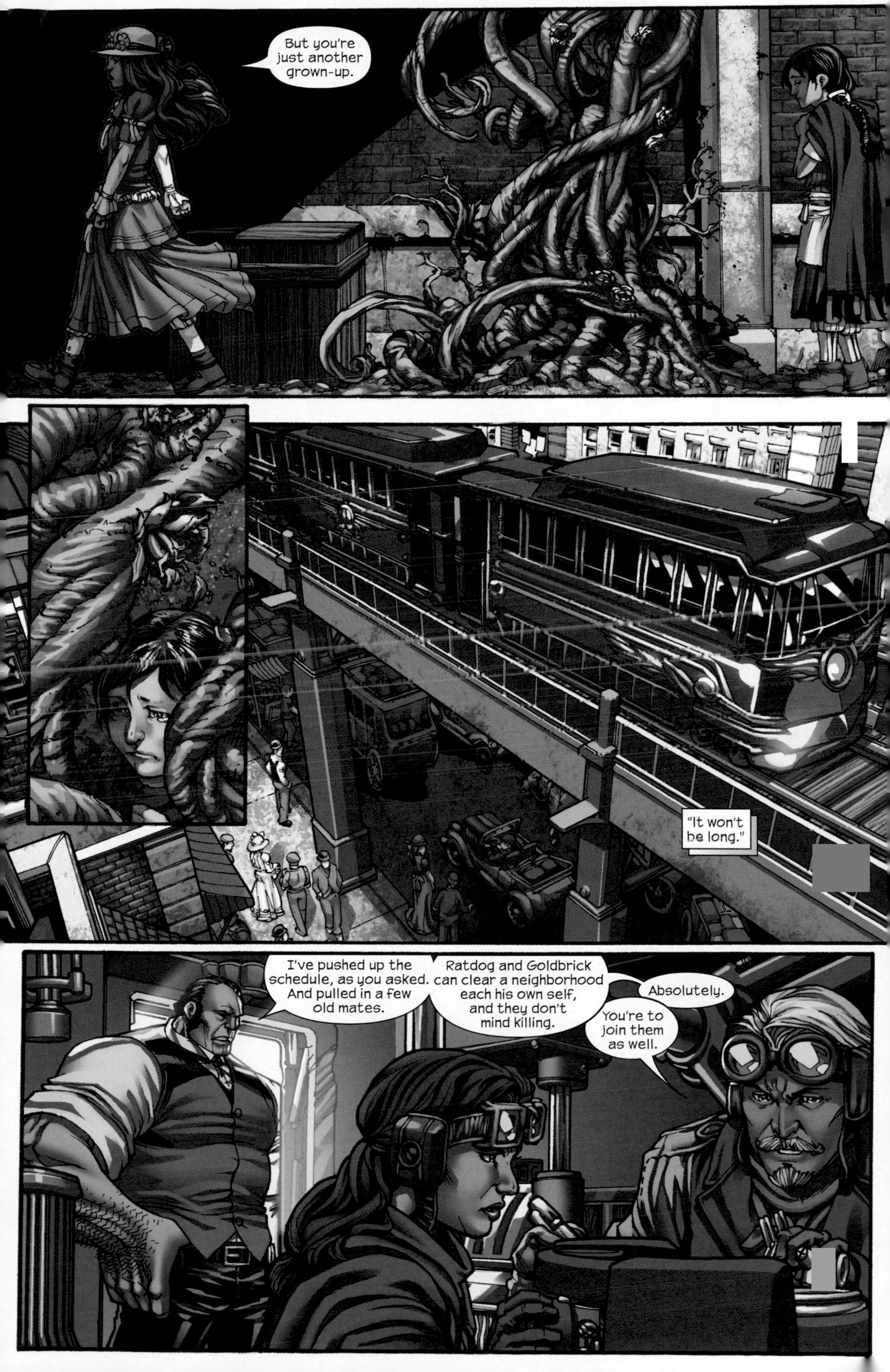
But you're just another grown-up.
"It won't be long."
I've pushed up the schedule, as you asked. And pulled in a few old mates.
Ratdog and Goldbrick can clear a neighborhood each his own self, and they don't mind killing.
Absolutely.
You're to join them as well.

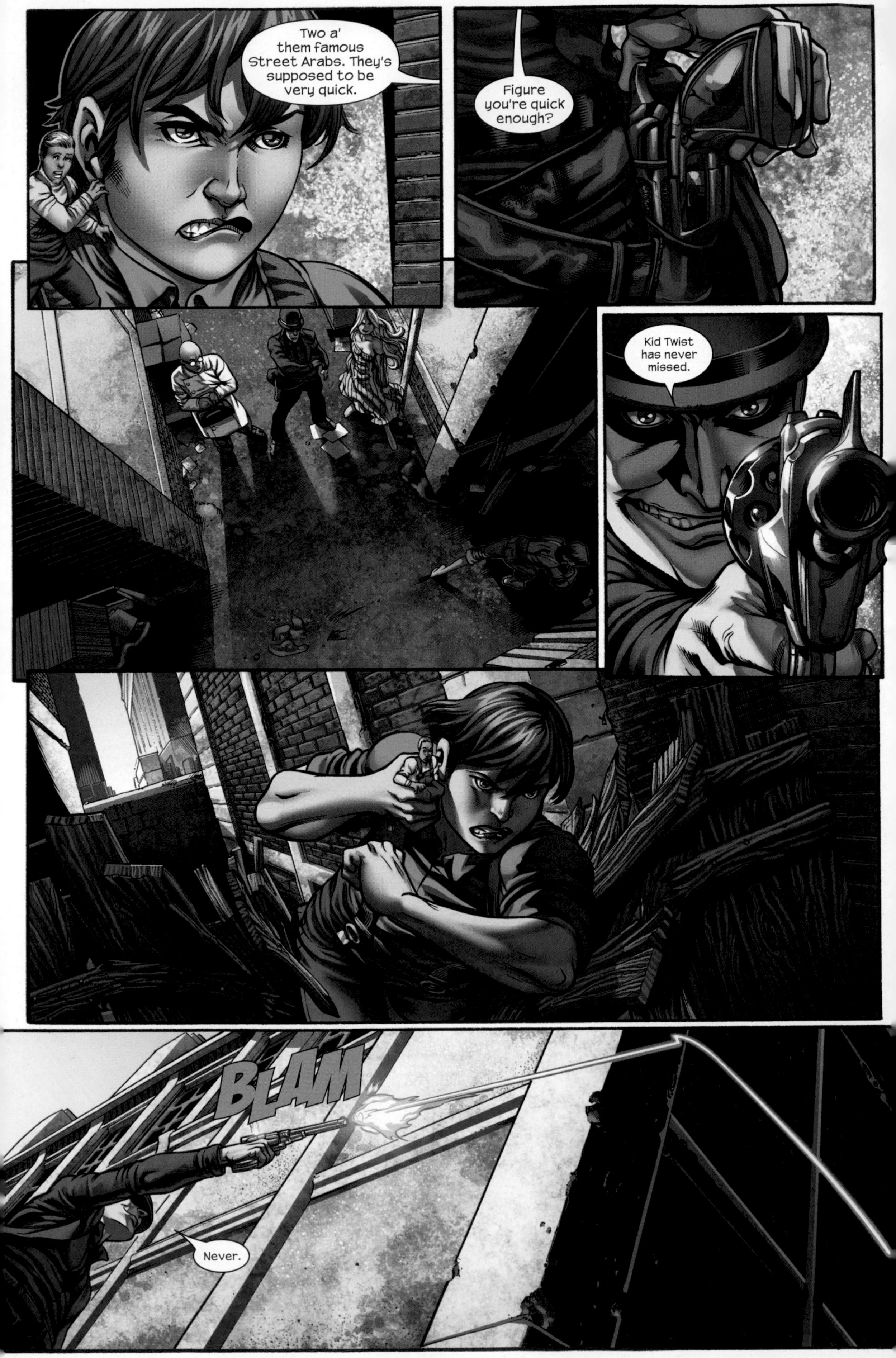
Two a' them famous Street Arabs. They's supposed to be very quick.
Figure you're quick enough?
Kid Twist has never missed.
BLAM
Never.

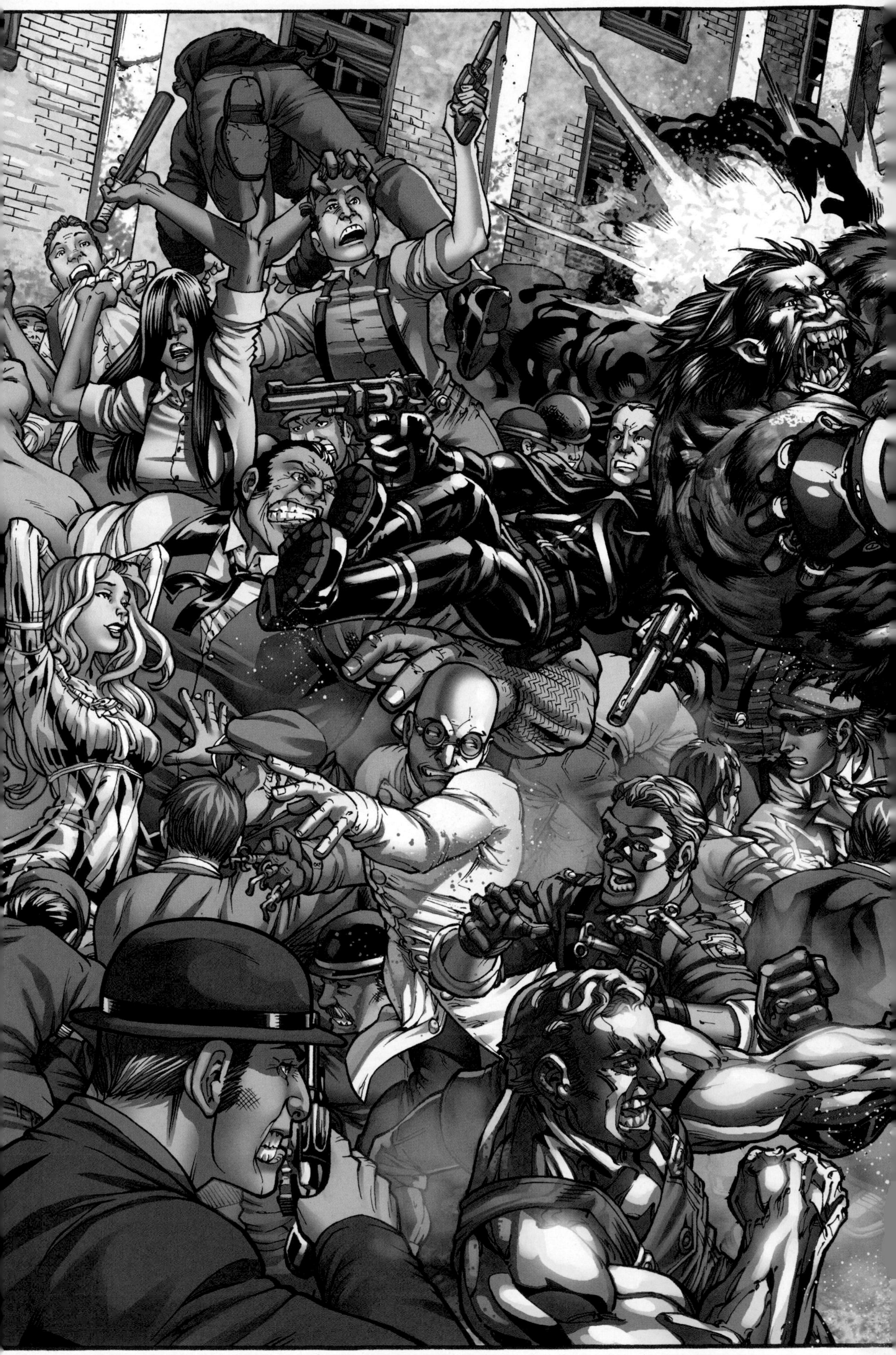

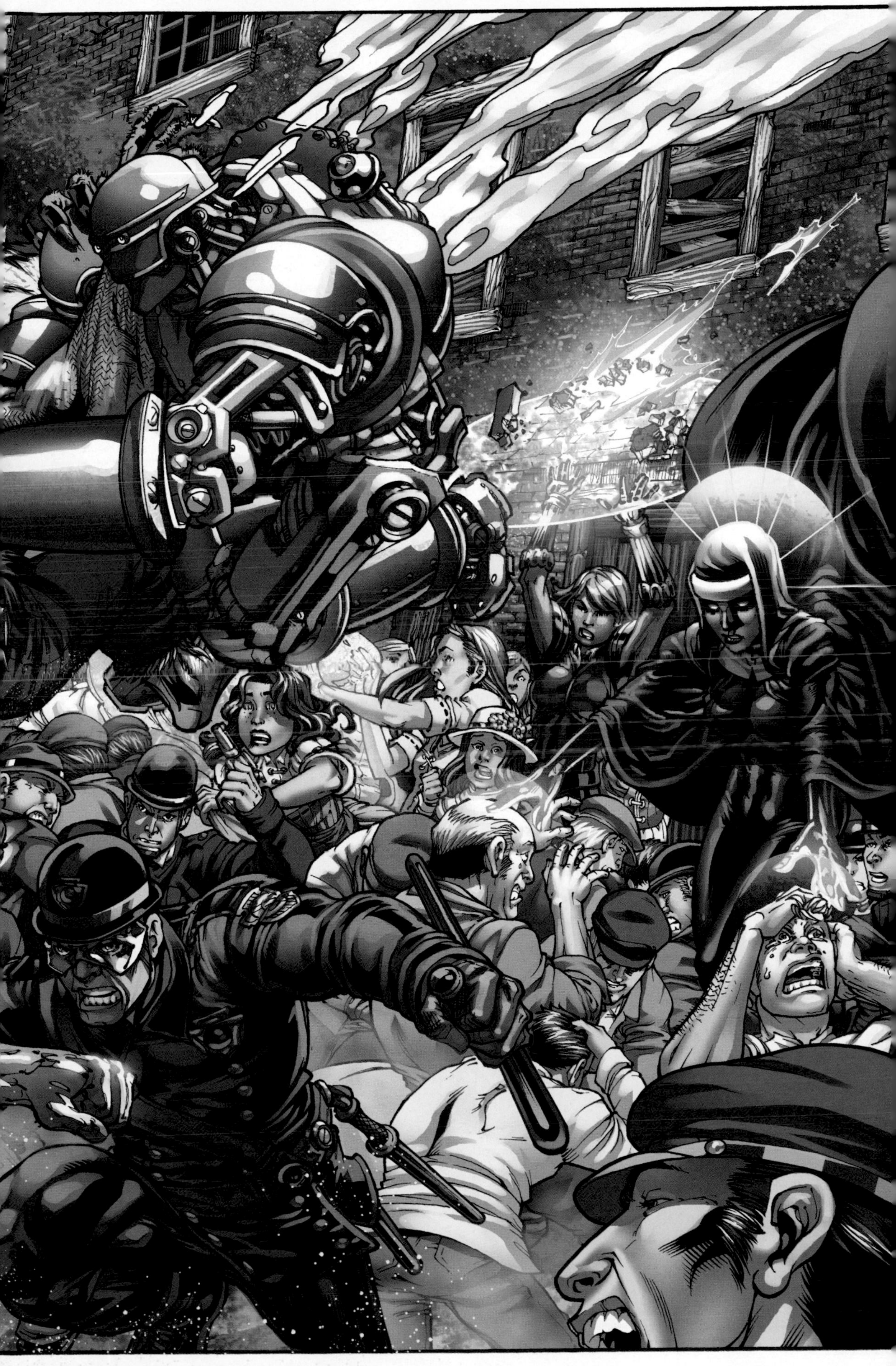

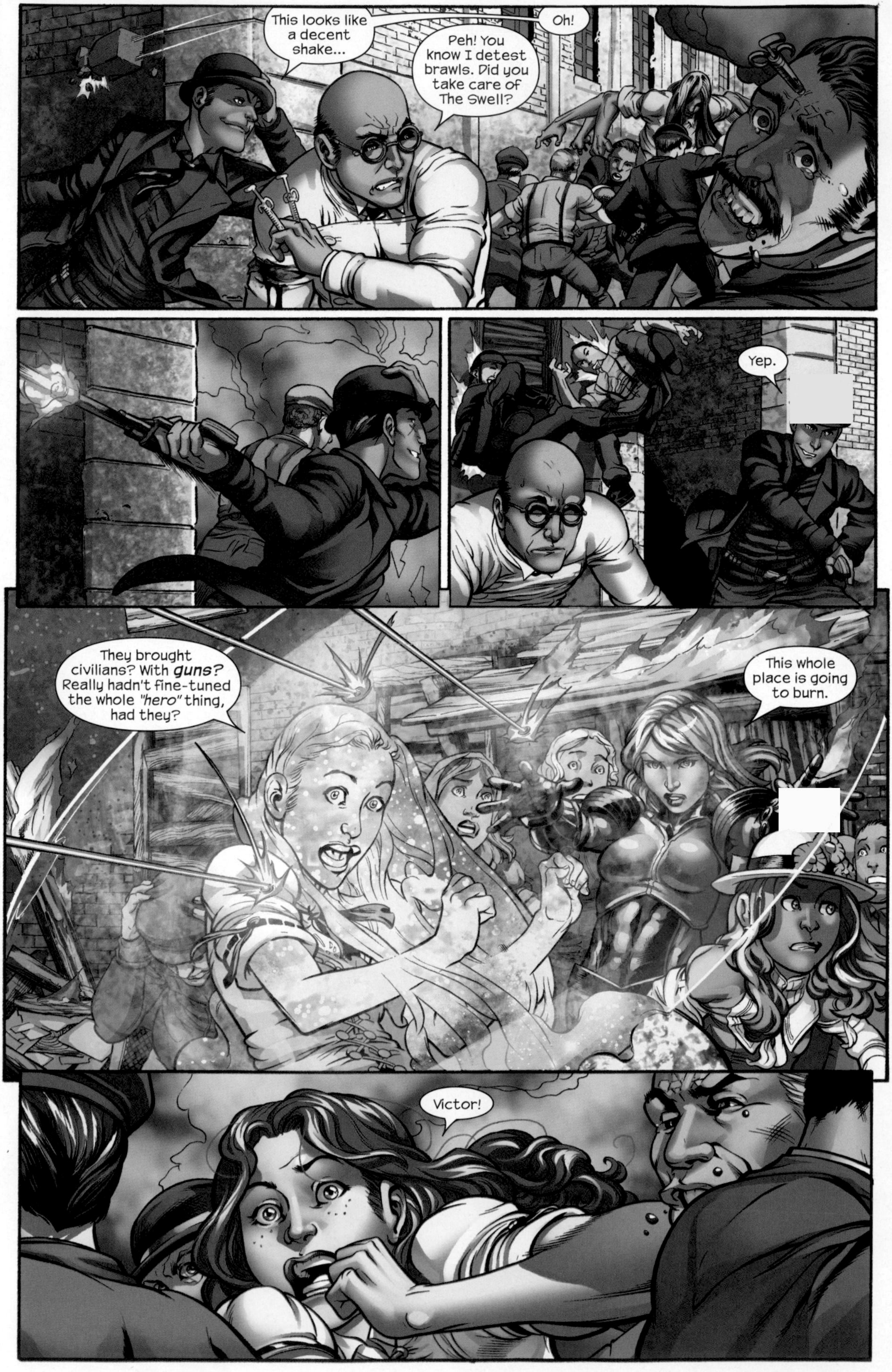
This looks like a decent shake...
Oh!
Peh! You know I detest brawls. Did you take care of The Swell?
Yep.
They brought civilians? With *guns*? Really hadn't fine-tuned the whole *"hero"* thing, had they?
This whole place is going to burn.
Victor!

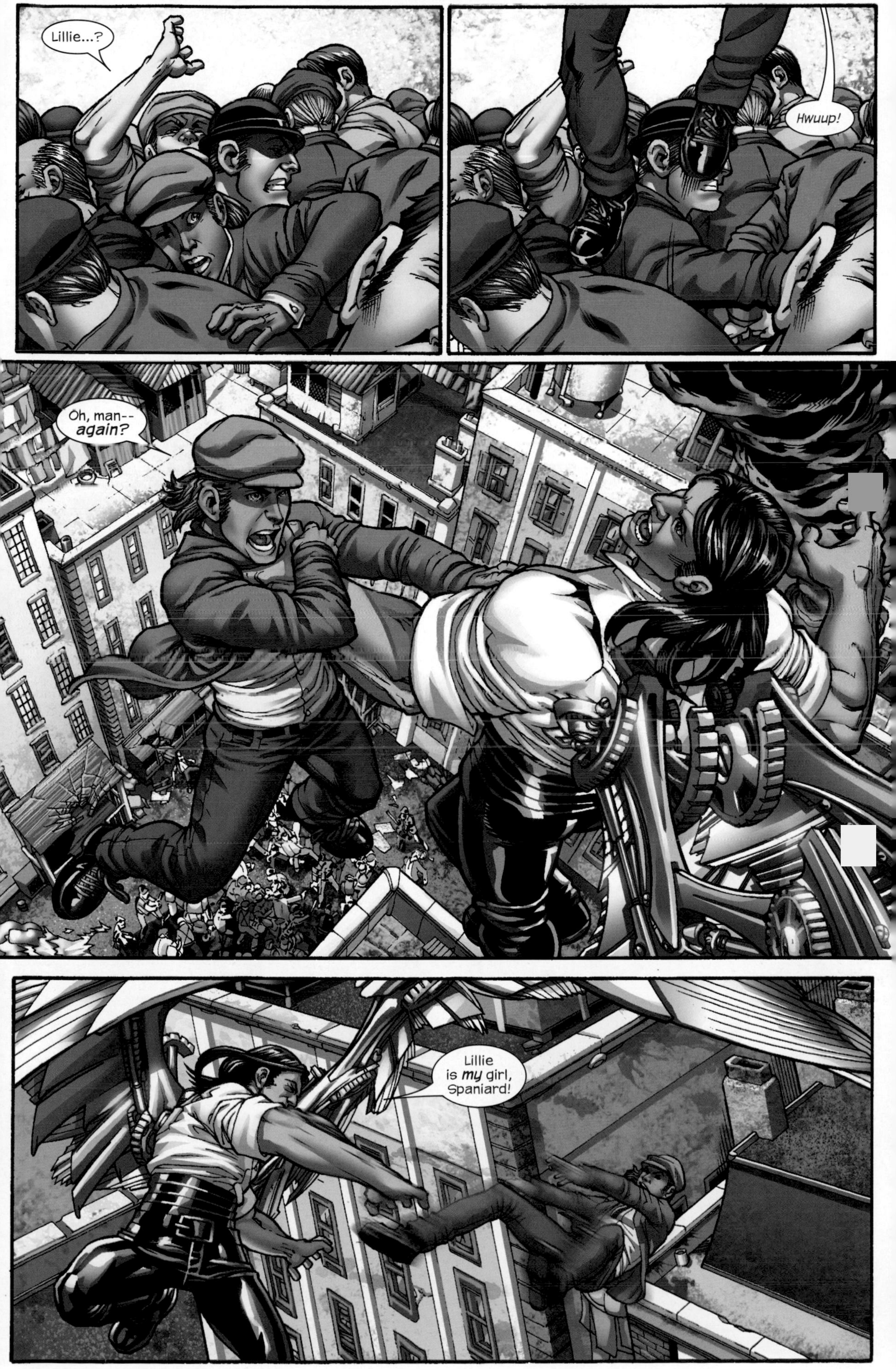
Lillie...?
Hwuup!
Oh, man-- again?
Lillie is my girl, Spaniard!

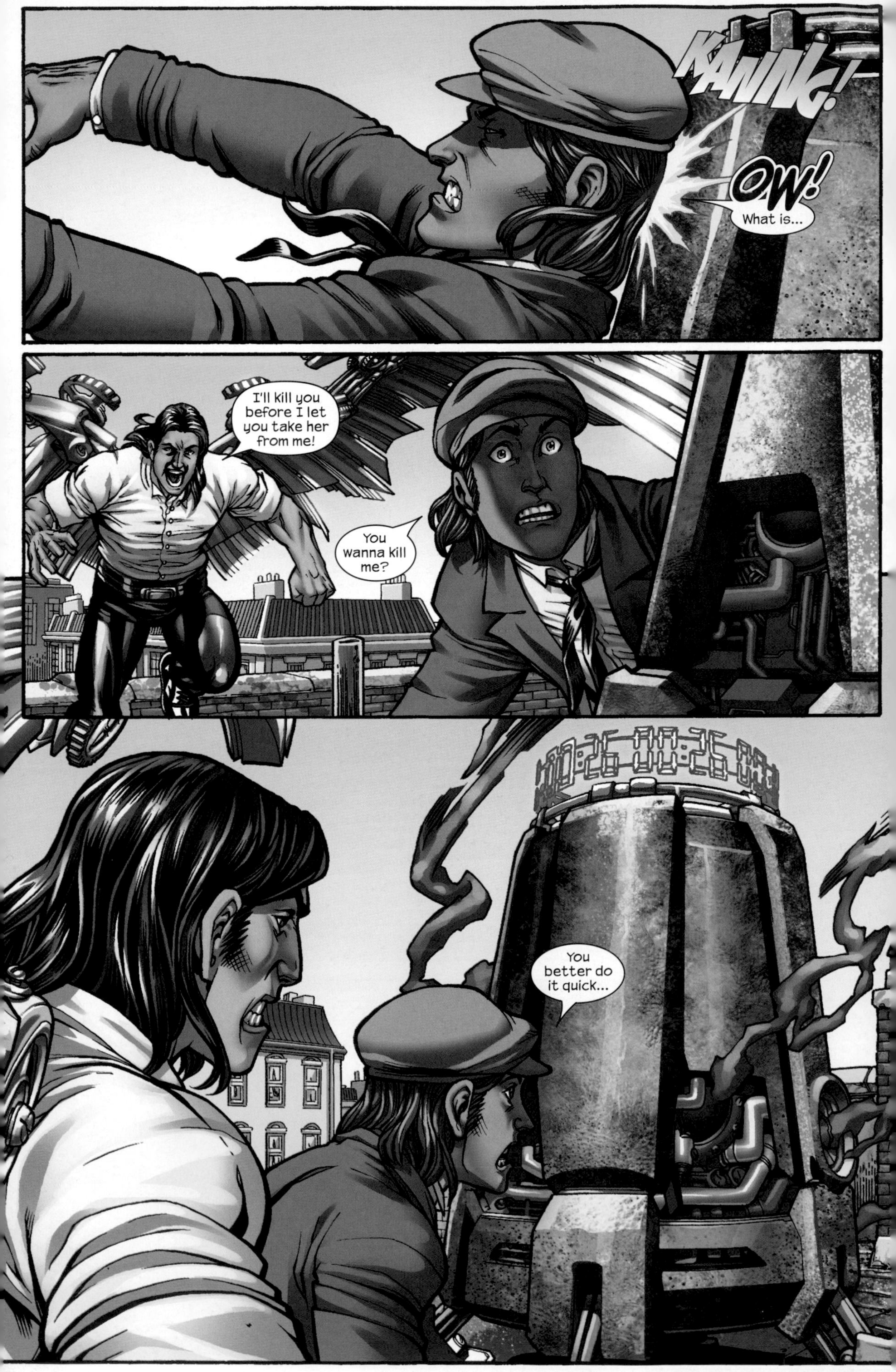
KANNG!
OW!
What is...
I'll kill you before I let you take her from me!
You wanna kill me?
You better do it quick...

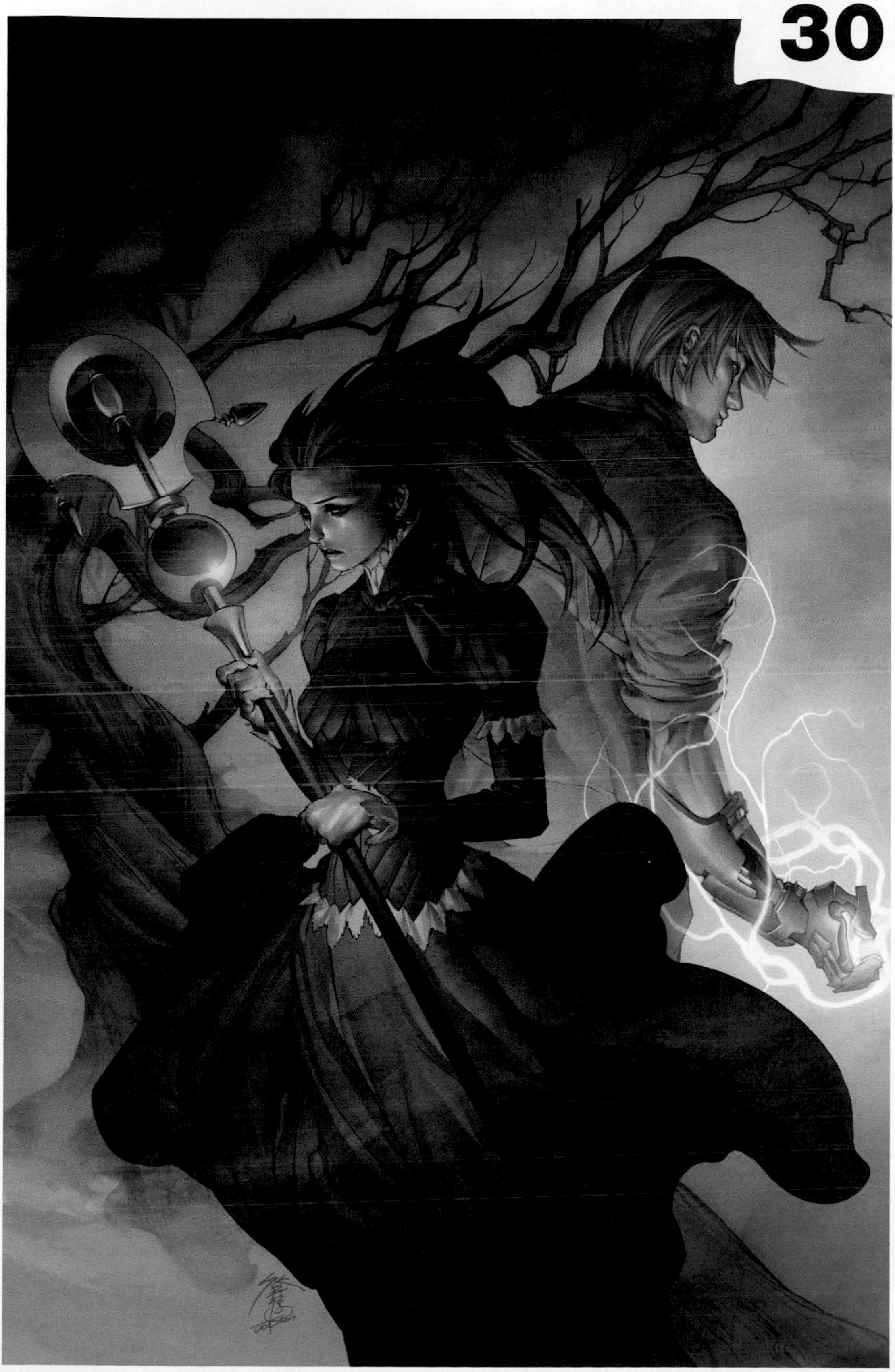

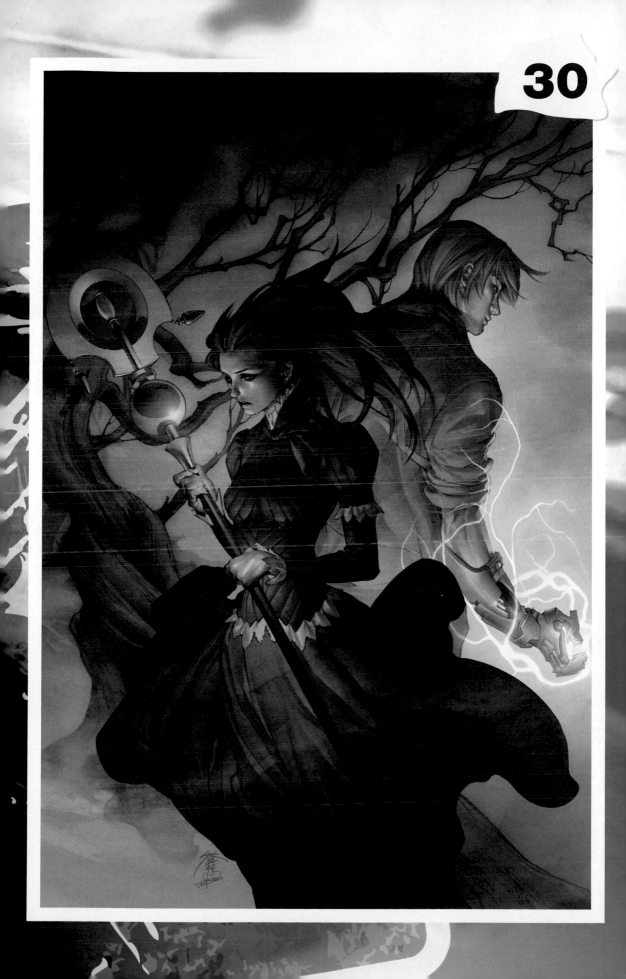

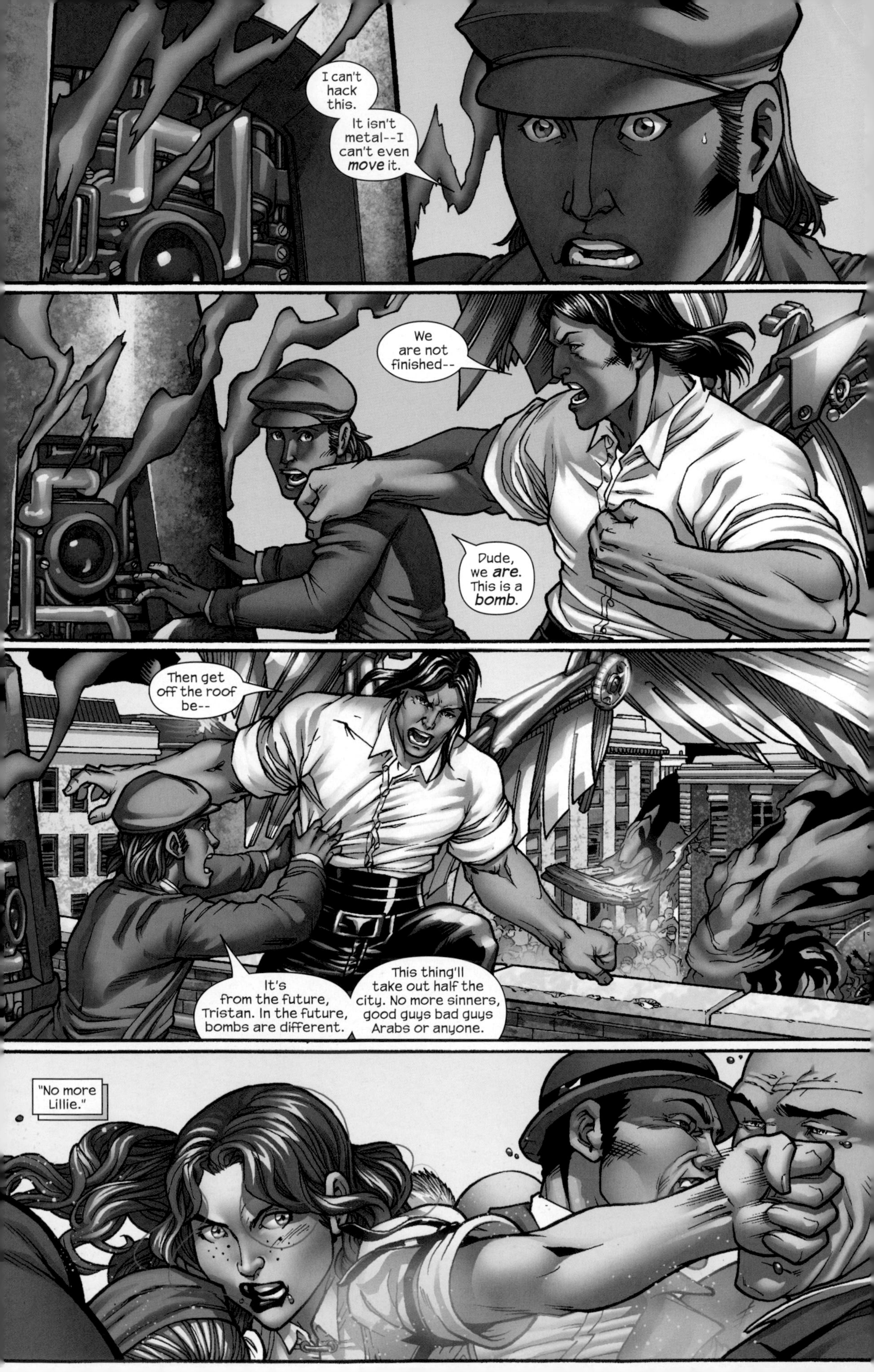
I can't hack this.
It isn't metal--I can't even *move* it.
We are not finished--
Dude, we *are*. This is a *bomb*.
Then get off the roof be--
It's from the future, Tristan. In the future, bombs are different.
This thing'll take out half the city. No more sinners, good guys bad guys Arabs or anyone.
"No more Lillie."

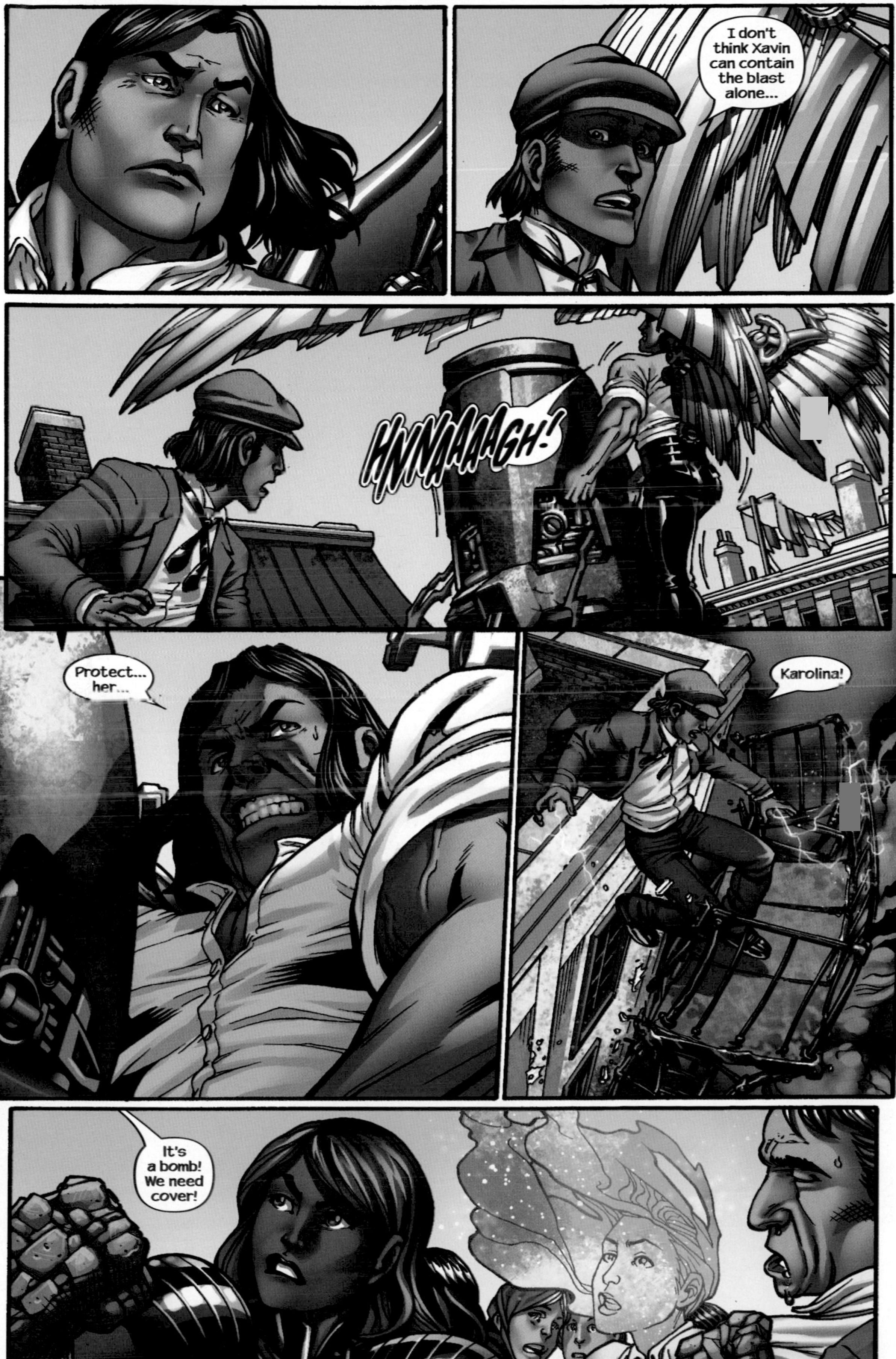
I don't think Xavin can contain the blast alone...
HNNAAAAGH!
Protect... her...
Karolina!
It's a bomb! We need cover!

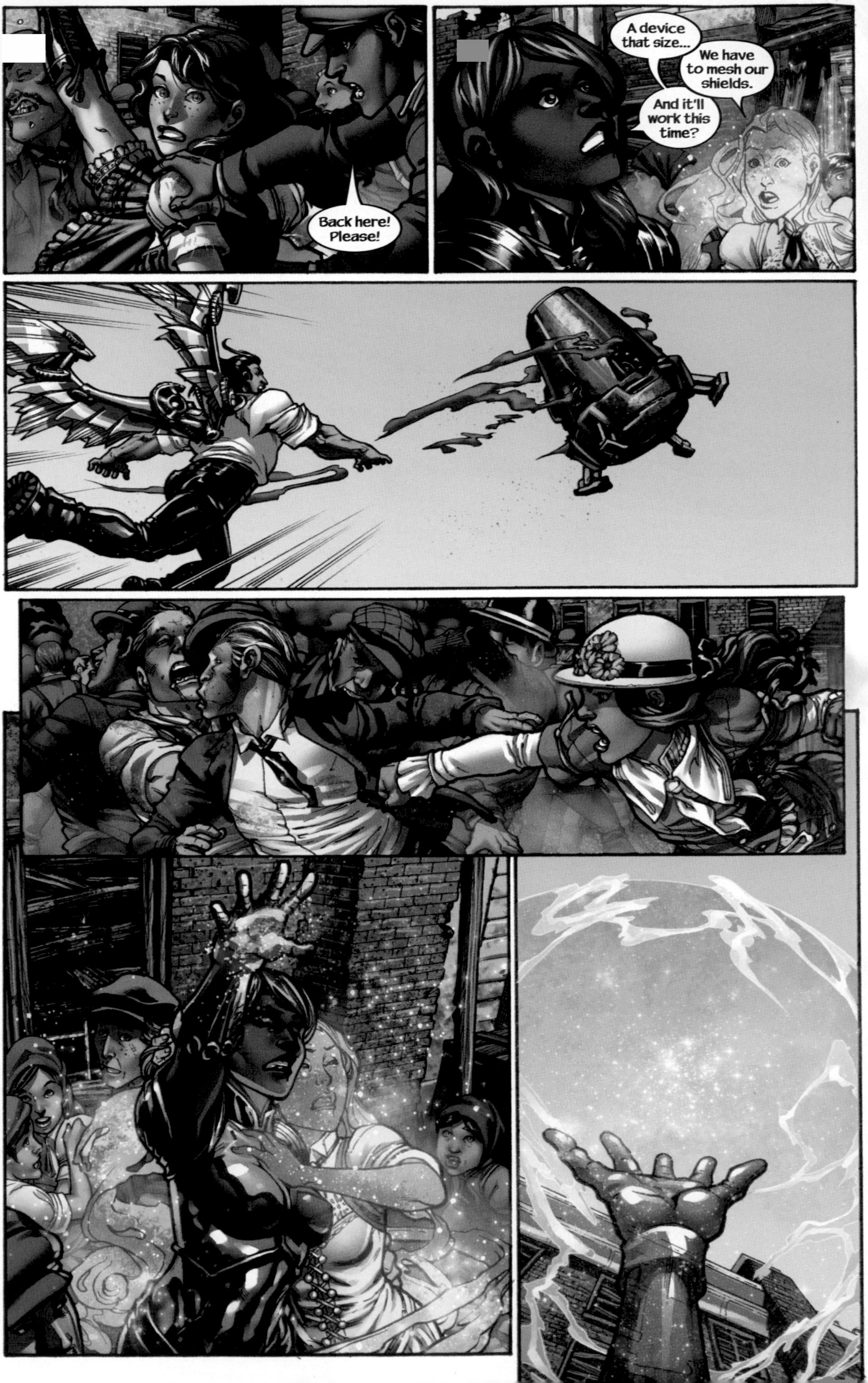
Back here! Please!
A device that size...
We have to mesh our shields.
And it'll work this time?

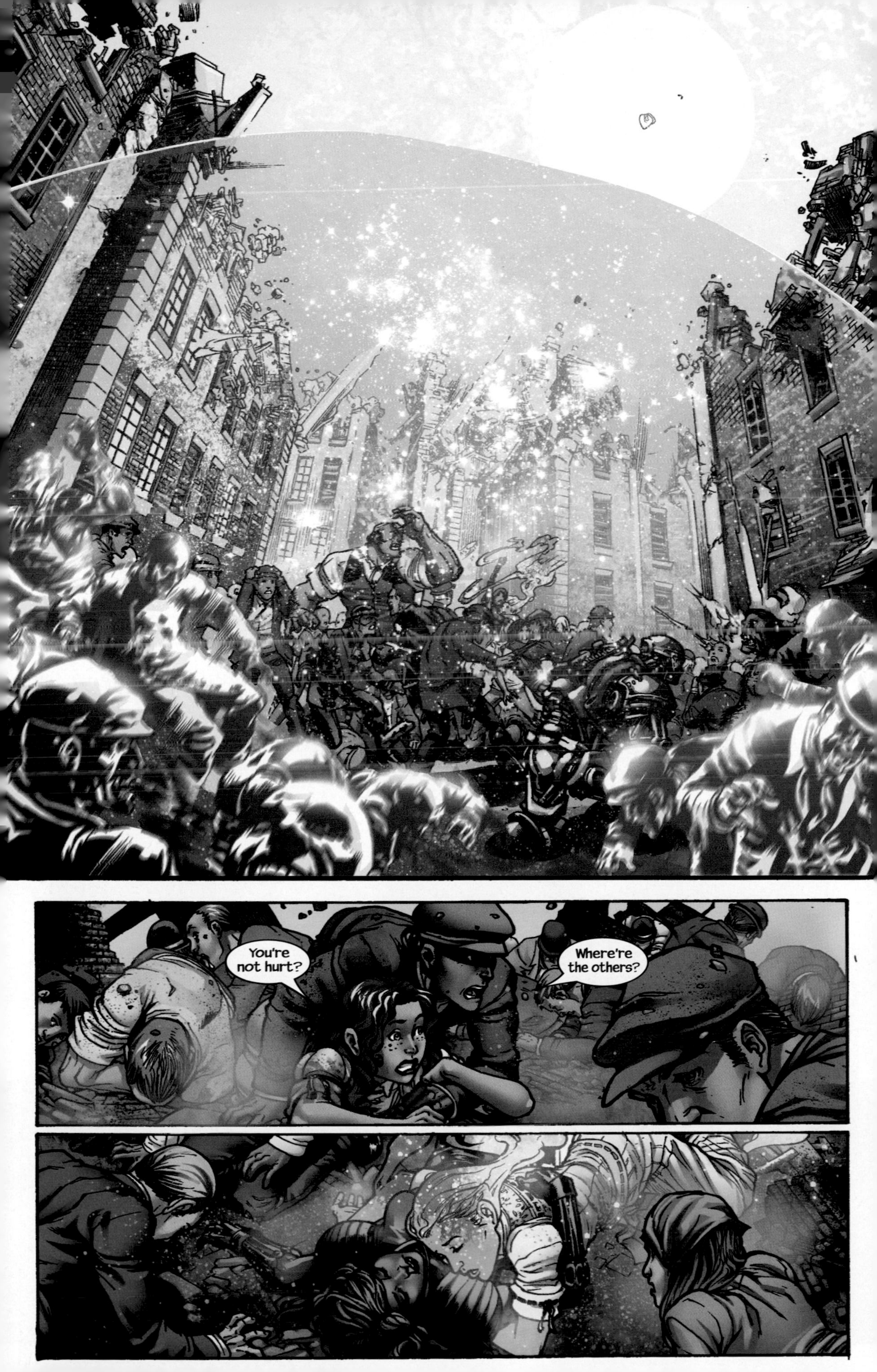
You're not hurt?
Where're the others?

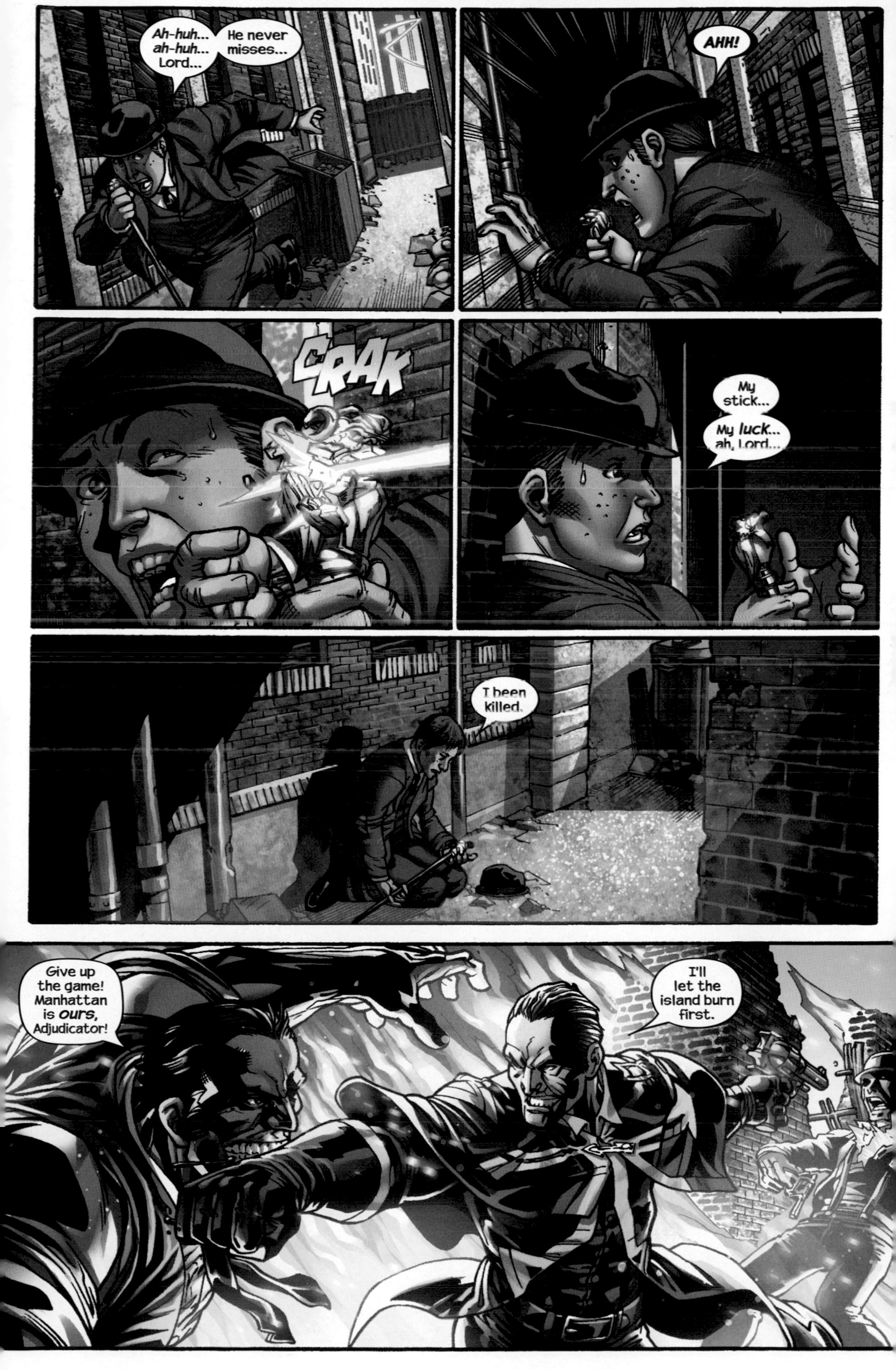
Ah-huh... ah-huh... Lord...
He never misses...
AHH!
CRAK
My stick...
My luck... ah, Lord...
I been killed.
Give up the game! Manhattan is ours, Adjudicator!
I'll let the island burn first.

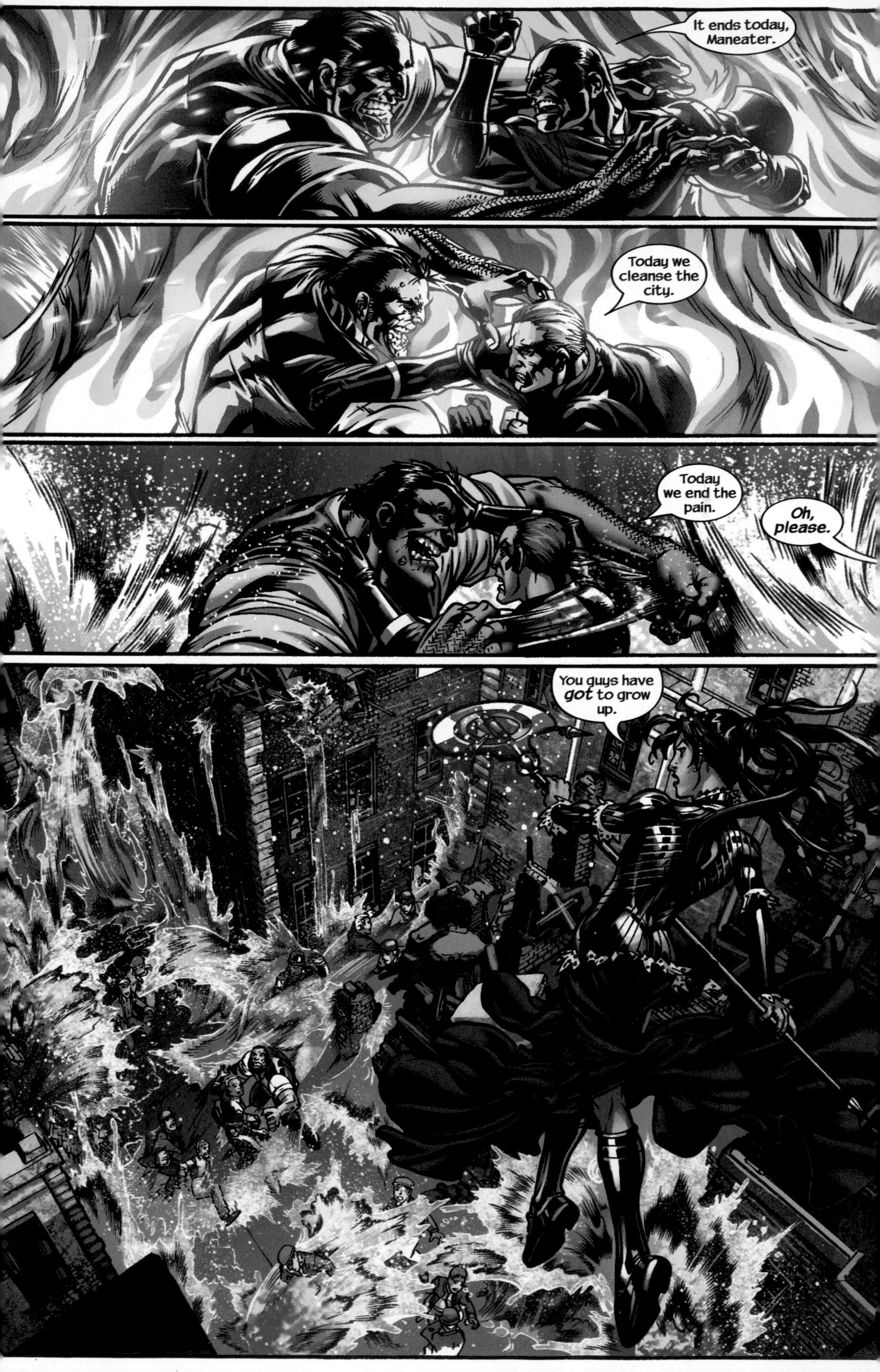

It ends today, Maneater.
Today we cleanse the city.
Today we end the pain.
Oh, please.
You guys have got to grow up.

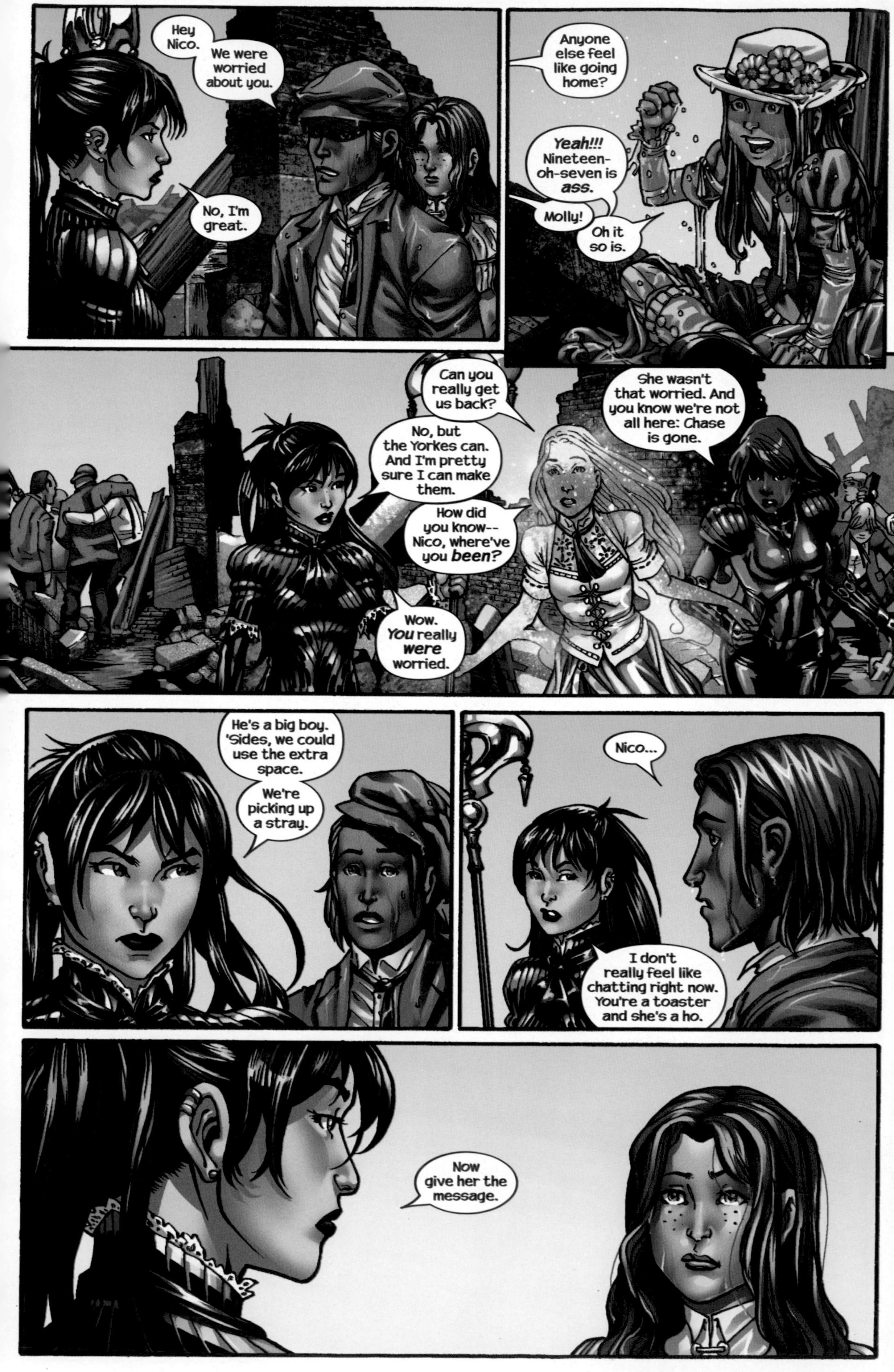
Hey Nico.
We were worried about you.
No, I'm great.
Anyone else feel like going home?
Yeah!!! Nineteen-oh-seven is ass.
Molly!
Oh it so is.
Can you really get us back?
No, but the Yorkes can. And I'm pretty sure I can make them.
She wasn't that worried. And you know we're not all here: Chase is gone.
How did you know-- Nico, where've you been?
Wow. You really were worried.
He's a big boy. 'Sides, we could use the extra space.
We're picking up a stray.
Nico...
I don't really feel like chatting right now. You're a toaster and she's a ho.
Now give her the message.

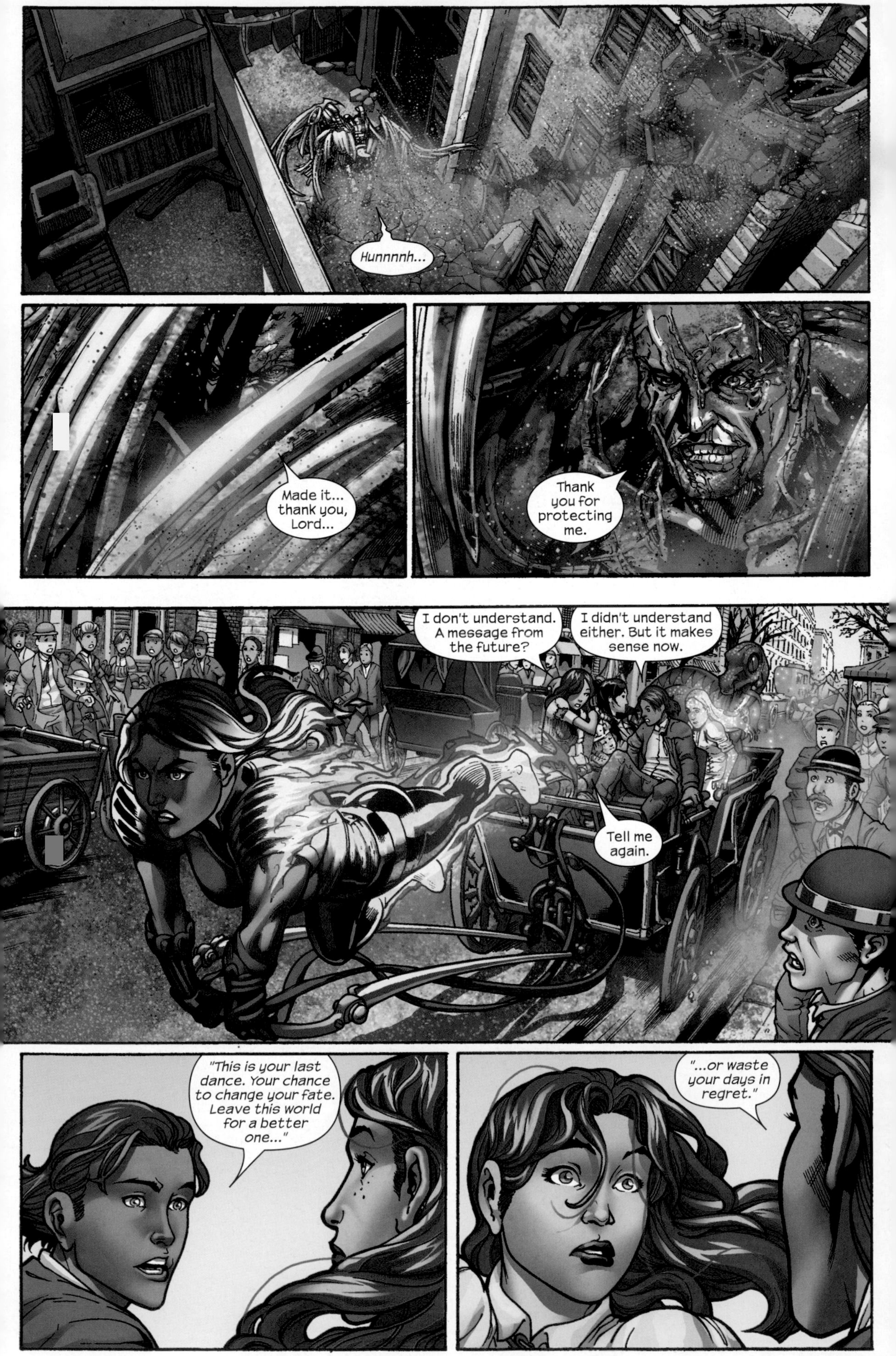
Hunnnnh...
Made it... thank you, Lord...
Thank you for protecting me.
I don't understand. A message from the future?
I didn't understand either. But it makes sense now.
Tell me again.
"This is your last dance. Your chance to change your fate. Leave this world for a better one..."
"...or waste your days in regret."

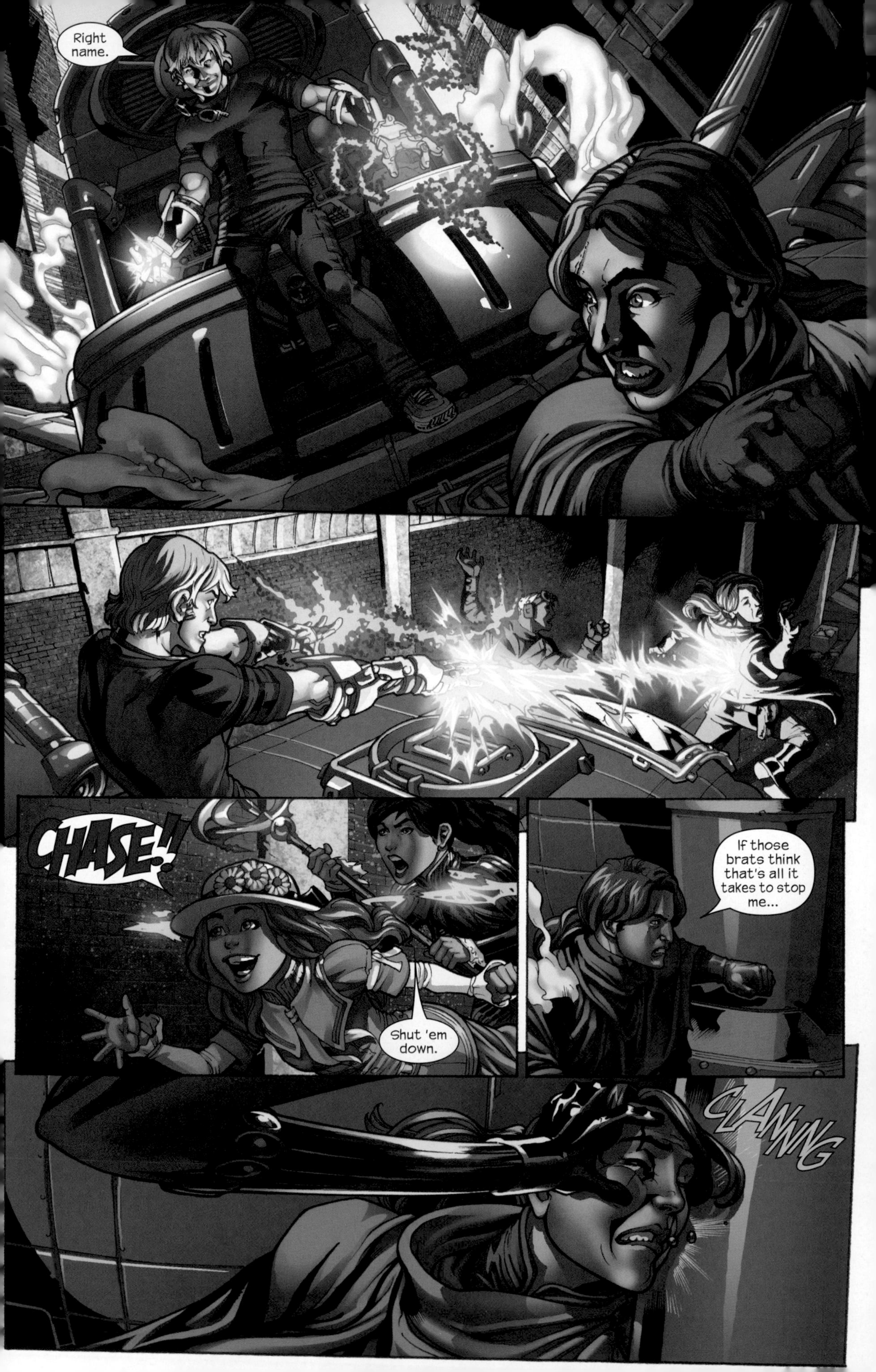
Right name.
CHASE!
Shut 'em down.
If those brats think that's all it takes to stop me...
CLANNNG

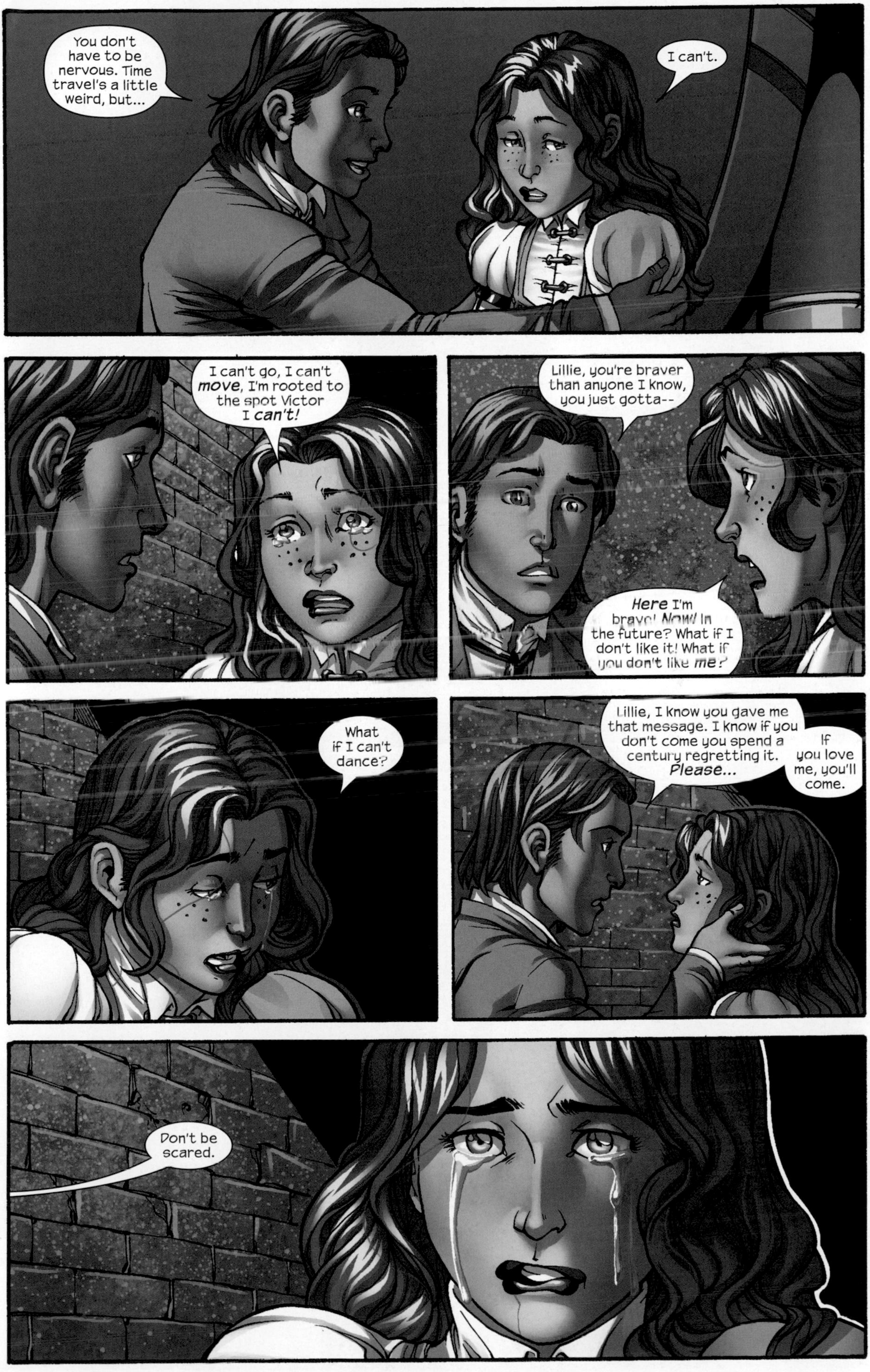
You don't have to be nervous. Time travel's a little weird, but...
I can't.
I can't go, I can't *move*, I'm rooted to the spot Victor I *can't!*
Lillie, you're braver than anyone I know, you just gotta--
Here I'm brave! *Now!* In the future? What if I don't like it! What if you don't like *me*?
What if I can't dance?
Lillie, I know you gave me that message. I know if you don't come you spend a century regretting it. *Please...*
If you love me, you'll come.
Don't be scared.

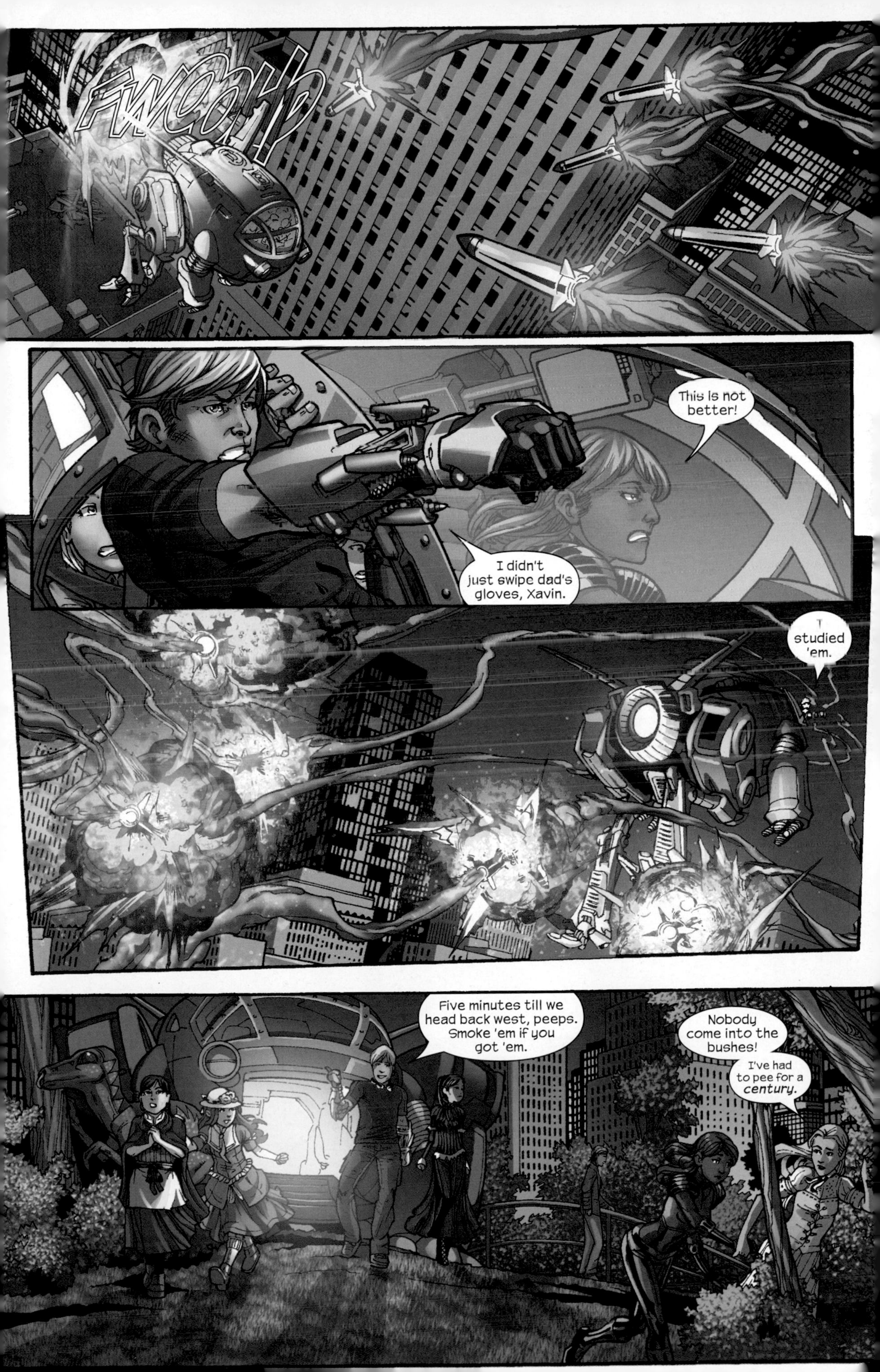
FWOOOM
This is not better!
I didn't just swipe dad's gloves, Xavin.
I studied 'em.
Five minutes till we head back west, peeps. Smoke 'em if you got 'em.
Nobody come into the bushes!
I've had to pee for a century.

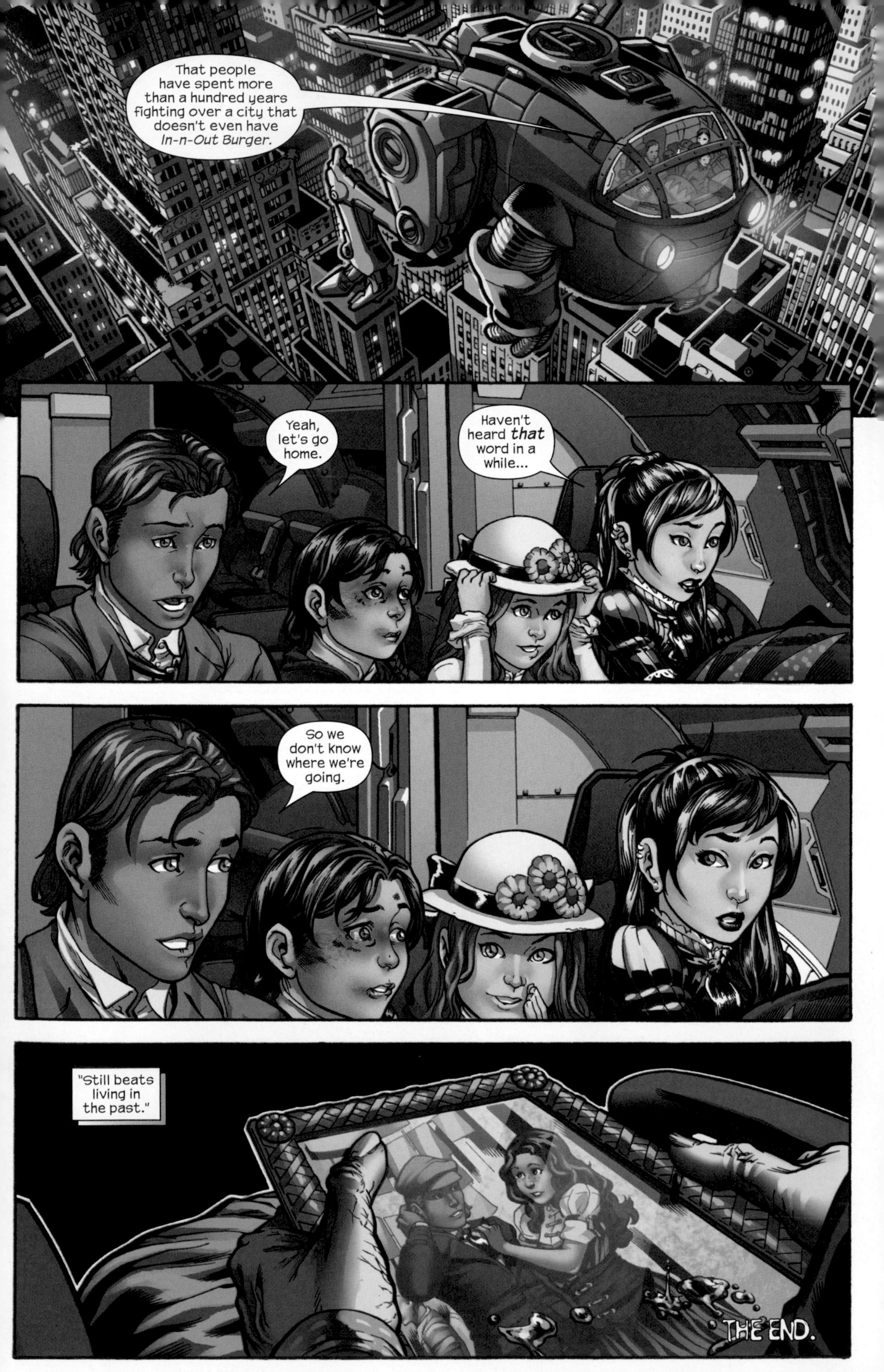
That people have spent more than a hundred years fighting over a city that doesn't even have *In-n-Out Burger*.
Yeah, let's go home.
Haven't heard ***that*** word in a while...
So we don't know where we're going.
"Still beats living in the past."
THE END.

30

NICO & KAROLINA

Dark grey-
Black

White

See through
Black

White

grey

Black

Edwardian
Style.

Sleeves/Trim
lighter than
Skirt and Bodice

Brass
Buttons

Hairstyle
only lasts
till she lets glow.

collar White or
Cream

She'll
roll up
the Sleeves
when she
says she's
Hot

Two part
Skirt.

Not sure
How much
color we
get in
1907?

White
or
Creme

Brown?

CHASE

NICO

CHARACTER SKETCHES
BY MICHAEL RYAN

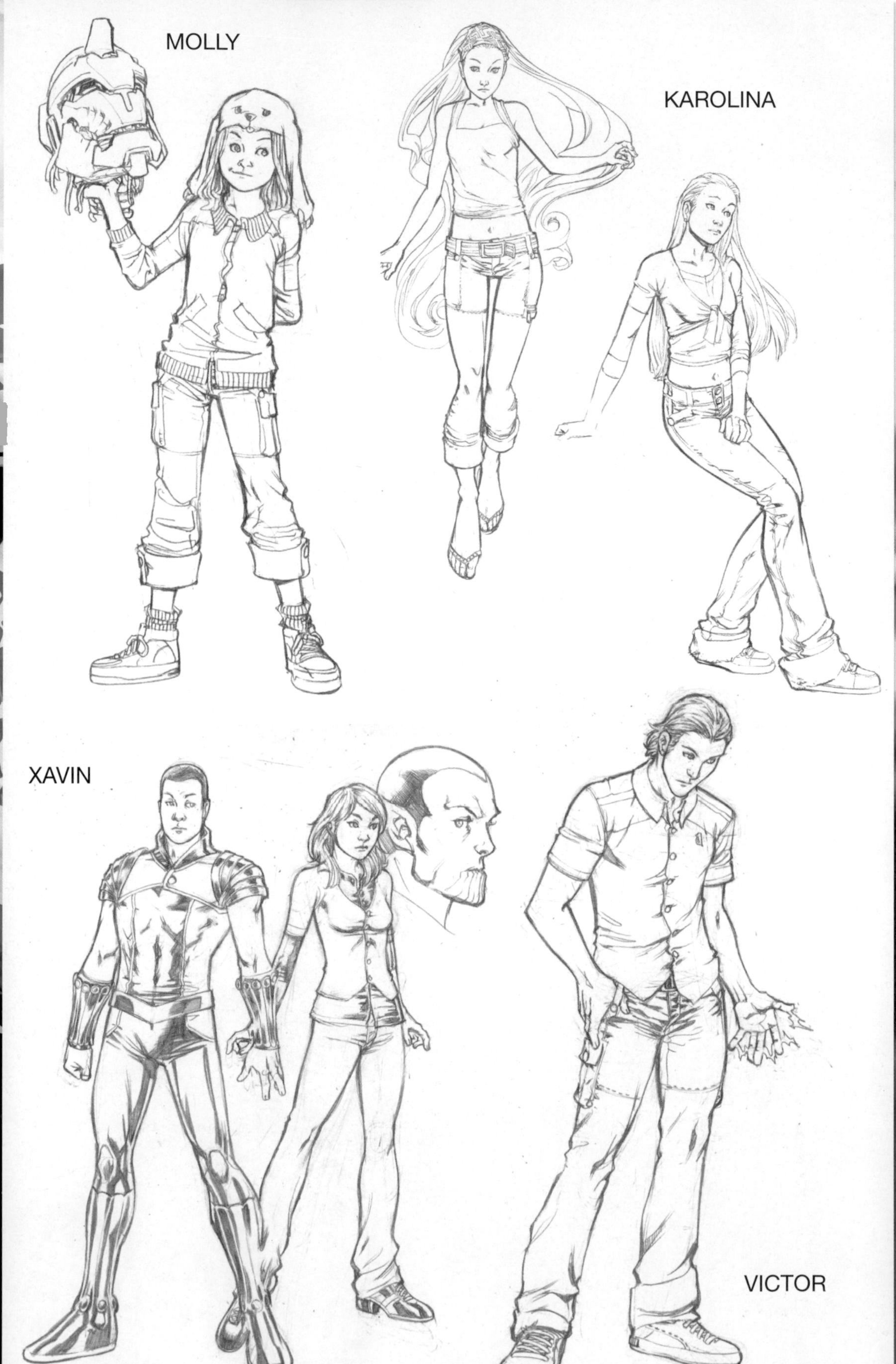
MOLLY
KAROLINA
XAVIN
VICTOR